CITY OF THE SILENT

CITY OF

THE CHARLESTONIANS

THE SILENT

OF MAGNOLIA CEMETERY

Ted Ashton Phillips, Jr.

Edited by Thomas J. Brown

Foreword by Josephine Humphreys

Afterword by Alice McPherson Phillips

THE UNIVERSITY OF SOUTH CAROLINA PRESS

Published by the University of South Carolina Press
Columbia, South Carolina 29208

www.sc.edu/uscpress

Manufactured in the United States of America

19 18 17 16 15 14 13 12 11 10   10 9 8 7 6 5 4 3 2 1

Library of Congress Cataloging-in-Publication Data

Phillips, Ted.
  City of the silent : the Charlestonians of Magnolia Cemetery /
Ted Ashton Phillips, Jr. ; edited by Thomas J. Brown.
    p. cm.
  Includes index.
  ISBN 978-1-57003-872-3 (cloth : alk. paper)
    1. Charleston (S.C.)—Biography. 2. Magnolia Cemetery (Charleston, S.C.)
3. Charleston (S.C.)—Genealogy. 4. Registers of births, etc.—South Carolina—
Charleston. 5. Magnolia Cemetery (Charleston, S.C.)—Guidebooks. 6. Charleston
(S.C.)—Buildings, structures, etc. I. Brown, Thomas J., 1960– II. Title.
  F279.C453P48 2010
  975.7'915—dc22   2009034347

CONTENTS

ILLUSTRATIONS

FOREWORD

Josephine Humphreys

When I think about Ted Phillips, I hear him saying, "Hey, Doll," which was how he usually started up a phone conversation. After that he might say, "Let's have lunch at Martha Lou's," "Want to run up to Magnolia this afternoon?," or one time, "Let's go to Bishopville and look for Lizard Man." I've never known anyone so steadily enthusiastic about local exploration. And I've never had a better friend.

I didn't know him in 1988, when he first called and introduced himself as "LaVonne's son." LaVonne and I are the same age, so I automatically cast myself as a person of the older generation with regard to Ted . . . but that didn't last long. Ted's friendships cut across lines of age. In fact they cut across all lines. He knew famous people, and he knew convicted felons, many of whom he had met in his capacity as public defender; and when someone hailed him on the streets of Charleston, there was no telling who it might turn out to be.

When he called me that day in 1988, he said he was getting married soon and wanted my help. "I want to give my groomsmen copies of your novel," he said. "Will you autograph the books if I bring them to you this afternoon? There are fifteen."

So we spent an hour together in my living room in a sort of ceremony. It wasn't just a matter of getting fifteen books signed. Ted wanted me to know something about each person for whom I was signing a book. So he would pass me the novel, and I would hold it while he told me where he'd met the friend, his talents and personality and character, and some funny story about the time they got in trouble together somewhere. Then I would sign and inscribe. This seemed awkward to me at first, but by the time I had finished, I understood this was the way books should be inscribed. Some of those groomsmen were Ted's childhood schoolmates, while others were friends he'd made in college or somewhere along the way. I don't think Ted ever let friendships lapse. Eventually the fifteen groomsmen spread out across the world, but they kept coming back to visit over the years. Meanwhile, Ted stayed home. So did I. The hometown had a grip on both of us.

We had some common interests. We loved books, junk stores, gossip, history, and jokes; southern towns and cigarettes and examples of great courage. Politically we were allied along the southern-liberal axis that often brings people together in our town. We never argued; we laughed more than grown-ups are supposed to. Sometimes on Saturdays we went to auctions at Roumillat's on the Savannah Highway, where Ted mainly bought books and paintings, and I bought sillier, junkier things. We egged each other on. Ted bought a huge box of costume jewelry for his little girls. I bought kitchen props used in the movie *Lolita.* Once when I couldn't make it to the Saturday auction, he bought me a camel saddle that had been a gift from Anwar Sadat to Strom Thurmond.

Ted had such great loves in his life. His wife, Janet, and their girls, Sarah and Alice, came up in every conversation I ever had with him, because they were constant presences in his heart. He unabashedly loved his mother and father, his brothers and his sister, and his town. As a student, he had spent a summer vacation as a tour guide, driving tourists around in a horse and carriage, telling the stories of Charleston.

I was bowled over when I found out that Ted had a consuming interest, if not an obsession, with the great sprawling riverside cemetery called Magnolia—because I shared that obsession. I'd loved Magnolia since my early years, when I went with my parents to tend the graves of various old dead loved ones, and I'd wandered its paths and climbed its trees and written about it in a novel, but I never knew Magnolia the way Ted did. The cemetery was his novel, or at least his collection of strange and wonderful stories. He was famous for the Magnolia tours he conducted for friends, and for friends of friends, even for tourists he happened to run into. When I went with him, I often had the feeling that we were in our element. But I never thought of his interest (or mine) as morbid. Death wasn't the fascination here; life was. In a sense, Ted was a custodian of those lives, as he researched and collected the details, reconstructing stories that might never have been known otherwise, certainly not by me. We walked the sandy paths as if along Church Street or Tradd Street, Ted pointing out who was where, and who was who, and what the secrets and scandals had been, what the great accomplishments were.

One day, in the cemetery's big old ledgers (which he never tired of poring over), Ted found an unusual entry. A one-year-old child had died in 1883 and was buried in an un-marked grave. His name was "King of the Clouds." Born in "the Dakotas," died of "fever," the brief handwritten entry read, as short and mystifying a story as was ever written. We couldn't flesh it out with research, except to speculate that maybe the parents of King of the Clouds had come from the Dakotas with one of the traveling Wild West Shows that occasionally passed through Charleston. But beyond that we could only imagine the story. We should have a gravestone made, Ted said, so we did. When I go to Magnolia now, I pay my respects to my own predecessors, and to Ted Phillips, and to King of the Clouds. I know we are connected.

INTRODUCTION

Thomas J. Brown

The founding of Magnolia Cemetery was the first capital investment in what would later become the staple commodity of Charleston, the aura of local memory. Long before tourist groups in horse-drawn-carriages obliged resident motorists to deal with the complications of living in a historic showcase, Magnolia sought to combine a commemorative spectacle with an institution that would serve basic human needs. The cemetery made this marriage work to an extent that provides a model for the living city, although that success of the cemetery came in unforeseen and traumatic ways.

The establishment of Magnolia was part of the development of nineteenth-century urban infrastructure in what was then the twelfth-largest city in the United States. As the Charleston artist Charles Fraser observed in his November 1850 dedication address, the opening of Mount Auburn Cemetery outside Boston in 1831 had "marked an era of taste in our country" that spread quickly to Laurel Hill Cemetery in Philadelphia (1836), Green-Wood Cemetery in Brooklyn (1838), Spring Grove Cemetery in Cincinnati (1845), and Hollywood Cemetery in Richmond (1848). The so-called rural cemetery movement reflected shifting religious and cultural ideas about death. The new institutions aimed to replace bleak and ominous church graveyards with sylvan spaces in which beautifully regenerating trees and flowers surrounded decorous memorials. The carefully wrought landscapes aspired to facilitate serene contemplation of the blissfully reposing dead and provide assurances of eternal life. Twenty-two-year-old Charleston poet Henry Timrod aptly declared in the ode he composed for the Magnolia dedication that the emerging idea of the cemetery was to "make it a place to love, and not to fear." These sentiments overlapped with social attitudes toward growing and increasingly heterogeneous cities. Critics argued that churchyards exposed burial sites and mourners to the convulsions and indifference of street life and that rural cemeteries situated the response to death in a more controlled private enclave.

The men who incorporated Magnolia in 1849 were committed to keeping Charleston up to date with the current trends of the age. None of the original directors—William D. Dukes, William D. Porter, George N. Reynolds, Frederick Richards, and William S. Walker—was a member of an old Charleston family. None was a member of the planter elite who owned fashionable town houses. Instead they were all leading figures in business and law. The first president, Edward Sebring, was president of the State Bank, a key financial booster of city development. The founders hired the young Edward C. Jones to design the grounds and buildings of Magnolia; he would soon earn his fame as the leading

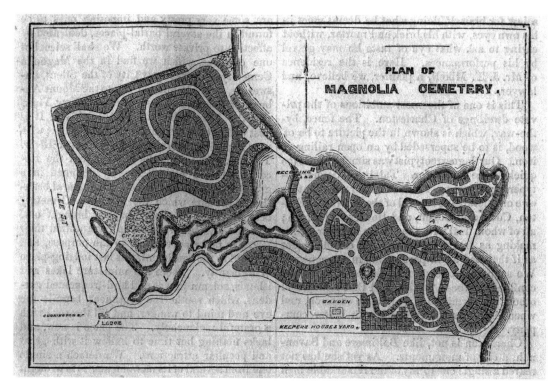

E. C. Jones's plan for the grounds of Magnolia Cemetery. Courtesy of the Thomas Cooper
Library, University of South Carolina

architect of Victorian modernity in Charleston, including such innovations as the first
department store in town.

These impulses collided with local interests in traditional patterns of burial, particularly in church graveyards. The conflict expressed itself most sharply when projected onto
debates about health policy. Proponents of rural cemeteries often claimed that urban interments were dangerous sources of miasma. These allegations were especially sensitive in
fever-ridden Charleston, and many church officials and members vigorously rejected them.
The opening of new cemeteries within the city limits had already been banned for three
years when Mayor Henry Laurens Pinckney called for prohibition of all urban burials in
1839 on the basis of "numerous and appalling facts . . . sustained by the concurrent opinion of the medical profession." Despite Pinckney's influence and the shadow of a recent
epidemic, however his bid to close the churchyards failed completely in the face of the
support the established practice drew from influential congregations. Several years later
Wentworth Street Baptist Church challenged the 1836 ban by establishing a new cemetery. Represented by Magnolia cofounder William D. Porter, who was coincidentally
corporation counsel for Charleston, the city sued to force the church to shut down its
graveyard. After appealing unsuccessfully to the state's supreme court, the congregation
wound up buying a large plot in Magnolia to relocate the bodies already interred and
secure room for the future. But the churches had shown that they would not easily yield
to the new nondenominational cemetery.

Subsequent proposals to close all churchyards after the 1858 epidemic illustrated the relations between Magnolia and its competitors. A sensational pamphlet echoed Pinckney's republished arguments and added that urban burials were increasing because church policies for reassigning burial space continually renewed the substantial remaining capacity of those facilities. From the opposing side, a memorial signed by 148 well-connected residents pointed out that the 1850s had been the worst decade for yellow fever in city history even though up to nine-tenths of all fever victims had been buried in Magnolia as a precautionary measure. The churchyards, these petitioners concluded, could not be at fault.

Under these circumstances Magnolia made limited early progress toward matching the churchyards as a repository of community memory. The fullest statement of this objective was the original poem "The City of the Silent," which William Gilmore Simms delivered at the November 1850 dedication. The poem presented a lengthy, recondite tour of the funereal shrines of various civilizations, culminating in Magnolia as the definitive expression of South Carolina history and culture. Simms envisioned the translation to the cemetery of the remains of Pinckneys, Gadsdens, and Rutledges and the raising of monuments to Isaac Hayne, John Laurens, Francis Marion, and other Revolutionary War heroes. Most timely was his suggestion that Magnolia would be an ideal final resting place for John C. Calhoun, whose death several months earlier had prompted many suggestions for public commemorations.

Consistent with Simms's prospectus, Magnolia began to cultivate a civic dimension during its first decade. The founders bought a touching slice of memory with the land from the Magnolia Umbra plantation. A young man setting out for the Mexican War from this estate had bid farewell to his mother at a large tree, under which he asked to be buried if he did not return. She complied with this request when he succumbed to disease at the end of the war, and the tree came to be a revered spot in the cemetery. Other sentimental associations gradually developed. Travel writers, who were important promoters of the rural cemetery movement, praised the beauty of Magnolia in several accounts of Charleston during the 1850s and also commented on the noteworthy tombs. Simms reported in a national magazine in 1857 that the grounds were splendidly suited "to fill the soul with a grateful melancholy" and predicted that the cemetery "lacks nothing but time to hallow it with great and peculiar attractions."

A few steps toward providing these great and peculiar attractions took place during the late 1850s. Richard Yeadon of the *Charleston Courier* launched a successful campaign to bring the remains of Hugh Swinton Legaré home from Mount Auburn, where he had been buried in 1843 after he died on a trip to Boston. Shortly before the highly publicized effort concluded with Legaré's reinterment in October 1857, the cemetery received its most distinguished addition to date when the family of Langdon Cheves determined to bury him at Magnolia. That decision probably reflected in part the plans of Cheves's daughter Louisa McCord to commission an exceptionally impressive monument featuring a statue by Hiram Powers, a desire that would prove frustratingly elusive for her. Meanwhile other public monuments appeared at the cemetery. The Washington Light Infantry dedicated a column entwined with ivy in honor of William Washington and his wife, who had given the corps its standard, the flag carried by Colonel Washington's partisan force at Eutaw.

A broken column honored Robert Barnwell Rhett's nephew William R. Taber after the *Charleston Mercury* editor died in a celebrated duel, though the family buried him in the Rhett vault at St. Philip's.

Although significant, these results fell short of what Simms had anticipated in 1850. The proprietors of the cemetery did not undertake to build any monuments, in contrast to the precedent of Mount Auburn, and no Revolutionary War heroes were moved to the cemetery. At its third meeting in January 1850 the board of trustees authorized William D. Porter to seek permission from the family of Gen. William Moultrie to reinter his remains in an appropriate place at Magnolia, which overlooked the Sullivan's Island site of Moultrie's famous palmetto fort. But the initiative failed, for Moultrie had been buried in an unmarked grave at Windsor Hill Plantation that could no longer be located. John C. Calhoun, the most prestigious corpse in the state, remained entombed in St. Philip's churchyard. In its first fifteen years the cemetery attracted relatively few of the citizens most widely associated with Charleston. During this period James L. Petigru, James Gadsden, Joel R. Poinsett, Mitchell King, Samuel Gilman, John Blake White, and James Adger were all buried elsewhere. Charles Fraser, orator at the dedication of Magnolia, was buried at St. Michael's. Even Henry Laurens Pinckney, the early champion of suburban interment, was buried at the Circular Congregational Church. Prominent Charlestonians, it seemed, were too strongly attached to the churchyards for Magnolia to win a conspicuous place on the collective imaginative map of the city.

The Civil War transformed Magnolia into a public shrine far more resonant than the historical theme park Simms had described. Confederate troops camped in the cemetery for three years and built breastworks in it for the defense of Charleston. They also turned to it to accommodate the shocking number of wartime burials, which Magnolia was better prepared to handle than any other graveyard in the Charleston area. More than eight hundred soldiers and sailors in Confederate service were interred at the property during the war, mostly in a starkly gridded new Soldiers' Ground that established a stern counterpoint to the gently curving lanes and idiosyncratic family tombs envisioned by the cemetery founders. The Confederate dead gravitated to Magnolia for reasons other than numbers and logistical convenience. Some bodies were unidentified and would otherwise have been candidates for burial in a municipal potter's field, an alternative that the war made politically unacceptable. And even the fallen who were well known and ceremoniously mourned, such as Confederate submarine developer Horace L. Hunley and Fort Sumter commander John Mitchel, Jr., had in many cases come to Charleston only as a result of the war and lacked the local ties that might have led to a churchyard burial. Some Confederates would later be reburied elsewhere by their families, but Magnolia provided a permanent manifestation of the temporary wartime community.

Most important for Magnolia, in the wake of the Civil War the bodies of dead soldiers became vital to American memory at Gettysburg, Arlington, and other locations, including Charleston. An early example of cemetery politics focused on the interment of several Union soldiers. The famous 54th Massachusetts regiment camped at Magnolia after the occupation of Charleston in February 1865, and Union commanders allowed the troops to cut down for firewood a grove of oak trees that had been a centerpiece of the landscaping design. The Magnolia founders had reserved this chapel grove as a public space and

A burial in the Soldiers' Ground. Courtesy of the Magnolia Cemetery Trust

permitted no burials in it, but abolitionist James Redpath led a northern group that, in the words of diarist Esther Hill Hawks, "selected the finest place in the Cemetery for our 'brave and honored dead' much to the evident disgust of a rebel who is still in charge of the grounds." The Magnolia board of trustees complained to the commanding officer, Gen. John P. Hatch, that the burials would invade private property and violate the consecrated purpose of the chapel grove. But Hatch ordered that the controversial graves would remain in their prominent location and that they would be protected by a high wooden palisade (also contrary to cemetery regulations). Only after another few years, when similar security concerns led to an overall regional consolidation of federal burials in a national military cemetery system, were the Union dead removed from Magnolia and taken to Beaufort National Cemetery.

In the meantime Magnolia had begun to emerge as a leading site of Confederate memory. The inaugural observance of Memorial Day at the cemetery on June 16, 1866, was among the most auspicious in the South, for Henry Timrod contributed to it an ode that would be widely admired for decades to follow:

> Sleep sweetly in your humble graves,
>   Sleep, martyrs of a fallen cause;
> Though yet no marble column craves
>   The pilgrim here to pause.
>
> In seeds of laurel in the earth
>   The blossom of your fame is blown,
> And, somewhere, waiting for its birth,
>   The shaft is in the stone!
>
> Meanwhile, behalf the tardy years
>   Which keep in trust your storied tombs,
> Behold! your sisters bring their tears,
>   And these memorial blooms.
>
> Small tributes! but your shades will smile
>   More proudly on these wreaths to-day,
> Than when some cannon-moulded pile
>   Shall overlook this bay.
>
> Stoop, angels, hither from the skies!
>   There is no holier spot of ground
> Than where defeated valor lies
>   By mourning beauty crowned!

Memorial Day soon expanded into an elaborate civic ritual organized by the Ladies Memorial Association. Businesses closed early every May 10, the anniversary of Stonewall Jackson's death, so white Charlestonians could gather at the cemetery at 5:00. For more than a half-century after the war, newspaper reports consistently estimated attendance to be two or three thousand. Exercises included prayers, hymns, instrumental music, readings of Timrod's ode, original poems, and frequently an oration. The focal point was the decoration of soldiers' graves. The young women of the Confederate Home School usually took a prominent part in the proceedings, and other community notables rotated through different roles. Some annual observances were particularly charged with emotion. Surely one of the most dramatic was the ceremony of 1871, when six thousand people gathered for the interment of the remains of eighty-four South Carolinians whom the

Ladies Memorial Association had brought home from the battlefield at Gettysburg. Rev. John L. Girardeau delivered a fiery anti-Reconstruction address in which he urged his listeners to resist what he described as the radicalism undermining family, church, and state and thereby ensure that the soldiers did not die in vain.

Similar commemorative impulses supplied, many times over, the monument that Timrod had foreseen in his ode. At the 1870 Memorial Day observance the Ladies Memorial Association laid the cornerstone for the "Defenders of Charleston" monument that would be unveiled at a state reunion of Confederate veterans in November 1882 in a ceremony that featured Gen. Wade Hampton as the main speaker. While that project was still in its early phases, the Washington Light Infantry dedicated a memorial to its war dead on June 16, 1870. Other monuments erected at Magnolia honored German soldiers, Irish soldiers, the Charleston Light Dragoons, Confederate generals from South Carolina, Confederate sailors, and the ironclads, forts, and batteries engaged in the defense of Charleston harbor. Markers for individual soldiers proliferated even more rapidly as Confederate veterans passed from the scene.

The extent to which soldiers' graves, Memorial Day, and Confederate monuments made Magnolia a representative expression of the Lost Cause was captured with sly satire by the most eminent travel writer to visit Charleston in the early twentieth century, Henry James. Acknowledging that it was by now a cliché to identify a cemetery as an illustration of the picturesque charm of an American city, James nevertheless put forward Magnolia as the epitome of the charm of the slaveholding South, "the charm, I mean of the flower-crowned waste that was, by my measure, what the monomania had most prepared itself to bequeath." At Magnolia that influence distilled an "irresistible poetry" from "the golden afternoon, the low, silvery, seaward horizon, as of wide, sleepy, game-haunted inlets and reed-smothered banks, possible site of some Venice that had never mustered, the luxury, in the mild air, of shrub and plant and blossom that the pale North can but distantly envy." Amid this magniloquent setting and the commensurably pious inscriptions on the stones, even James, whose brother had served in the 54th Massachusetts, could feel for an hour that he was "really capable of the highest Carolinian pitch."

The impact of the Civil War on Magnolia reached beyond the rituals and memorials to the daily administration of the cemetery. Antebellum sales of lots had been substantial but had not matched the large outlays for landscaping. After the war the corporation shared in the overall economic ruin of the white South. Many of the firms in which it had invested were now bankrupt. Like other enterprises, moreover, Magnolia would no longer be able to rely on slave labor—one of the first steps of the corporation had been the purchase of two slaves to work in the cemetery. At the same time, the proprietors faced heavy expenses to repair the damage caused by years of neglect and military use of the grounds. The financial rescue of Magnolia coincided with the political "redemption" of South Carolina. In June 1877 a group of thirty Charlestonians bought the cemetery for thirty thousand dollars from the original proprietors. The revitalization of the cemetery and realization of its original promise paralleled the self-conscious regeneration of the white South after Reconstruction.

The shareholders of the corporation included some of the wealthiest and most prominent citizens of Charleston. Among the initial directors were the bankers Andrew Simonds and James S. Gibbes. The second president of the cemetery, after twenty-seven years under Edward Sebring, was William C. Bee, who had long been the head of the Magnolia lot holders' association. The most important force in the new ownership was the merchant and banker George Walton Williams, who became president on Bee's death in 1882 and remained in that office until his own death in 1903. Williams had been interested in Magnolia since burying three children there during the yellow fever epidemic of August 1854, followed a year later by his first wife, and he illustrated the way in which deep private ties to the cemetery converged with a sense of public responsibility to the Confederate past. While he was the very epitome of a dynamic, forward-looking New South businessman, he was also the president of the gentleman's auxiliary association of the Confederate Home. That institution, like the Ladies Memorial Association so active at Magnolia, was presided over by founder Mary Amarinthia Snowden, whom Williams called "one of the most remarkable women Charleston ever produced." If the Lost Cause was not as central to Williams's view of Magnolia as it was for someone such as Snowden or Maj. Henry E. Young, a director of the new corporation and its attorney until his death, all agreed that remembrance of the Civil War gave Magnolia a distinctive and important place in the life of the community.

Similar considerations helped Magnolia attract an increasing share of the most prominent Charlestonians after the war. Some of these, such as James Conner and Wilmot Gibbes DeSaussure, were men for whom Confederate military service had been a significant interlude in a varied, active life. The unifying appeal of the cemetery was not, however, restricted to veterans. In the case of William Gilmore Simms, interred a few days before dedication of the Washington Light Infantry monument, burial in Magnolia brought to fulfillment an ideal of the cemetery as a site of South Carolinian nationalism that he had held since its dedication. For George Alfred Trenholm, who had signed the 1859 petition to protect the old churchyards, the experience of the war and service as Confederate secretary of the treasury perhaps pointed toward interment at Magnolia. William Aiken, Isaac Hayne, Alfred Huger, and A. G. Magrath were other Charlestonians whose political commitments indicate how the local elite increasingly came to be buried at Magnolia in the decades after the Confederate war.

As G. W. Williams appreciated, the future of the cemetery depended not merely on preserving shrines to the Confederacy or local notables but on providing valuable services to large numbers of ordinary people. His effective management soon restored the fortunes of Magnolia to the point that the corporation could pay the shareholders a modest annual dividend while the cemetery regained and expanded on its beauty, developing the landscape that Henry James found so evocative on his visit in 1905. Along the way cemetery officials dealt with such challenges as the cyclone of 1885, the earthquake of 1886, and the hurricane of 1893, all of which wreaked havoc but none of which exasperated Williams as much as the lot holders who neglected graves and failed to enter into arrangements with the cemetery for permanent maintenance. He also continued until the end of his tenure to complain about church graveyards, but Magnolia had secured a strong competitive position, aided by regulatory restrictions on recycling of urban burial space and by the sheer number of local interments. Williams's final report to the lot holders was a good measure of his success. He proudly noted that the cemetery had spared no expense in preparing for the tourists who would find Magnolia to be one of the most attractive places in Charleston when they visited the city for the South Carolina Interstate and West Indian Exposition of 1902. He reported that the number of people buried in the cemetery had almost doubled during his tenure and was now approximately eleven thousand, of whom about one thousand were Confederate dead.

By the twentieth century Magnolia came to reflect a broader range of lives led in Charleston. The cemetery commanded a high percentage of local burials, and it could satisfy the most discriminating expectation for permanent repose in a quintessential Charleston institution. As years passed, the Magnolia firmament extended well beyond Confederate luminaries. The Charleston Renaissance brought to the city a new creative spirit that rather pointedly ignored the Lost Cause, and many of its leading figures—including Alice Ravenel Huger Smith, Josephine Pinckney, John Bennett, and Albert Simons—would eventually rest at Magnolia. The civil rights movement produced outstanding Charlestonians more openly antithetical to the Confederate inheritance who would find a final home at Magnolia, most notably J. Waties Waring. Commemoration of the Confederacy did not disappear from the cemetery, as evidenced by the spectacular ceremonies surrounding the burial in April 2004 of the bodies of crew members recovered on the raising of the submarine *Hunley* from Charleston harbor. That aspect of local history, however, was now one of the many different parts of a past remembered at Magnolia.

Like the other great rural cemeteries, Magnolia offered a new definition of the relationship between public and private realms. Motivated less by municipal necessity than by civic self-expression, it opened a public space in which to conduct an essential activity that had long been fundamental to private institutions such as families and churches. The Magnolia initiative assumed that networks of kinship and religion and work and education came together in a coherent community that shaped the legacies of the people buried in the cemetery. At the same time, the rural cemetery conferred a kind of citizenship on the dead and suggested that those individuals could still embody the community in their various ways. The promoters of Magnolia Cemetery built wisely in centering their efforts on the close interconnection between personal and collective identity in Charleston. The local culture abounded in representative figures, and it fostered a reverence for the examples of previous generations. Through the powers of memory for which it is famous, Charleston continues to benefit from the contributions of its residents in the City of the Silent.

CITY OF THE SILENT

A BRIEF NOTE ON THE BIOGRAPHICAL SUBJECTS

Ted Ashton Phillips, Jr.

Magnolia Cemetery was founded in 1849 and has since received well over thirty thousand permanent residents. These residents have included great writers, artists, and politicians as well as bootleggers, slave traders, whores, and other socialites. Mostly, though, the cemetery is filled with ordinary people who slogged through life and made do under seemingly impossible conditions as they were assaulted by politics, history, natural disaster, and various and sundry varieties of pestilence. I know that every tombstone and every sunken unmarked grave represents the story of a life, most untold and likely to remain so. I do not have the time to tell every story. I would dearly love to.

Every mother's child who is buried here tells an instructive tale by his or her example. One prepublication reader of this work remarked that I seemed preoccupied with writers, artists, and politicians (or statesmen, to use their posthumous designation). It is true. My prejudice shows up in the finished work.

A bit of personal history is in order. I first became truly acquainted with Magnolia Cemetery in the summer of 1976 when my friend Tommy Rhett and I got jobs there as groundskeepers and assistant gravediggers. I have always been an obsessive student of Charleston history, even before I moved here with my family at the age of nine. By the nature of my job at Magnolia, I had the chance to read every tombstone on the property at least ten times in that first summer. I would be embarrassed to say how many times I have walked the entire cemetery since then.

I was thus intimately familiar with the major historical figures buried at Magnolia by the time I began this study in the spring of 1994. At the time I started, I thought this book would take about two months of my time to complete. The further I got into the research, the more I found that the people in the strange little crevices of history that everyone has forgotten are the interesting ones. Most devoted students of American history can tell you who Robert Barnwell Rhett was, or Langdon Cheves, George Alfred Trenholm, J. Waties Waring, even Burnet Maybank. They held high office; they did remarkable things; their works live after them. No biographical study of Magnolia would be complete without them.

But what of Frank Hogan, Daisy Breaux Calhoun, Mary Wilkerson Pinckney Lee, Henrietta Pignatelli? Who could ever make up such stories, or forget them, or fail to include them in such a history?

Mourners at the Simonds tomb, ca. 1893. Courtesy of the Historic Charleston Foundation

These unexplainable sidelights of history are often the most illuminating and, to me at least, fascinating, in the history of Magnolia Cemetery and of Charleston.

When I began this study and survey, there was no map of the interesting folks in Magnolia. Ultimately, the subjects I have included have been those lives that interest me. Some of the people were friends of mine: Albert Simons, Beatrice St. Julien "Kitty" Ravenel, Mary Vereen Huguenin, Louie Jenkins, Frank Munnerlyn. A good chunk of this book was written on Kitty Ravenel's desk, which I bought at her estate sale. That same desk had been her mother's (possibly her grandmother's) and had thus been the birthplace of *Architects of Charleston*, *Charleston Murders*, and *The Arrow of Lightning*. Nice desk. Frank Munnerlyn is a classic example of a person who might not otherwise have made a history of *anything*. But I loved him. He was born and died at 95 Church Street, across the street from my parents. He lived two houses down from Catfish Row, knew Sammy Smalls (Porgy) well, and was a contemporary fellow insurance agent of DuBose Heyward. When I queried him about the greatest Charleston writer that side of Josephine Humphreys, he merely shook his head sadly and said, "Poor DuBose just couldn't sell insurance, didn't have it in him."

I have found the characters in this book by hook and by crook, by chance and design. A shocking number of the more famous and/or interesting people in Magnolia are buried in unmarked graves: William Elliott, Wilmot Gibbes DeSaussure, Fannie Mahon King, Antoinette Rhett, Nelson Mitchell, and the infamous William C. Corrie. I found them by checking the computerized record of interments. Many others were found by cross-indexing such great works as C. Vann Woodward's *Mary Chesnut's Civil War*, Chalmers

Davidson's *The Last Foray*, the *Dictionary of American Biography*, and *Appleton's Cyclope-dia*. I have lived in terror of missing some major figure, but, after all, what are new and revised editions for?

I repeat, these are the people who interested me. These are also the people who have left enough records around to be written about. There are many tantalizing details that will be left, I hope and know, for some future historians to figure out. When word got out that I was doing this sort of history, the little old genealogist ladies besieged me with tales of great-great-aunts, of the sort who wrote two recipes for *Charleston Receipts* or who founded short-lived societies for the worship of unknown Confederate/Revolutionary dead. Most of those aunts are not found in this book. Some of them are. For all those whom I missed who were worthy of incorporation in this work, so sorry, mea culpa. For those kinfolk who find that Uncle Jim or Aunt Nettie is an unincluded character, I plead ignorance. Daisy Breaux Calhoun is only an Aunt Nettie with enough money and moxie to be writ large. Uncle Jim is a William C. Corrie without the genocidal streak. My book and I miss them and would genuinely like to make their acquaintance. Originally, I hoped that this work could be a true *Spoon River Anthology*–like history of Charleston. I soon realized that the history of a white, upper-class cemetery like Magnolia automatically excluded at least half of Charleston's history, the African Americans. Right across the street from Magnolia are the graves of such distinguished figures as Septima Clark, Congress-man and Lieutenant Governor Alonzo Ransier, the Reverend Daniel Jenkins, Ambassador Theodore Crum, and many other major figures of African American history. I thought to expand my study and include their histories but decided I wanted to finish this book in my lifetime. They await another pen—I hope not for long.

This is my big ball of string: hemp rope is tied to silk is tied to twisted muslin. I invite you to unwind it, feel it, sew your own garment. I have endeavored to present the history of these people in the best and truest light possible given the time that I write in, the avail-able scholarship, and my own predilections.

These are teeny-tiny sketches of lives that are often huge, confusing, and more fun than I dared to intimate. My fondest hope is that it will be a seedbed for future biographers. So many of these few did unforgettable things and yet are forgotten. Remember, please.

Main entrance to the cemetery in the early 1890s. Courtesy of the Historic Charleston Foundation

BIOGRAPHICAL PROFILES

WILLIAM AIKEN, JR. (1806–1887)

Planter and Politician   MAP LOCATION: SOUTHWEST 1

William Aiken, Jr., became heir to a huge fortune at the age of twenty-five when his father died in a railroad accident. William Aiken, Sr., had been president of the South Carolina Canal and Railroad Company and had successfully built what was then the longest rail-road in the world, from Charleston to the Savannah River at Hamburg, South Carolina, near Augusta. William Aiken, Jr., soon began to enlarge on that legacy. He developed a magnificent rice plantation on Jehosee Island near Charleston that was touted as a model in an extensive article in the magazine *DeBow's Review.*

Aiken served in the South Carolina House of Representatives from 1838 to 1841, when he was elevated to the South Carolina Senate. In 1844 he was elected governor of South Carolina, in which position he sought to develop the economic interests of the state, most particularly (naturally enough) the interests of the railroads. He was elected to the U.S. Congress for three consecutive terms from 1851 through 1857, missing election as speaker of the U.S. House in 1856 by the narrowest of margins. After declining to seek reelection he remained a consistent antisecession voice until the South and the North were actually at war. Once the war began, however, he gave tremendous financial support to the Confederate cause and received Jefferson Davis at his magnificent home in Wraggsboro, now known as the Aiken-Rhett House.

After the war, Aiken was briefly detained by Federal authorities but was almost immediately released. He was elected to his old seat in the U.S. Congress in 1865 but was denied the office when the Republican majority withheld representation from the former Confederate states. Aiken was an original trustee of the Peabody Educational Fund and was an untiring advocate for reconciliation of the Union after the war.

MARY WILSON BALL (1892–1984)

Artist   MAP LOCATION: NORTHEAST 1

Miss Ball was a member of the Charleston Etchers' Club, whose members were as important in the world of visual arts in the Charleston Renaissance as their friends in the Poetry Society were in the world of writing. She displayed a talent for art early in life and studied under the most important Charleston artist of her time, Alice Ravenel Huger Smith, as well as under the renowned artist and teacher Arthur Dow of Columbia University. For much of her career she worked in Washington, D.C., as a cartographer with the Department of the Army and the Bureau of Public Roads. She returned home for the last years of her life and helped organize an annual art show of the Charleston Artist Guild on the gates of St. Philip's Church. Her watercolors, etchings, and oils continue to be much prized by collectors.

WILLIAM WATTS BALL (1868–1952)

Newspaper Editor   MAP LOCATION: NORTHEAST 2

William Watts Ball was an upcountryman and unapologetic reactionary whose antidemocratic views marked him as a dinosaur in his own time. By the end of his life he was the very journalistic symbol of the Old South, and at his death even the New York *Times* acknowledged that he was the last of the great editorial personalities.

W. W. Ball was born in Laurens, South Carolina, and educated in the private schools of Laurens and at Adger College in Walhalla, South Carolina. He entered South Carolina College at the age of fifteen and graduated in 1887 with honors. He taught school and studied law for a time. In 1890 he bought the Laurens *Advertiser* with borrowed money, and his career in journalism was set. In 1895 he accepted the editorship of the then-floundering Charleston *Evening Post*. Once the *Evening Post* was on its feet again, Ball left in 1897 to become editor of the Greenville *News,* but not before he married a wealthy and beautiful Charleston girl, Fay Witte, daughter of Charles Otto and Charlotte Sophia (Reeves) Witte. Ball didn't last long in Greenville. Within a year he was let go. He commenced a six-year period in which he wandered from Philadelphia to Laurens to Jacksonville, Florida, and from job to job as lawyer, editor, and reporter. Finally, he was able to return to Charleston in 1904 as J. C. Hemphill's assistant editor at the *News and Courier.*

Ball left Charleston again within five years to accept the position of managing editor of the Columbia *State.* When its editor-in-chief William Elliott Gonzales became ambassador to Cuba in 1913, Ball took charge of South Carolina's most important newspaper. He held that position through many tough times until he was named the first dean of the University of South Carolina School of Journalism in 1923. Although he had actively sought the position, the relatively sedentary life of an academic began to wear on him after a life in the rough and tumble of newspaper work. When the job of editor of the *News and Courier* became open in 1927, it was no surprise to anyone that W. W. Ball was offered and accepted the post. He would remain editor of the *News and Courier* until his final illness.

Ball only hardened in his reactionary opinions in Charleston. He was an ardent opponent of Prohibition, the New Deal, universal suffrage, and civil rights. These editorials were often reprinted in Northern newspapers. Ball also published a number of pamphlets, including *A Boy's Recollection of the Red Shirt Campaign of 1876 in South Carolina* (1911), *A View of the State* (1913), *An Episode in South Carolina Politics* (1915), and *Essays in Reaction* (1923).

His most important work and the only real book he published in his lifetime was *The State That Forgot: South Carolina's Surrender to Democracy* (1932). There he gave vent to his most extreme antidemocratic, white supremacist views. He maintained that South Carolina had been going downhill since adoption of the constitution of 1868, and he saw no hope of recovery. He was a man who believed in government by the aristocracy. He never wavered in his conviction that South Carolina's government was doomed to failure after the property requirement was removed from suffrage and after the governor, presidential electors, and U.S. senators were directly elected by the people instead of by the General Assembly.

Ball became as much a fixture in Charleston as the Battery. He delighted in infuriating his enemies and in making new enemies of the right sort. He was nevertheless always an extremely popular man about Charleston, well known for his priceless supply of anecdotes and his courtly Southern manners.

After Ball's death, one of his protégés, Anthony Harrigan, edited a collection of his writings, *The Editor and the Republic* (1954). John D. Stark has written a magnificent biography of Ball, *Damned Upcountryman: William Watts Ball* (1968).

Rufus Calvin Barkley (1829–1898)

Engineer and Entrepreneur   MAP LOCATION: SOUTHWEST 2

Rufus Barkley used his native mechanical ability and steady ambition to become one of Charleston's great entrepreneurs of the postbellum period. He was born in Fairfield County, South Carolina, and raised in and around Winnsboro, where he received his early education in the public schools. He apprenticed himself at a factory in Baltimore and there learned the trades of machinist and boilermaker. At the end of his apprenticeship he learned that men of his training were needed in his home state for the operation of the railroad. He returned to South Carolina and ran one of the early engines for the South Carolina Railroad for several years. At the outbreak of the Civil War, he became an engineer on the blockade runner *Nashville* until the vessel was captured and Barkley was imprisoned at Fort Lafayette, New York.

At the end of the war, Barkley was a founder of Cameron & Barkley, a builder of machinery. Through ups, downs, and the changes of time, Cameron & Barkley has remained one of Charleston's (and the Southeast's) most vital businesses, diversifying over time as a distributor. The Barkley family bought out the Camerons in the nineteenth century, and only in the late 1970s did Barkley's great-grandson sell the family-owned business to its employees.

Towards the end of his life, Barkley turned to public service. He served for a number of years as alderman for Ward Eight and afterward for three terms in the South Carolina House, where he achieved remarkable influence in a short time. The *News and Courier* noted at his death that as head of an informal group of former upcountry members known as the "Scatterword Alliance" he had often managed to carry his point in "even the most bitter of anti-Charleston legislatures."

JOHN BENNETT (1865–1956)

Renaissance Man   MAP LOCATION: NORTHEAST 3

John Bennett came to Charleston as a renowned writer and stayed to serve as godfather of what became the Charleston Renaissance. Born in Chillicothe, Ohio, shortly after the end of the Civil War, he enjoyed taunting his Southern friends with tales of Northern superiority, though in fact he had a good deal of Virginian gentry in his ancestry. By the time he arrived in Charleston in the late 1890s, he had already published his best-known work, *Master Skylark,* first serially in *St. Nicholas Magazine* (1896–1897) and then in book form. The story of a boy in Shakespeare's time, the novel became an enduring popular favorite; a month before Bennett's death, a national magazine listed it among the one hundred best children's books of all time.

Visiting Charleston in the winter of 1898, allegedly for his health, Bennett quickly improved upon a correspondence with Susan Smythe, daughter of Augustine T. and Louisa (McCord) Smythe, that had begun four years earlier after they met at a summer resort when Bennett was twenty-nine and Miss Smythe was sixteen. Bennett became enamored of the city and the fair maiden, whom he married in 1902. Both loves grew and stayed with him to the grave.

Bennett developed a consuming passion for the legend, lore, and history of his adopted home. In 1906 he published *The Treasure of Peyre Gaillard,* which is both a fine mystery and a quiet inside joke at the expense of Lowcountry history and historians. His novella *Madame Margot* (1921) is the story of a black Lowcountry conjurer who, Faust-like, traded her soul so that her daughter might become white and a proper member of Southern society. *Madame Margot* was quite scandalous for its time. In 1928, he consolidated many of his children's tales into the book *The Pigtail of Ah Lee Ben Loo,* which achieved enormous commercial success.

Bennett's masterwork was *The Doctor to the Dead: Grotesque Legends and Folktales of Old Charleston* (1946). In it, he distilled half a lifetime of tales, legends, and ghost stories about the underworld of Charleston's African-American culture into one very strange, frightening work. There is nothing quite like it in American literature.

John Bennett's importance to Charleston's culture cannot be overemphasized. He was an accomplished silhouettist, one of the founders of the Charleston Etchers' Club, and most important, a founder of the Poetry Society of South Carolina. He was the mentor and champion of the Charleston Literary Renaissance and of its principal writers. Among his many protégés were DuBose Heyward, Hervey Allen, Josephine Pinckney, Alexander Sprunt III, Beatrice Witte Ravenel, Beatrice St. Julien Ravenel, Ned Jennings, Elizabeth O'Neill Verner, and Elizabeth Verner Hamilton. He was forever encouraging and generous to young writers, often to the detriment of his literary productivity. His best friend and constant correspondent was Yates Snowden. Their letters have been published as *Two Scholarly Friends: Yates Snowden–John Bennett Correspondence, 1902–1932,* edited by Mary Crow Anderson (1993). Harlan Greene's *Mr. Skylark: John Bennett and the Charleston Renaissance* (2001) is an excellent biography.

John Bennett, *The House of the Doctor to the Dead*, etching, ca. 1925. Courtesy of Harlan Greene

SAMUEL MURRAY BENNETT, JR. (1896–1973)

Actor   MAP LOCATION: SOUTHWEST 3

A native Charlestonian, Murray Bennett became a successful actor on the Broadway stage. After serving with the Navy in 1919, he began studying at the American Academy for Dramatic Arts in New York. His first Broadway role was in *The Green Goddess* with George Arliss in 1921. He had a string of successful appearances capped by thirteen months in the first Broadway run of Tennessee Williams's *Cat on a Hot Tin Roof.*

After his retirement from the stage, Bennett devoted much of his time to poetry. His *Invisible Pursuit* was published in 1961 with a laudatory introduction by Archibald Rutledge.

THOMAS BENNETT, JR. (1781–1863)

Governor of South Carolina   MAP LOCATION: SOUTHEAST 1

Thomas Bennett, Jr., was born with a respected name, a handsome face, a fortune, and the high regard of the community. He added to these burdens his charm, artistic talent, discerning intellect, and wide circle of friends. His tragic flaw as a politician was his sense of fairness and compassion and an abiding respect for the meaning of the U.S. Constitution. It was a cruel fate that made Gov. Thomas Bennett one of the central characters of the Denmark Vesey insurrection. His governance during that period effectively ended a rapidly rising political trajectory and left him with a personally tragic situation which no doubt haunted a sensitive man like him for the rest of his life.

Thomas Bennett, Jr., was the son of a successful lumber and rice mill owner. Early on his father made Thomas a partner in the business, and Thomas, Jr., proved worthy of his father's confidence in every way. Young Bennett was a magnificent architect, as two of his surviving buildings demonstrate. The lone remaining wall of Bennett's Rice Mill at the foot of Society Street is still considered one of the finest examples of nineteenth-century American industrial architecture extant. The home Bennett built for himself on what was then a remote spit of land he named Bennettsville is today considered one of the finest surviving nineteenth-century homes in a city that has much to boast about in regard to nineteenth-century domestic architecture.

Bennett was well read and extremely respected in his home city. He was elected to the South Carolina House from 1804 to 1805 and again from 1808 to 1817. During this time he was elected intendant (mayor) of the city of Charleston from 1812 to 1813 as well. He was no back-bencher in the South Carolina House, as he was elected speaker from 1814 to 1817. He was elected to the South Carolina Senate in a special election in 1819 and served in that body until he was elected governor of South Carolina in 1820 as a Democrat-Republican. Bennett's administration was relatively uneventful until the Denmark Vesey insurrection.

The facts of the Vesey insurrection (or attempted insurrection) were never quite clear in 1822 and remain murky now. While some historians have suggested that the rebellion was entirely a fabrication of slaveholders determined to use its ruthless suppression to instill obedience, the scholarly consensus is that there was indeed a plot led by Denmark Vesey, a former slave who had won enough money in a local lottery to purchase his freedom. Vesey and his fellow conspirators evidently planned for slaves in the city and surrounding rural areas to kill their masters on the morning of Sunday, July 14, 1822, fight their way to the docks, and sail to freedom in Haiti. The plot catered to all the worst fears of whites who lived in a sea of slaves.

When a frightened domestic first betrayed the plot to authorities, it seemed incredible. Gov. Bennett, in particular, could hardly believe it. Among those named as Vesey's inner circle were several of Gov. Bennett's bondsmen. Rolla Bennett, identified as one of Vesey's top lieutentants, was the governor's most trusted servant, the man to whom he entrusted the safety and lives of his wife and children when he went to Columbia on government business. Gov. Bennett reluctantly ordered the arrest of the slaves in his household.

The city intendant, James Hamilton, Jr., acted swiftly to quash the rebellion and relieve the widespread panic among whites. With the backing of state attorney general Robert Hayne, city authorities quickly constituted a court that held trials in secret at the city workhouse. Gov. Bennett hired one of the leading lawyers in town, James Axson, to defend his property. But Rolla Bennett boldly confirmed the allegations on the witness stand. Looking directly at his stunned master, he acknowledged that it had been his responsibility to see to the murder of Gov. Bennett, though he indicated that he had expected a fellow conspirator to take care of the deed. Rolla was among the thirty-five African Americans, including Vesey, hanged for participation in the planned insurrection; another thirty-seven were exiled from the state. One of the most significant events to take place in Charleston during the forty years before the Civil War, the Vesey incident led to a wide range of measures designed to strengthen the security of whites.

Gov. Bennett, meanwhile, continued to dig himself into a deeper political hole after the executions. Whites dismissed as naive his expressions of confidence in African Americans' loyalty. He also drew criticism for sharing with his brother-in-law, U.S. Supreme Court Justice William Johnson, a concern about the lack of due process accorded the alleged conspirators. In a letter to Thomas Jefferson, Johnson lamented that "this last summer has furnished but too much cause for shame and anguish. I have lived to see what I never believed it possible I should see—courts held with closed doors, and men dying by scores who had never seen the faces nor heard the voices of their accusers." Gov. Bennett made a similar point in a message to the legislature proposing reform of the judicial procedures for handling similar cases, but the legislature tabled his message and declined to have it printed. Attacked from all quarters as soft on a satanic conspiracy virtually hatched in his household, Gov. Bennett found his political career at a practical end. He served another term in the South Carolina Senate from 1837 to 1839, but he never regained the high place he had reached before the Vesey insurrection.

Bennett maintained his commitment to charitable endeavors. He was most interested in the fate of the Charleston Orphan House and demonstrated the depth of his feeling by adopting a young German orphan, Christopher Gustavus Memminger, into his own home. Memminger grew up to be secretary of the treasury of the Confederacy.

Bennett's son **Washington Jefferson Bennett** (1808–1874) took over his father's business and achieved great success himself. When Robert E. Lee made a tour of the South at the end of his life, he stayed with W. J. Bennett for three days. Bennett's greatest efforts were on behalf of the public schools of Charleston and the Charleston Orphan House, for which he supervised the construction of a new building in 1853–1855 to replace the Orphan House built by his grandfather in the 1790s. Like his father, W. J. Bennett adopted an orphan, Andrew Buist Murray, who became one of the leading citizens of Charleston. Murray also became Bennett's son-in-law. They are buried in the same plot, just across the causeway from W. J. Bennett's father.

OLIVER JAMES BOND (1865–1933)

President of the Citadel   MAP LOCATION: SOUTHWEST 4

With the possible exception of Gen. Charles Summerall, no man has had as much impact on the history of the Citadel as Col. O. J. Bond. Under his leadership, the Citadel was transformed academically and moved from the Marion Square facility to its present location. Col. Bond was associated with the Citadel for over fifty of his sixty-eight years. In addition, he was a novelist, poet, and historian.

Bond was born in Marion, South Carolina, and educated in the public schools of Marion and Chester. He entered the Citadel in the fall of 1882 as a member of the first class to matriculate since the closing of the school at the end of the Civil War. After graduating with the class of 1886 he became assistant professor of mathematics. He would remain connected to the Citadel continuously until the end of his life.

In 1908 Col. Bond was made superintendent of the Citadel, a title changed to president in 1921. Col. Bond remained president until 1931, when he became dean upon the election of his hand-picked successor, Gen. Charles P. Summerall. Largely through the efforts of Col. Bond, the Citadel campus was moved in 1922 from Marion Square to the spacious campus it occupies today on the banks of the Ashley River. The administration building of the Citadel was named Bond Hall in 1933 in honor of his half-century of service to the institution.

In addition to his work as a teacher and administrator, Col. Bond had a literary turn of mind. He published the novel *Amzi* (1904) while he was still a professor of mathematics. After his death, his collected poems were published as *Magnolia Gardens and Other Verse* (1936). *The Story of the Citadel,* a history of the institution to which he had devoted so much of his life, was published the same year.

WILLIAM HIRAM BRAWLEY (1841–1916)

Legislator and Jurist   MAP LOCATION: SOUTHWEST 5

The career of William H. Brawley demonstrated the experiences, connections, and decisions that often led to political and judicial power in the nineteenth century, or the twenty-first. Born in Chester, South Carolina, he was educated in local schools and at South Carolina College. He enlisted in the 6th South Carolina Volunteers and saw action from Fort Sumter until he lost his left arm at the Battle of Seven Pines in May 1862. During his recuperation, he operated his family farm before running the blockade to England in April 1864. He then studied law in Europe for a year.

Brawley returned home in November 1865 and was admitted to the bar in the following year. He served as solicitor of the Sixth Circuit from 1868 until 1874, when he moved to Charleston. There he was associated with two of the leading lights of the local bar, W. D. Porter (who was his father-in-law) and later Joseph Barnwell. Brawley served in the South Carolina General Assembly from 1882 to 1890. He was the chairman of the Judiciary Committee in the S.C. House of Representatives and was considered one of the leaders of that body when he was elected to the U.S. Congress in 1890.

Brawley went against the sentiments of his fellow Southerners in Congress on the silver question. He was the only Southern congressman to vote against the Bland Silver Bill, and he similarly broke ranks on the repeal of the Sherman Silver Purchase Act. In recognition of Brawley's talents and proadministration views, President Cleveland appointed him in 1894 to the position on the United States District Court that had become vacant upon the elevation of Judge Charles Simonton to the U.S. Court of Appeals for the Fourth Circuit. Judge Brawley was a highly respected, conservative jurist. He remained on the bench until his retirement in 1911.

ARTHUR LEROY BRISTOL (1886–1942)

Naval Officer   MAP LOCATION: SOUTHEAST 3

Arthur L. Bristol was a pioneer in naval aviation and the third active-duty admiral to die in World War II. He was born in Charleston and graduated from the High School of Charleston. He attended the College of Charleston for one year before he received an appointment to the United States Naval Academy. He graduated from Annapolis in 1906 and was commissioned an ensign.

Bristol saw duty all around the world for the Navy. After serving in World War I, he taught at the Naval War College in the early 1920s and was then attached to the American embassy in Brazil. In 1928 he became a naval aviator and took command of the aircraft

Stereograph of Magnolia Cemetery in the 1870s by Kilburn Brothers, a New Hampshire photography firm. Courtesy of the South Caroliniana Library, University of South Carolina

squadrons of the Asiatic Fleet. He was naval attaché to the American embassy in London in 1934 until he took command of the *U.S.S. Ranger,* the first ship specifically designed to be an aircraft carrier. He was commander of the naval air station at San Diego from 1936 to 1939. He assumed command of the aircraft scouting force in the Atlantic in 1940 and soon became commander of the support force escorting convoys across the Atlantic. He continued in that post until he suffered a fatal heart attack.

ALEXANDER HENRY BROWN (1809–1879)

Lawyer   MAP LOCATION: SOUTHEAST 4

Alexander H. "Sandy" Brown rose up from a relatively impoverished youth to become one of the great admiralty lawyers of his day. Born in Charleston, he was largely self-educated and in his youth sailed "before the mast" on merchant ships between Charleston and Europe. These experiences were later to prove extremely valuable in his legal career. His first law partner was Stephen Elliott, later bishop of Georgia. He then practiced with W. D. Porter until the beginning of the Civil War. Brown also planted. He owned Hillsborough Plantation on the Ashley River and is listed as owning fifty-three slaves in the census of 1860.

Brown served a term as sheriff of Charleston District before the Civil War and was a delegate from St. Andrew's Parish to the convention that passed the Ordinance of Secession. Brown was a signer of the document. He served as colonel of a regiment of reserve forces during the Civil War and as provost marshal of the city under Gen. John C. Pemberton. Mary Chesnut mentions in her diary that Sandy Brown stabbed William Izard Bull in a brawl in 1862. After Reconstruction, Gov. Hampton appointed Brown one of two trial judges for the county. He retained his judgeship until his death.

CHARLES PINCKNEY BROWN (1825–1864)

Signer of the Ordinance of Secession   MAP LOCATION: SOUTHEAST 5

Charles Pinckney Brown was born in Charleston, the son of Charles Tennent Brown and Sarah Eliza (Smith) Brown. He attended the Cotes School, but he was unable to attend college because of financial reverses in his family. Brown was a delegate to the secession convention from St. James' Goose Creek and signed the Ordinance of Secession. He enlisted in the Confederate Army in 1862 and was killed at Drewry's Bluff, Virginia, while serving as a sharpshooter in Company A, Twenty-Seventh Regiment of the South Carolina Infantry. He was buried in Petersburg, Virginia, but his remains were moved to the plot of Dr. E. B. Joye in Magnolia Cemetery on July 12, 1868. He lies today in an unmarked grave.

HENRY BROWN (1828–1907)

Developer of the Bell Buoy   MAP LOCATION: NORTHWEST 1

Henry Brown was an immigrant who served his adopted country in two wars and made sea travel much safer by his invention of a vastly improved bell buoy. Born in Drobak, Norway, Brown sailed at the age of sixteen for New York, where he obtained a smattering of education before he returned to the sea. He was a volunteer in the U.S. Army in the Mexican War and the U.S. Navy in the Civil War. He served under Farragut and Porter and commanded a ship by the end of the war.

After the Civil War, Capt. Brown became commander of the *Alanthus,* a Lighthouse Department buoy tender stationed in Charleston. While commanding the *Alanthus,* he suffered an extraordinary embarrassment that led to his invention. His superior officer Admiral Blenheim was on board and anxious to get back to Charleston when a dense fog settled over the harbor in very calm seas. Under these conditions, the old "bell and can" type of bell buoy, which was merely a bell hung on a metal float, would not ring. In fact, it took a good amount of agitation on the sea to force the clapper to ring the bell at all. Despite his knowledge of the area, Capt. Brown was forced to anchor, wait for a lifting of the fog, and face the ire of Admiral Blenheim. When the fog finally lifted, the bell buoy marker Capt. Brown had been looking for was found to be only a few feet from where the *Alanthus* was anchored.

Capt. Brown determined to make a bell buoy that would ring in relatively calm seas. To that end, he devised a closed bell with a heavy ball bearing rolling about on a radially grooved metal disk. His invention was such an improvement that it was almost immediately adopted in ports around the world. It remained the standard bell buoy until fairly recently. Capt. Brown was much beloved in the community not only for his ingenuity but for his courtly good manners and cheerful humor. As he grew older, the government granted him a sinecure as "buoy master" that he held until his death.

George Dwight Bryan (1845–1918)

Mayor of Charleston   MAP LOCATION: SOUTHEAST 6

George Dwight Bryan bore the burden of personifying the aristocratic Broad Street Ring in late-nineteenth-century Charleston politics. The son of U.S. District Court Judge George S. Bryan, he entered the U.S. Naval Academy in Annapolis but resigned in March 1861 to return home. He was appointed a midshipman in the Confederate States Navy and rose to the rank of captain before he was captured off Brazil. He was imprisoned in Fort Warren in Boston until the close of the war.

Bryan took up the study of law and was admitted to the bar in 1867. He became corporation counsel of the city of Charleston, a position he retained until he was picked by the local elite to succeed Mayors William Ashmead Courtenay and Christopher S. Gadsden. A racially integrated local party inspired by Henry George's tax theories, the United Labor Party, put up a candidate, but Bryan was elected mayor by an overwhelming majority in 1887.

Mayor Bryan's term was relatively uneventful, but long-simmering resentments and the continuing economic stagnation of the city proved to be his undoing. The rise of the populist Benjamin R. Tillman was also disastrous for Bryan's political fortunes. Tillman used hatred of the Charleston aristocrats to build class envy throughout the state. His old friend from the legislature, John Ficken, successfully used these resentments and the growing working-class and ethnic population of Charleston's upper wards to defeat Mayor Bryan in his bid for reelection.

Bryan returned to the practice of law until his appointment by President Cleveland to the post of collector of customs for the port of Charleston, which he held from 1894 to 1898.

William Izard Bull (1813–1894)

Planter and Politician   MAP LOCATION: SOUTHWEST 6

William Izard Bull was the grandson of South Carolina's first U.S. senator, Ralph Izard, and the descendant of the William Bulls who had been the only native-born governors and lieutenant governors under British rule. He attended the College of Charleston until ill health forced him to withdraw in his junior year.

Bull represented St. Andrew's Parish in the South Carolina House of Representatives from 1836 to 1847 and served in the South Carolina Senate from 1848 to 1864. While in the Senate, he was chairman of the commissioners of the new state capitol. During the Civil War, Bull served as a colonel on Gen. Beauregard's staff, with Gen. Johnson Hagood on James Island, and under numerous commands in North Carolina until the end of the war. Mary Boykin Chesnut reported in a tantalizing entry of her Civil War journal that Bull was stabbed in a brawl by his fellow St. Andrew's Parish planter Alexander H. Brown.

The most dramatic incident associated with Bull was his burning of his ancestral plantation, Ashley Hall on the Ashley River. His son William Izard Bull, Jr., recounts the story:

> When the City was evacuated he had not sufficient notice to save any of his personal property from Ashley Hall, so, rather than that the enemy should plunder it, he set fire with his own hands to the home of his ancestor, that venerable mansion which was so dear to his heart (and honor be to him for it). The Yankees, when they saw what he had done, posted a notice in the neighborhood: $5000 for Bull's head.

Bull lost the plantation after the war and died in genteel poverty in Charleston in 1894. He was originally buried in the family cemetery at Ashley Hall Plantation, but the entire cemetery was moved to Magnolia in 1904.

Among those moved was **William Bull** (1748–1799), who was a member of the Colonial Commons House of Assembly, His Majesty's Council, and the Provincial Congress of 1774–1776.

Andrew William Burnet (1811–1896)

Signer of the Ordinance of Secession   MAP LOCATION: SOUTHWEST 7

Andrew William Burnet was a wealthy planter and lawyer who became a signer of the Ordinance of Secession. He was a nephew of Chancellor Henry William DeSaussure and a kinsman of the "Firebrand of Secession," Robert Barnwell Rhett, through his marriage to Ann Burgh Smith. Burnet was an 1830 graduate of South Carolina College and a student at Yale Law School. Though he was admitted to the South Carolina bar in 1839, Burnet never actively pursued a career in law. Instead he concentrated his energies on his plantation Woodbourne on the Combahee River. He also served in the state House of Representatives from 1850 to 1854. By the time of the Civil War, he owned 176 slaves.

Daisy Breaux Calhoun (1864–1949)

Socialite   MAP LOCATION: SOUTHWEST 8

Daisy Breaux Calhoun lived the life that today's international socialites only aspire to. She married three wealthy men, each of whom built her the biggest, grandest house in town. She buried each one before she married the next. She was a successful businesswoman, author, and collector of celebrity friends. She knew six presidents. Her autobiography drops the names of more European nobility per paragraph than are on any full page of *Burke's Peerage*. Yet for all her vivacity, beauty, and famous charm, she finally sleeps alone in an oddly configured plot a hundred yards from her first husband. She was one of Charleston's great "characters."

Her father was an Irish immigrant and Pennsylvania Roman Catholic politician, Capt. Cornelius McCarthy-Moore Donovan O'Donovan, who fell in love with Julia Josephine

Villa Margherita in the early 1890s, shortly after its completion.
Courtesy of the Charleston Museum

Marr, daughter of a Scottish Presbyterian minister. The twin gifts of blarney and an eye for the main chance ran through the life of their daughter, whom they called Daisy rather than using her full name of Margaret Rose Anthony Julia Josephine Catherine Cornelia Donovan O'Donovan. Her natural father died on a trip to Texas, and her mother eventually remarried a wealthy Louisiana lawyer-planter, Gustave A. Breaux, who promptly gave Daisy his surname.

Educated in the school of Madame Carnaty and at the Convent of the Visitation in Georgetown, D.C., Daisy made her debut at Avery Island, Louisiana. Soon afterward she met young Andrew Simonds, Jr., whose family was among the wealthiest in postwar Charleston. They owned the First National Bank of South Carolina among other business interests and were accepted within the highest echelons of Charleston society despite the fact that they were originally from Abbeville. The two were soon married at St. Louis Cathedral in New Orleans. Daisy described the ceremony with typical modesty as "one of the most artistic affairs of the time, indeed it would have been so at any time, with a cortège picturesque in the extreme and ten lovely girls as attendants, all of whom have since taken conspicuous places in the social world."

After an extensive European honeymoon the couple settled in Charleston, where Andrew Simonds, Sr., had provided a large nineteenth-century mansion at the corner of Church and South Battery as a wedding present for the happy couple. Daisy Breaux Simonds was never one to leave well enough alone. As she later explained in her autobiography, "the house itself did not please me. It was not in keeping with the more stately homes on the Battery. According to Charleston fashion there were no communicating rooms, each room being a single unit and opening onto a hall." What's a girl to do? After Andrew Simonds, Jr., became president of the First National Bank, his wife had the old house torn down and a new one built. She reported that "the erection of this new home, later known as the Villa Margherita, gave me the joy of artistic expression. It was built from my original plans, inspired by early studies in France, and drawn to scale by an architect."

Mr. and Mrs. Simonds entertained lavishly at the Villa Margherita. Mrs. Simonds took Charleston by storm, redecorating the St. Cecilia Ball and putting on artistic performances in her palatial home. She and her husband soon had a daughter, Margaret. All was not perfect happiness in paradise, however. In the words of Mrs. Simonds, her husband "was not domestic, and 'home life' was not in his line." After Andrew's fondness for the good life led to a nervous breakdown, Daisy Breaux Simonds eventually had him placed in an asylum near Washington. She visited him only occasionally in the few years he had left, for "the doctors assured me that my presence only increased his nervousness and filled him with a restless desire to leave the sanitarium with me." Meanwhile, she continued with an active social life, planning parties and entertainments and even writing plays.

When Andrew finally died in 1905, Daisy found that he had left her only a life estate in his properties. She found further that her lavish lifestyle had somewhat depleted Andrew's fortune. In an effort to reverse the flow of money, she opened the Villa Margherita as an inn, and it became one of the most fashionable hostelries in the South. Sinclair Lewis wrote part of *Main Street* there. Thomas Edison, Henry Ford, Charles MacArthur, Ben Hecht, and other celebrities of the time stayed there.

For the irrepressible Daisy, tragedy was but a stepping stone, and romance was never far away. She caught the eye of a wealthy New Jersey banker, Barker Gummeré, president of the Trenton Trust and Savings Bank. They were soon married, and she was off on another exotic honeymoon to Europe and North Africa. On their return, the Gummerés moved into his home in Trenton. Daisy's artistic urges started up again, and she designed and built "Rosedale House" on fifty-seven acres partly in and partly outside Princeton, with an extensive view of the valley. She once again threw herself into society and found time to write four plays: *The Favorite, The Tale of Two Shawls, Dream of Fair Women,* and *The Marriageable Mother.* While living in Princeton, she renewed her old friendship with former President Cleveland and made the acquaintance of the president of Princeton University, Woodrow Wilson. But tragedy revisited Daisy's life, as Barker Gummeré died in 1914, a scant two years after building Rosedale House and seven years to the day after he made the acquaintance of the future Mrs. Gummeré.

After Mr. Gummeré's death, Daisy founded a school to insure the proper education of her daughter Margaret. The School of Four Seasons met part of the year in Rosedale House, and part of the year in Daisy's second home in Charleston at 53 East Bay Street. Once Margaret had completed her course Daisy closed the school and moved to Washington, D.C., where Margaret could make a proper debut. Of course the move meant she needed to design a new house. First called "the Widow's Mite" and then "the Might," the townhouse on the former site of the offices of the Spanish Embassy was small but "so in conformity with the fine mansions around it as to lose nothing in dignity." Daisy considered it "one of the choicest bits of Washington architecture." Construction costs on "the Widow's Mite" proved to be exorbitant, and Mrs. Gummeré was forced to consult a prominent Washington lawyer, Clarence Crittenden Calhoun, to get the contractor to adjust his price. Capt. Calhoun won her suit and her hand. They were married in 1918.

A new husband of course meant a new house. Before long Mrs. Calhoun was busy with the design and building of what she planned as her most lasting monument, Rossdhu Castle, named after the ancestral Scottish home of the Calhouns. Rossdhu was set on a hundred acres just outside Washington in Chevy Chase, Maryland. The Calhouns had plans for it to become a national Scottish museum after their deaths and even acquired the sword of the Pretender Charles Stuart, "Bonnie Prince Charlie," from Lord Garioch.

Daisy was also once again busy in international society. She founded and headed the Woman's National Foundation, intended to be the focus of "dynamic woman power," which Mrs. Calhoun felt was just then ascendant. Unfortunately, the Foundation foundered due to petty jealousies engendered by some perfectly horrible women who somehow got on the board. Mrs. Calhoun compared her plight to that of President Harding, who was "too anxious to serve his friends and in the end some of his friends most illy served him." She also compared herself to Joan of Arc and the embattled founders of various patriotic societies and other national and political movements. "Indeed," she reflected, "the pioneers in anything usually met a sad fate." Undaunted, she folded the Woman's National Foundation and started the Woman's Universal Alliance. One of the principal goals of the new organization was the erection of a Mothers' Memorial in memory of the good work that mothers do everywhere. Mrs. Calhoun exclaimed that "next to religion itself, motherhood has been the greatest influence on the lives of humanity."

In 1930, Daisy published her memoirs, the aptly named *Autobiography of a Chameleon*, under the names Daisy Breaux and Mrs. Cornelia Donovan O'Donovan Calhoun. There is nothing quite like this work. In it she chronicles her quite amazing life in a style at once condescending and unintentionally hilarious. Her encounters with Presidents Cleveland, Theodore Roosevelt, Taft, Wilson, Harding, and Coolidge, not to mention Czar Nicholas II, Marie of Rumania, and the Prince of Wales, make for truly fascinating reading.

At the time she wrote her autobiography, all was right in Daisy's life. Plans were proceeding apace for the Mothers' Memorial and the National Scottish Museum; Rossdhu was a showplace; and her daughter was happily married to the commodore of the Carolina Yacht Club in Charleston. Then Clarence Crittenden Calhoun died, and everything began to fall apart. Daisy's frenetic spending and entertaining finally drained the three fortunes she inherited. She sold Rosedale and lost control of the Villa Margherita. Rossdhu Castle fell into a ruin and was eventually lost to heavy mortgages. Even Bonnie Prince Charlie's sword had to be sold to satisfy creditors. Needless to say, the Woman's Universal Alliance collapsed, as did the plans for the Mothers' Memorial. She published another book, *Favorite Recipes of a Famous Hostess* (1945), but it did little to revive her fortunes.

Daisy Breaux Calhoun lived her last few years in Charleston with her daughter. When she died, there was no room for her in the Simonds family plot. She was buried a few hundred feet away, alone at last.

James Butler Campbell (1808–1883)

Lawyer and Legislator   MAP LOCATION: SOUTHEAST 7

James B. Campbell was one of Charleston's most brilliant lawyers and a leader of the Unionist movement. At his death, he was despised by white South Carolinians because of his active support of black suffrage and solicitation of black votes. He was a most contrary man.

Campbell was born in Oxford, Massachusetts. He traced his ancestry to a Campbell supporter of the Stuarts who fled to this country in the early eighteenth century. He attended Brown from 1822 to 1826, but he did not receive a degree until that university bestowed upon him an honorary Doctor of Laws in 1870. He moved in 1826 to Edisto Island, where he taught the children of wealthy plantation owners. At the same time, he began to read law under that most distinguished son of Edisto, Hugh Swinton Legaré. He moved to Charleston in 1831 and was admitted to the bar in 1832. Probably through his connections with Legaré, he became involved in Unionist politics. He was a delegate to the Unionist convention in Columbia in 1832 and served as confidential agent and Washington correspondent of the Union committee of South Carolina. At the invitation of President Andrew Jackson, he resided at the White House and became an intimate of the president and also of a boyhood acquaintance, Daniel Webster, with whom he maintained an active correspondence until Webster's death.

On his return to Charleston, Campbell established a reputation as a leading light in one of the most brilliant bars in the country's history. Around 1837, he solidified his position among the Charleston elite by marrying Anna Margaret Bennett, daughter of former governor Thomas Bennett, Jr., and Mary Lightbourn (Stone) Bennett. He eventually became a member of virtually every exclusive group in Charleston: the Hibernian Society, the South Carolina Society, the St. Andrew's Society, and the New England Society. He was president of the latter organization for the last fourteen years of his life.

Campbell was elected to the South Carolina House in 1850 and reelected through 1855. He fought for Unionist ideals in the House and proposed the Convention Bill, which brought the question of secession to an unsuccessful vote of the people in the early 1850s. He was suggested as a candidate for the secession convention of 1860, but he declined candidacy. Campbell was devoted to the South, but more devoted to the Union. He felt that secession and civil war were acts of state suicide and made his views known. When South Carolina was irrevocably in the conflict, Campbell ran for and was elected to the South Carolina House in 1862. There he became the leader of the anti–Jefferson Davis faction. He remained in the South Carolina House until 1866, when he was elected to the U.S. Senate by the provisional government of South Carolina. He was denied his seat even though he had courageously remained a Unionist throughout the Civil War, albeit a Unionist in the legislature of a state in rebellion.

Campbell was a great good friend of Wade Hampton and backed his election in the "Redemption" of 1876. Both men were supporters of black suffrage, though Campbell carried his support further than Hampton. Campbell was elected to the South Carolina

Senate in 1877 and served through the end of his term. He sought black support in the election of 1878 and fought Charleston Democratic rules designed to keep blacks from the polls. As a result he lost the Democratic nomination for his South Carolina Senate seat. He ran as an independent and was named the head of the ticket by the Republican Party, anathema to white South Carolinians. He blamed his loss in the general election on ballot box fraud (probably correctly). Forever after, he was estranged from the Democratic Party and the white electorate. Campbell ran for the U.S. Congress in 1882 as the candidate of the Republican and Greenback-Labor Parties and lost. His alliance with post-Reconstruction Republicans caused South Carolina whites to label him a traitor to his race.

In 1882 Campbell was made a South Carolina commissioner to Washington. He died there a year later of congestion of the lungs. It is said that among his last words were: "I wish to be buried in Charleston, because the people of that city speak so kindly of the dead."

Campbell's daughter, **Celia Campbell,** (1842–1887), was known as "Charleston's Florence Nightingale." Educated in Charleston, she traveled in Europe for several years to expand her horizons. Upon her return she established the House of Rest for the care of indigent women and children. She recognized that women thrown upon their own resources often had no other choice but prostitution, and she saved hundreds of women and their children from that fate. Tireless in the solicitation of support from her friends, she collapsed in 1887 while receiving a donation for charitable institutions damaged by the earthquake and died twelve days later. A window in Grace Episcopal Church was dedicated to her memory. She and her father lie together around the curve from her grandfather, Gov. Thomas Bennett, Jr.

WILLIAM CARRINGTON (1812–1901)

Silversmith and Jeweler   MAP LOCATION: SOUTHWEST 9

Why is some of Louis Comfort Tiffany's finest work found in Charleston? When Tiffany was working and prolific, Charleston was poor, hardly the high-end market for a Yankee jeweler whose name became synonymous with extravagance. The answer was in Tiffany's shared apprenticeship with William Carrington.

Carrington was a native of Connecticut and met Tiffany when they apprenticed for a Mr. Benedict in New York. Carrington moved to Charleston as early as 1830 and possibly worked for James Eyland, a Charleston jeweler. By 1835 he had formed W. Carrington & Co., which survived in various permutations into the early years of the twentieth century. He assured his place in Charleston society in 1845 when he married Harriet E. Simonds. The new Mrs. Carrington was a relation of John C. Calhoun and of Charleston's banking Simonds family.

There is a tremendous amount of silver bearing Carrington's hallmark. Although some of it is thought to have been crafted by Carrington, much was probably manufactured in the North and stamped here for sale in the jewelry shop of Carrington and his later partner Stephen Thomas.

Carrington's friendship with Tiffany produced tangible results for Charleston. Among the acknowledged Tiffany works in Charleston are the windows in St. Michael's Church, those in the F. S. Rodgers mansion on Wentworth Street (Atlantic Coast Life), and the tombstones of Charles O. Witte and Thomas R. Waring in Magnolia Cemetery.

Carrington's son, Waring P. Carrington, married Martha, the daughter of George W. Williams. For their wedding present they received from Mr. Williams a check for $75,000, which went towards the construction of 2 Meeting Street. From the Carringtons the lucky couple got the gift of a two-year grand tour of Europe along with eleven Tiffany windows that still grace the present-day Two Meeting Street Inn.

EDWARD BURNHAM CHAMBERLAIN (1895–1986)

Naturalist   MAP LOCATION: SOUTHWEST 10

E. Burnham Chamberlain was one of Charleston's early important environmentalists and naturalists. He was born in Charleston and educated at the High School of Charleston, the College of Charleston, and the National Museum in Washington, D.C. He also studied under Arthur T. Wayne of the Charleston Museum, one of the great ornithologists of his day.

After serving with the Charleston Light Dragoons in the Mexican border campaign of 1916 and as an infantry officer in World War I, Chamberlain joined the staff of the Charleston Museum in 1924 and eventually became the curator of vertebrate zoology. He had a wide variety of scientific interests and was a noted authority in the study of mammals, reptiles, amphibians, and especially birds. In 1949, Mr. Chamberlain collaborated with his lifelong friend Alexander Sprunt on *South Carolina Bird Life,* which remains the definitive work on ornithology in this state.

Mr. Chamberlain lobbied tirelessly for the passage of hunting laws and the establishment of wildlife preserves. He was active in the Audubon Society and served as coordinator and statistician for the annual bird counts.

LANGDON CHEVES, SR. (1776–1857)

Statesman   MAP LOCATION: SOUTHEAST 8

Langdon Cheves was a towering intellect who rose from obscurity on the frontier of South Carolina to become a public figure second only to Calhoun in importance in the state. Daniel Elliott Huger called him the most self-willed man he ever knew. That will carried Cheves to the pinnacle of success in several fields.

Cheves was born in the stockade in the Bulltown section of Long Canes, in which his family had sought refuge during the Cherokee uprising of 1776. His father, Alexander Chivas (Cheves), was a Scottish immigrant to South Carolina in the 1760s who had married Mary Langdon, daughter of a Scotch-Irish farmer-physician from Virginia. Alexander Cheves remained loyal to the British during most of the Revolutionary War. His shifting allegiance cost him his fortune, as American forces burned his house and stores and the British government refused to compensate him for his losses due to his unsteady loyalty. To rebuild his fortune the widowed Cheves moved to Charleston, where he opened a mercantile establishment on King Street. Young Langdon, who had received a rudimentary education in the Ninety-Six District, benefited from a trifle more schooling in Charleston before he was put to work in a store at the age of twelve.

The diligent young Cheves earned the plaudits of his employer and attracted the notice of others in Charleston. He read constantly and eventually studied law in the office of William Marshall. Admitted to the bar in 1797, Cheves set up an office with Robert Turnbull near the corner of Meeting Street and St. Michael's Alley. He struggled in his first few years of practice, but his assiduous preparation and native intelligence soon earned him the largest clientele in Charleston. In 1801 he wrote to his partner at the time, Joseph Peace, "I have no holiday, not even the Sabbath, never one day in which to rest from my labors." Such complaints were akin to crocodile tears, for Cheves was becoming one of the wealthiest and most respected lawyers in town. That respect was manifested in his election to the Charleston City Council in 1802 and to the South Carolina House of Representatives later the same year. The strain of overwork and the pressing obligations of his law practice caused Cheves to decline to offer for reelection in 1804.

Cheves was so burdened with his work that his health began to suffer, and he was advised to travel in the North. On his return home, he chaperoned sixteen-year-old Mary Elizabeth Dulles on her return from her boarding school in Philadelphia to her home in Charleston. Mary was the daughter of Joseph Dulles, a prominent Irish immigrant merchant. (His descendants included John Foster and Allen Dulles.) They were married at her parents' Church Street home on May 6, 1806. Mary was the great and only love of Cheves's long life.

The rejuvenated Cheves ran successfully for the state House of Representatives in 1806. He played prominent roles in the reapportionment of state legislative districts and in public protests against the attack of the British ship *Leopard* on the *U.S.S. Chesapeake*. In his 1808 reelection he once again led the ticket. He was appointed chairman of the powerful Ways and Means Committee but resigned when his fellow legislators elected him attorney general of the state in December 1808.

Cheves's major political achievements followed his election to the U.S. House of Representatives in 1810. War fever was running high when he took his seat in the new Congress. Cheves moved into a boardinghouse whose lodgers became known as the War Hawks: Cheves, John C. Calhoun, and William Lowndes of South Carolina; Henry Clay of Kentucky; and Felix Grundy of Tennessee. They were often joined in their meals and deliberations by Madison's secretary of state, James Monroe. Appointed to the Ways and Means Committee and the important Select Committee on Naval Affairs, Cheves used his positions to fight for greater appropriations for the U.S. Navy and militate for war. He continued to concentrate on military funding and international trade restrictions after the United States declared war in June 1812. Reelected against a Federalist challenge, Cheves's solicitude for his merchant constituents distanced him from the embargo policy of the party, but the situation worked out well for him when Clay resigned as House speaker to join the delegation that would negotiate a peace. The minority New England Federalists backed Cheves for the leadership position, and their support together with that of

Charles Fraser, *Langdon Cheves* (1818).
Courtesy of Henry Middleton Cheves
and the Gibbes Museum of Art /
Carolina Art Association

Southern Democrat-Republicans was enough to give Cheves a comfortable margin of victory. As speaker, Cheves oversaw the lifting of the embargo and continued to focus on financial issues that had occupied him since the beginning of the war. President Madison offered to appoint him secretary of the treasury in 1814, but Cheves stood by his expressed intention to return to Charleston at the end of the term.

But Cheves was not destined for a sedentary life. When he finished leading the extraordinary House session that met in the General Post Office and Patent Office after the burning of Washington, he was elected to the board of the Charleston branch of the second Bank of the United States (BUS). He soon became chairman of that board. One week later he was elected one of the associate judges of South Carolina. In this position he acted as both a civil and a criminal judge and, sitting with the other judges *en banc,* as one of the members of the state Supreme Court. During his tenure as judge he wrote an important opinion establishing judicial review of South Carolina legislative enactments.

Cheves would have been content on the bench for the remainder of his life, but national events once again conspired to take him away from his native state. With the BUS in danger of bankruptcy, its governing board turned to Cheves in 1819 to make things right. A little later, President Monroe offered him a vacant seat on the U.S. Supreme Court. Cheves would have much preferred the court position, but he had already committed himself to the bank and so declined the nomination.

As president of the BUS, Cheves immediately instituted cost-cutting measures. He cut his own salary and limited the power of Southern banks to issue notes. These measures were extremely unpopular across the country, but they worked. Those who had been most critical of his early actions at the bank praised his statesman-like conduct and extraordinary efficiency. He continued to serve as president of the BUS until he retired in January 1823 and was replaced by Nicholas Biddle.

Cheves next served as commissioner for the United States in a proceeding to settle property disputes arising from the War of 1812 with Great Britain. Most of the disputed claims arose from the British seizure of slaves from the South. Cheves was relentless in his efforts and largely successful, but he resigned as commissioner a month before a final settlement was reached because of temporary ill health and probable disgust at the slow progress of the negotiations.

By that time, Cheves had established himself as a gentleman farmer in Lancaster, Pennsylvania, where one of his most ardent admirers was his congressman, the young James Buchanan. After a few years of quiet retirement in Lancaster, Cheves became homesick and at long last returned to South Carolina in 1829. There he landed in the midst of the Nullification controversy. He tried to remain aloof from the dispute before ultimately coming down somewhat diffidently on the Unionist side, which ensured the permanence of his retirement from political office. For most of the 1830s he concentrated on building a fortune for his ever-growing family. He bought a great deal of valuable rice land along the Savannah River that he eventually consolidated as Delta Plantation. There he focused his razor-sharp mind on the minutiae of agriculture in the same way that had earlier brought him such extraordinary success in law, politics, and banking. He turned this same practical eye to farming cotton on lands near St. Matthews, South Carolina, inherited through his wife's family, which he rechristened Lang Syne Plantation.

Cheves's last important public service came in 1850, when he served as a delegate to the Nashville Convention called to test secessionist sentiment in the South. There Cheves argued vehemently against submission of the Southern cause to Yankee domination but also cautioned against single-state action, warning that only united Southern action could save the slave South.

Langdon Cheves did not live to see the war for southern independence or its consequences for the son and grandson who carried his name into battle. He spent his last years in the Columbia home of his devoted daughter Louisa Cheves McCord. He died on June 26, 1857. Even one of his occasional opponents, Benjamin F. Perry, acknowledged that "South Carolina never produced an abler, purer, or more unostentatious son."

Langdon Cheves, Jr. (1814–1863)

Father of the Confederate Air Force   MAP LOCATION: SOUTHEAST 8

Langdon Cheves, Jr., lived up to the brilliant heritage bequeathed him by his father and namesake. He had an incredibly rich and inventive mind that he put to good use for his state and the Confederacy. Unfortunately, his life was cut short under the most tragic of circumstances while he was commanding Battery Wagner, which he had sited, designed, and built.

Langdon Cheves, Jr., was born in 1814 in Philadelphia, where his family had refugeed because of the British capture of Washington during his father's tenure as speaker of the U.S. House of Representatives. He received his early education in Philadelphia and an appointment to West Point but was expelled for infractions of dress regulations. He graduated from South Carolina College in 1833 and, after reading law for a time, was admitted to the South Carolina bar in 1836. He was commissioned advocate general of the South Carolina Militia in 1836 and saw service in the Seminole War. In 1841 he moved to Savannah, where he successfully ran his father's plantations along the Savannah River (chiefly Delta Plantation). He inherited Delta Plantation at his father's death and was listed in the 1860 census as owning 289 slaves.

Cheves was widely read and an original thinker. Professor Joseph LeConte, a scholar of natural history at South Carolina College before the Civil War, would later describe a vigorous debate over Robert Chambers's *Vestiges of the Natural History of Creation* (1844) in which Cheves anticipated Darwinian arguments for the theory of evolution in opposition to LeConte's support for Agassiz's view of creation according to a preordained plan.

As the conflict between the South and the North grew, Cheves cast his lot with the secessionists. He was a delegate to the secession convention from St. Peter's Parish and a signer of the Ordinance of Secession. He then threw his engineering genius and worldly goods into the cause of the Confederacy. In 1862 he designed and built the first war balloon for the Confederacy at Chatham Armory in Savannah. Legend has it that he gathered the silk for the balloon's skin from the dresses of patriotic Confederate women. In fact, he merely purchased from the firm of E. L. Kerrison (forerunner of Kerrison's Department Store) a large amount of silk that had been meant for ladies' dresses. In any case, the balloon was used to great advantage by the Confederates at the Seven Days' Battle in Virginia before it was captured by the Yankees. For his actions, Cheves is called the "Father of the Confederate Air Force."

Cheves also assisted Gen. Thomas F. Drayton in repairing and building forts around Savannah and Hilton Head, and he was placed in charge of the design and building of the fortifications on Morris Island in Charleston harbor. From this effort came the forts at Cummings Point and Battery Wagner. Cheves was killed in the fort he had designed and built, Battery Wagner. Robert Gilchrist described Cheves's death on July 10, 1863, in his *Confederate Defence of Morris Island* (1884):

> Captain Cheves, son of the late Judge Cheves, to whose engineering skill and untiring zeal Fort Wagner was to be thenceforth famous in history, was sitting in his quarters overwhelmed with grief at the tidings just brought to him of the death of his nephew, Capt. Chas. T. Haskell. But as the sound of approaching battle grew louder, he roused himself to action, and stepping across the threshold of his door, towards one of the magazines, he was stricken to death by a fragment of the first shell hurled at Fort Wagner.

Killed on the same day, Capt. Cheves and Capt. Haskell were both buried in the Cheves family plot at Magnolia Cemetery.

The Cogswell Family

Printers and Citizens   MAP LOCATION: SOUTHWEST 11

Cogswell is one of Charleston's famous names and for good reason. The members of the Cogswell family have distinguished themselves in almost every variety of endeavor in this city for the last couple of hundred years.

Most people know the Cogswell name as the last one in Walker, Evans and Cogswell, for decades the premier printing firm in Charleston. The predecessor firm of Evans and Cogswell printed the Ordinance of Secession as well as Confederate money, bonds, and government documents. A longstanding local joke has been that the modern WECCO kept the plates for the Confederate money locked in an accessible vault . . . just in case.

Benjamin F. Evans (1831–1873) married Julia Eliza Cogswell, the sister of his partner Harvey Cogswell (1831–1922). Their names are the Evans and Cogswell of the eventual firm name. Benjamin Evans was born in Georgetown and formed the company of Evans and Cogswell with his brother-in-law in the late 1850s after an earlier venture with Joseph Walker as Walker, Evans and Company. During the Civil War, Evans ran the blockade to London, where he was able to procure enough equipment and trained lithographers to continue running the printing factory. Its function was vital to the Confederacy. The company was moved from Charleston to Columbia late in the war and was largely destroyed by Sherman's troops. Much of Charleston's treasure had been transferred to Columbia by Charlestonians rightfully fearing the vengeful wrath and terrorism of Sherman's March. Military imperatives saved Charleston, but much of her heart was destroyed with her upstate storehouse.

Benjamin Evans died young. His brother-in-law, Harvey Cogswell, combined again with the Walker family to form Walker, Evans and Cogswell. Though C. Irvine Walker headed the company in the late nineteenth century, for most of the twentieth century the firm had a William H. Cogswell I, II, or III as president.

Julius Elisha Cogswell (1865–1956) distinguished himself outside the family business. He was a member of the Washington Light Infantry for seventy years and Register of Mesne Conveyance (recorder of deeds) for sixty-three years. The job of register is an elective one, renewable every four years. Thus, "Uncle Julius" (as he was universally known) was, if not the longest, certainly one of the longest holders of an elective office in human history.

Julius Chesnee Cogswell (1896–1947) was a great war hero. A graduate of the Citadel class of 1917, he was a Marine and eventually rose to the rank of captain. During World War I, he was regularly cited for conspicuous gallantry and was awarded many medals: the Distinguished Service Cross, the Navy Cross, Silver Star, Bronze Star, French Croix de Guerre, Presidential Unit Citation, Purple Heart with three stars, and Victory Medal with two stars. He died almost thirty years after the war of the lingering effects of his wounds.

William H. Cogswell III (1922–1994) brought Walker, Evans and Cogswell into the modern era. It was his decision that led to the transfer of the company from its traditional home near the corner of Broad and East Bay to North Charleston. The extraordinarily valuable real estate left behind became luxury condominiums. The machinery of the company went to the Smithsonian.

James Conner (1829–1883)

Lawyer and Confederate General   MAP LOCATION: SOUTHWEST 12

James Conner served his state as U.S. attorney, Confederate States attorney, brigadier general in the Confederate States Army, acting major general, and attorney general of South Carolina. He was born in Charleston, the son of Bank of Charleston president Henry Workman Conner and Julia (Courtney) Conner. He graduated from South Carolina College in 1849 in the same class as Charles Simonton. He read law under Charleston's most distinguished lawyer, James Louis Petigru, and was admitted to the bar in 1852. Conner wrote three important law books in the 1850s: *A Digest of the Cases Decided in the Law Court of Appeals of the State of South Carolina, 1835–1854* (1855); *A Digest of Equity Reports of the State of South Carolina, from the Revolution to December 1856* (with C. H. Simonton); and *The History of a Suit at Law* (1857).

Conner rapidly attained a large practice and reputation as an outstanding lawyer. In 1856, he was named U.S. attorney for South Carolina. In this position, he prosecuted several cases that brought him tremendous attention. The case of the *Echo* and the proceedings against William C. Corrie for his command of the *Wanderer* both involved violations of the federal law barring participation in the Atlantic slave trade. Another politically charged case was the prosecution of Judge T. J. Mackey for his part in William Walker's filibustering expedition. In December 1860, Conner again came into the national spotlight when he and U.S. District Judge Andrew Gordon Magrath resigned upon learning of Abraham Lincoln's election as president. Conner became part of a delegation of three men sent to urge the state legislature to call a convention to consider secession from the Union, and he served as the lawyer for the convention that was called. He did not sign the Ordinance of Secession, but he had much to do with its drafting and his father did sign the document.

Conner immediately began to devote himself to the military preparedness of the Confederacy. He was named Confederate States attorney for South Carolina, but only held the title as he prepared the Washington Light Infantry (of which he was captain) for battle. He was promoted to major in July 1861 after distinguished service at Manassas. He declined to be promoted over a superior officer in Hampton's Legion and was transferred to the Twenty-Second North Carolina Regiment, where he was promoted to colonel of the cavalry. He was severely wounded in the leg at the Battle of Mechanicsville on June 26, 1862. He refused a promotion to brigadier general because he felt it was improper to hold that rank while he was recuperating.

After his return, Conner was commissioned brigadier general in June 1864. He commanded McGowan's and Lane's Brigades and eventually attained the rank of acting major general. Over the course of the war he served in the battles of Fort Sumter, Manassas, Yorktown, New Stone Point, West Point, Seven Pines, Mechanicsville, Chancellorsville, Riddle's Shop, Darby's Farm, Fussell's Mill, Petersburg, Rearn's Station, Winchester, and

Cedar Creek. At the last of these engagements, he suffered a second wound to his left leg that necessitated its amputation and ended Conner's service in the Confederate Army.

After the war, Conner resumed the practice of law, primarily as a railroad attorney. He went into practice with W. D. Porter from 1868 to 1874. During that time, he was general counsel for the South Carolina Railroad and the Greenville and Columbia Railroad Company.

Conner played a key role in the "Redemption" of South Carolina in 1876. A leader in opposing the "straight out" strategy, he felt that the Democratic party should gradually absorb its Republican opposition in the contests for state legislature. Elected chairman of the South Carolina Democratic Committee, Gen. Conner again opposed the nomination of a full slate of state officers at a second convention of the party. When he lost on this question, Conner accepted the party nomination for attorney general. Thereafter he was the primary aide to Wade Hampton. Such was the secrecy of the deliberations at this time that Gen. Conner and his followers met in a brothel to make their strategy for the election of 1876. During the campaign Conner was in command of the white rifle clubs in the state.

After the Democrats were securely in power, Conner resigned as attorney general in December 1877 because of poor health. He died in Richmond at the home of his father-in-law in 1883.

William C. Corrie (1818–1870)

Slave Smuggler   MAP LOCATION: SOUTHWEST 13

Captain Corrie, as contemporaries called him, earned his title in the most sensational illegal slave importation scheme in American history. He began his business career in his home city of Charleston and was a successful salesman at a dry-goods store on King Street. Around 1840 he moved to Washington, D.C., where he soon mastered the trade in political influence. One member of Congress reported that as a lobbyist Corrie enjoyed "more power than all the South Carolina delegation put together." Handsome and socially polished, Corrie was a fixture on the Washington social circuit, though he was given to boasting of the exact amount he had paid for each vote he bought.

In 1858 Corrie purchased the *Wanderer,* one of the fastest schooners of its day, from Louisiana plantation owner and New York sportsman Col. John Johnson. The *Wanderer* was capable of reaching twenty knots, but it was too large for the racing regulations of the New York Yacht Club, which may have explained Johnson's willingness to sell the new vessel to Corrie. Then, too, Johnson may have known that Corrie was part of a group led by the wealthy Georgia rice planter Charles Lamar that intended to flout the federal prohibition of the Atlantic slave trade. Corrie supervised the refitting of the ship for this purpose and served as commander on the voyage that left Charleston on July 3, 1858. Arriving at the Congo River in mid-September, Corrie memorably explored the African coast and made business calls in the uniform of the New York Yacht Club, to which he had been elected on Johnson's nomination after buying the *Wanderer.* He left with about 490 slaves packed closely on the decks, of which almost one-sixth died on the return voyage. After landing at Jekyll Island, Georgia, the 409 survivors were quickly sold to buyers in the Savannah River basin.

This venture violated federal laws that defined the Atlantic slave trade as piracy and provided not only for confiscation of the ship but also for execution of participants in the scheme. Lamar's local influence and the political cross-currents in Georgia eventually frustrated federal prosecution efforts in Savannah. But Corrie recognized that Charleston was an even safer political haven in this situation, and he bolted home as soon as authorities began to act. His calculations were correct, as federal district court judge A. G. Magrath refused to permit prosecutors to take Corrie to Savannah for trial. After several procedural rounds, Magrath ended the case against Corrie by ruling that the purchase of slaves in Africa for resale in the United States did not constitute piracy even though Congress had said that it did.

William Ashmead Courtenay (1831–1908)

Mayor of Charleston   MAP LOCATION: SOUTHWEST 14

William Ashmead Courtenay was the first true representative of Charleston's old elite elected mayor after the Civil War. He inherited a city government plagued with enormous debts. During his two terms, Charleston experienced two of her worst natural disasters, the cyclone of 1885 and the earthquake of 1886.

William A. Courtenay was born in Charleston of Irish stock. The little formal education he received was between the ages of twelve and fifteen at the academy of Dr. J. C. Faber. He then began to work. In 1850 he and his brother, Samuel Gilman Courtenay, started a book shop and publishing company with which W. A. Courtenay was associated until 1860. He took advantage of the resources of the bookstore to educate himself. Through the bookstore he also became acquainted with Charleston's antebellum literary lights, W. G. Simms, Henry Timrod, W. J. Grayson, and others.

In the fall of 1860 Courtenay became business manager for R. B. Rhett, Jr.'s fiery pro-secession newspaper, the Charleston *Mercury*. While working for the *Mercury*, he did an extensive survey of the damage caused to Charleston by the fire of 1861, which destroyed nearly a third of the city. In late 1861, he joined the Confederate Army, serving until the end of the war and eventually achieving the rank of captain.

After the war, Capt. Courtenay like most in the South was destitute. He took advantage of the destroyed railroads by moving to Newberry, South Carolina, and running a carriage cargo service from Newberry to Orangeburg until rail service was restored in 1866. He returned to Charleston in 1866 and started a shipping and commission business that together with his management of steamship lines to Baltimore, Philadelphia, and New York made Courtenay a small fortune.

Courtenay was active during Reconstruction in the Washington Light Infantry, which was reformed as a "rifle club," a paramilitary organization used to help force "redemption" of the state in 1876. He served as president of the Charleston Chamber of Commerce in the 1870s and became one of the leaders of the "Broad Street Ring" that was to rule Charleston intermittently up to the present day.

William Ashmead Courtenay (standing) in the early 1870s as commander of the Washington Light Infantry Rifle Club. Seated are two antebellum captains of the militia company, Magnolia Cemetery co-founder William D. Porter and Lewis M. Hatch (holding cap). Carte-de-visite by S. T. Souder, Charleston. Courtesy of the South Caroliniana Library, University of South Carolina

He challenged the upcountry-born mayor William W. Sale in the election of 1879 and won, promising to put the city on a more prudent business footing. During his first term the South Carolina Railway failed and the city of Charleston, which held six million dollars worth of the railway's bonds, was extremely stretched financially. Courtenay led the city in penny-pinching measures that greatly reduced services to the poor but which kept the city out of bankruptcy. He did, however, find the money for extensive paving in granite Belgium block of Charleston's chronically poor streets. He added the flagstone sidewalks still in evidence around the city. He saw to the creation of Colonial Lake. He renovated the interior of City Hall, removing the classical Adam interiors designed by Gabriel Manigault and replacing them with the high Victorian interior that remains today. He also professionalized the Charleston Fire Department.

Courtenay's greatest challenges came with the natural disasters of 1885 and 1886. In August 1885 a hurricane with winds up to 125 miles per hour hit Charleston, causing extensive damage to almost all Charleston buildings. About one quarter of Charleston houses lost their roofs. The city was just beginning to recover from the cyclone of 1885 when the earthquake of 1886 jolted the city on the evening of August 31, 1886. This shock was the most severe felt by an American urban center until the San Francisco earthquake of 1906. A city whose buildings were valued at twenty-four million sustained almost six million dollars in damage. Panic swept Charleston as aftershocks continued for days. People of all classes slept in parks, afraid to enter their quake-damaged dwellings. Courtenay was returning from a visit to England when the earthquake struck and didn't arrive in the city until September 7. Immediately upon his return, he took charge of the recovery efforts and was largely successful in calming fears and seeing to the reconstruction of Charleston's built environment.

Courtenay's tireless work was not without cost. The *News and Courier* opposed his penurious fiscal policies. His relationship with the Broad Street Ring that had brought him to power became strained. In early 1887 he announced his resignation as mayor due to "nervous strain" and "overwork." Mayor Pro Tem Christopher S. Gadsden served out the remaining months of Courtenay's term. Courtenay bought the *News and Courier*'s rival, the Charleston *World,* and used it to gain some measure of revenge on the Broad Street Ring by backing the successful mayoral candidacy of John Ficken against the incumbent George Dwight Bryan in 1891.

Several years after his resignation, Courtenay organized the Courtenay Manufacturing Company and established a cotton mill at Newry in Oconee County along the line of William Gregg's operation in Graniteville. He named the town of Newry for his ancestral home in Ireland. After his retirement from management of the cotton mill, Courtenay retired to Columbia, where he lived with his daughter for the remainder of his life.

In 1895 Courtenay lobbied successfully for the creation of a South Carolina Historical Commission, of which he was made chairman. He was always interested in South Carolina history and literature. It was largely through his efforts that an edition of Henry Timrod's complete poems was published. Profits from the sale of the book financed the monument to Timrod in Washington Park.

The bronze bust of Courtenay atop his monument in Magnolia Cemetery is by the noted Virginia sculptor Edward Valentine.

GEORGE IRVING CUNNINGHAM (1835–1902)

Mayor of Charleston　　　　　　　　　　　　　MAP LOCATION: SOUTHWEST 15

George I. Cunningham was twice elected mayor of Charleston as a Republican during Reconstruction and also served honorably in several other positions of public trust.

Cunningham was born in Monroe County, Tennessee, in 1835. His father was a minister of the Church of Christ and died when Cunningham was only twelve. When Cunningham was seventeen, he came to Charleston and was soon employed in the cattle and butchery business. He made a success of himself and began buying up real estate, eventually owning most of Daniel Island.

When Union troops took over city government, Gen. R. S. Canby appointed Cunningham one of six white aldermen to serve on City Council with seven African Americans. Cunningham ran for mayor in 1873 as a Republican and defeated the incumbent Democrat, John Wagener. The *News and Courier* predictably cried fraud and sought an investigation. But Mayor Cunningham surprised many with his coalition-building style of government. In addition, his prudent and flexible fiscal management actually led to a reduction in the city's indebtedness. Such was the success of his administration that Mayor Cunningham again defeated John Wagener in 1875. The *News and Courier* reversed field and praised Cunningham's management of the city.

In addition to his duties as mayor, Cunningham served as chairman of the Board of Commissioners of Charleston County from 1872 to1879. After his last election to that position, Cunningham never ran for public office again. He was, however, the recipient of a number of plum patronage jobs. He was appointed U.S. marshal in 1889 and held the office until 1894. In 1897 he was appointed postmaster of Charleston, a position he held until his death in 1902. He died respected for his honesty and integrity, even by his political enemies. He was the first white Charlestonian to show that the races could work together for the common good.

WILLIAM COOMBS DANA (1810–1880)

Clergyman   MAP LOCATION: NORTHWEST 2

William Coombs Dana gave the initial blessing at the opening of Magnolia Cemetery. A leading figure in the distinguished clerical fraternity of antebellum Charleston, Dana was descended from Huguenots who emigrated to England and then to Massachusetts, where author Richard Henry Dana, Jr., and other members of the family would gain distinction. His father was the influential New England clergyman and sometime Dartmouth College president Daniel Dana. William C. Dana's education was obtained at the most eminent schools of the day: Phillips Andover Academy, Princeton, and the Columbia Theological Seminary. He came to Charleston in late 1835 and assumed the pastorate of Central Presbyterian Church in February 1836. He spent the remainder of his life at the church, which he built into one of the strongest and most intellectual of the antebellum era.

The Reverend Doctor Dana published several works in addition to his sermons and other religious writings. He translated Fénélon's *On the Education of Daughters,* and he wrote an account of his travels in Europe and a biography of his father.

WILMOT GIBBES DeSAUSSURE (1822–1886)

Community Pillar   MAP LOCATION: SOUTHEAST 9

Wilmot Gibbes DeSaussure was considered in his day one of the great men of Charleston. He was a force in the Charleston bar, a noted historian, an accomplished legislator, a brigadier general of the South Carolina Volunteers in the Civil War, and a leader in numerous civic and fraternal organizations.

Wilmot Gibbes DeSaussure was the son of Henry A. DeSaussure and the grandson of Chancellor Henry William DeSaussure, first director of the U.S. Mint. DeSaussure was educated in Charleston schools and graduated from South Carolina College in 1840. Soon afterward he was admitted to the bar and became a law partner of his father. In his practice he rapidly began to fill the shoes of his distinguished forebears. He was also elected to the South Carolina House of Representatives from 1848 to 1850 and again from 1854 to 1864. In 1857 he helped prepare a revision of the rules of the House and Senate.

DeSaussure was a longtime member of the Fourth Brigade, South Carolina Militia. After Major Anderson abandoned Fort Moultrie for the relative safety of Fort Sumter, DeSaussure was placed in command of Moultrie. He was a colonel in the artillery at Cummings Point at the time of the firing on Fort Sumter on April 12, 1861. Upon the resignation of Gen. James Simons II, DeSaussure acceded to the post of brigadier general of the Fourth Brigade. Gen. DeSaussure was in command of the reserve forces guarding Charleston for the duration of the war. After the resignation of Gen. Gist, DeSaussure became adjutant general of South Carolina.

Gen. DeSaussure was the head of an extraordinary number of fraternal and social organizations. In 1875, he was elected grand master of Masons of South Carolina. He was invested with the Thirty-third Degree of the Ancient and Accepted Scottish Rite of Freemasonry in 1874 and was one of two active members of the supreme council at Washington for the state of South Carolina. In addition, he was grand master of Odd Fellows of South Carolina and grand sire of the Independent Order of Odd Fellows of the United States. At the time of his death, Gen. DeSaussure was president of the Society of the Cincinnati, the St. Andrew's Society, the Charleston Library Society, and the Huguenot Society. He had founded the last of these organizations with Daniel Ravenel and was its first president.

DeSaussure wrote widely on topics of interest in all of his associations. He died in Ocala, Florida, where he had gone to recuperate from his final illness. He is buried in an unmarked grave.

James W. Duckett (1911–1991)

President of the Citadel   MAP LOCATION: SOUTHWEST 16

James W. Duckett was the second president of the Citadel with an earned Ph.D. He was born in Greenwood, South Carolina, and was a 1932 honor graduate of the Citadel. He received a master's degree from the University of Georgia in 1934 and a doctorate from the University of North Carolina in 1941. He was a member of the Citadel faculty from 1934 to 1941, when he went on active duty with the Army Chemical Corps. He earned the Legion of Merit and the Army Commendation Medal and rose to the rank of lieutenant colonel. After World War II, he rose to the rank of full colonel in the Army Reserve. He was also a member of the South Carolina Militia, in which he was promoted to major general in 1966.

Gen. Duckett served his alma mater in a number of positions: professor, chairman of the Education Department, registrar, dean of admissions, dean of the college, and vice-president. In 1970 Gen. Duckett became president of the Citadel, a position he held until his retirement in 1974.

Benjamin Faneuil Dunkin (1792–1874)

Jurist   MAP LOCATION: SOUTHEAST 10

Benjamin Faneuil Dunkin was a Yankee who came to South Carolina and became an important force in law and politics for the remainder of his long life. Dunkin was born in Philadelphia, the son of Edward Dunkin, an Irish immigrant, and Susan (Bethune) Dunkin, who was of an old Boston family. He graduated from Harvard College in 1811 in the same class as Alfred Huger, Edward Everett, and Samuel Gilman. Soon afterward, he removed to Charleston to teach in the school of his cousin Benjamin Faneuil Hunt. His teaching career was interrupted by the War of 1812, in which he served as an adjutant in the Third Regiment of the South Carolina Militia.

At the conclusion of his service, Dunkin read law in the office of William Drayton. He entered the bar in 1814 and soon established a large and lucrative practice. In 1820, he was elected to represent St. Philip's and St. Michael's (Charleston) in the state House of Representatives. He increased his influence by his service and was elected speaker of the House in 1828. He retired from the House in 1836.

Dunkin began his judicial career in 1837 when he was elected chancellor of South Carolina to succeed the retiring Henry William DeSaussure. Extraordinarily respected in that position, Dunkin remained chancellor until 1865, when he was elected chief justice of the Supreme Court. He retained that post until he was deposed by the Reconstruction government in 1868.

Dunkin was always involved in affairs, governmental and otherwise. He was a founder of the New England Society of Charleston and a long-time member of the boards of both the Medical College of South Carolina and the South Carolina College. He was elected a representative to the secession convention in 1860 from Prince George Winyah Parish and was a signer of the Ordinance of Secession.

Dunkin made a fortune before the war through legal fees, success as a planter, and an advantageous marriage. At the outbreak of the Civil War, he owned 263 slaves as well as plantations on the Waccamaw and the Pee Dee and a mansion on Warren Street valued at $90,000. Samuel F. B. Morse and Charles Fraser both painted portraits of Dunkin and his wife. The Fraser miniatures are in the collection of the Gibbes Museum.

Anne Carson Strohecker Grimball Watt Elliott (1894–1980)

Educator   MAP LOCATION: SOUTHWEST 17

Anne Elliott was a gifted teacher who founded the Watt School and lived to see it merged with her son's school, Gaud, and Porter Military Academy to become Porter-Gaud School. She came from a family in which education was extremely important. She was born in

Charleston, the daughter of Henry and Anne (Carson) Strohecker. Her brother, Henry Strohecker, Jr., was to become principal of the High School of Charleston. She graduated from Memminger Normal School and took classes at the College of Charleston before beginning her career as a teacher at local public schools.

She was first married to Berkeley Grimball, but his early death in 1928 left her a young widow with a six-year-old son. She soon married Harvey Watt, a Canadian-born banker. With the Depression, Mr. Watt was out of work, and Mrs. Watt opened the Watt School in 1931 in their home at 170 Broad Street. The Watt School was originally for grades one through three but eventually expanded to include a fourth grade. The excellence of Mrs. Watt's instruction led to the growth of the Watt School in both size and reputation. After World War II, Mrs. Watt's son, Berkeley Grimball, bought the distinguished Gaud School from its founder, Henry Gaud, Sr., and Watt School became more and more a "feeder school" for Gaud.

In 1964, Porter Military Academy, Gaud, and Watt were merged as Porter-Gaud School and moved to a new combined campus on Albemarle Point. Mrs. Elliott (for by then Mr. Watt had died and his widow had married Exam A. Elliott) became first-grade teacher and director of primary grades until her retirement in 1967.

Today, Porter-Gaud School is considered one of the finest secondary schools in the country. A room in the Berkeley Grimball Fine Arts Center is named in memory of Mrs. Elliott.

William Elliott (1788–1863)

Planter and Author   MAP LOCATION: SOUTHWEST 18

William Elliott was an extremely wealthy plantation and slave owner, a politician, an agricultural experimenter and theorist, and the author of a South Carolina literary classic.

Elliott was born in Beaufort, the son of William Elliott and Phoebe (Waight) Elliott. He achieved great success at Harvard, as evidenced by his class rank (second) and early membership in Phi Beta Kappa. Although Elliott left college before graduation due to the death of his father and his own poor health, Harvard granted him a bachelor's degree in 1810 and a master's degree in 1815. By that time Elliott had been elected to the South Carolina House of Representatives, where he served from 1814 to 1815 and 1826 to 1829. He was elected to the South Carolina Senate from 1818 to 1821 and again in 1831. As a Unionist, Elliott was violently opposed to Nullification and thus at odds with most of his constituents. He resigned his seat and assured his political oblivion with the publication of a pamphlet, *Address to the People of St. Helena Parish* (1832), in which he attacked his constituents and their views.

After his retirement from politics, Elliott concentrated on the economic improvement of his area. By inheritance and marriage, he owned a tremendous amount of land and slaves. Among the plantations he owned were Myrtle Bank, Bee Hive, Hope, Ellis, Shell Point, The Grove, Bay Point, Middle Place, Newberry, and Oak Lawn. He also owned Farniente, his summer resort in Flat Rock, North Carolina, and a house in Beaufort. In 1860, Elliott owned over two hundred slaves.

Illustration from the 1859 edition of William Elliott's *Carolina Sports by Land and Water.*
Courtesy of the South Caroliniana Library, University of South Carolina

Elliott advocated crop diversification and increased industrialization. He served as president of the Beaufort Agricultural Society and vice-president of the South Carolina Agricultural Society. He was appointed by the governor as South Carolina representative to the Paris Exhibition of 1855, where he addressed the Imperial Agricultural Society of France. He published a number of articles under the name of Agricola that were collected in 1852 as *The Letters of Agricola.* He also wrote a five act-drama, *Fiesco,* published in 1850.

The work for which Elliott is best known is *Carolina Sports by Land and Water* (1846). Originally, the work was a series of articles published under the pseudonyms Piscator and Venator. The story of the catch of the devilfish has been widely anthologized, and the book has been in print sporadically since it was first published. The book was republished in 1994 with a new introduction by the eminent historian Theodore Rosengarten, who emphasizes the ambivalent feeling Elliott evinces towards slaves and slavery in his narrative. Elliott knew that this was the work for which he would be remembered. He wrote to his wife, "I think that if anything will live after me, it will be these 'Sports'. . . . at the worst they can only drop into oblivion, but should they acquire notoriety, it will be a sort of legacy of honor to my posterity who need not be ashamed of claiming descent from old 'Venator.'"

Elliott died in 1863 at the Mills House Hotel in Charleston and is buried in an unmarked grave near his daughter. His grandsons, the Gonzales brothers, founded *The State* newspaper in Columbia as an anti-Tillman organ. N. G. Gonzales, first editor of *The State,* was murdered by Ben Tillman's nephew, Lt. Gov. James Tillman, in front of the state capitol. Ambrose Elliott Gonzales was a well-known explicator of the Gullah language. William Elliott Gonzales was ambassador to Cuba under President Wilson.

JOHN EWAN (1786–1852)

Silversmith   MAP LOCATION: SOUTHEAST 11

Charleston was a city of enormous wealth at various periods of its existence. When Charlestonians were rich, they bought silver. During the second quarter of the nineteenth century John Ewan was able to prosper for a while and leave a large amount of Charleston silver for us to enjoy.

Ewan was born in New York and possibly spent time in Jamaica, where some of his silver has been found. He was in Charleston by 1823, for in that year Peter Mood, Jr., announced that he and Ewan were in business together as P. Mood & Co. By 1825 Ewan had his own shop at 203 King Street.

There is much of Ewan's work still extant. Because he advertised regularly that he was willing to remake old silver to the latest designs, there is some thought that his output and his willingness to melt down old Charleston pieces might account for the paucity of eighteenth-century Charleston silver.

His presumed son, **William H. Ewan** (d. 1860), is buried in the same plot. E. Milby Burton and Warren Ripley's *South Carolina Silversmiths* (revised edition, 1991) notes that he "must have been a most prolific worker, judging from the amount of silver still in existence that bears his mark."

Both Ewans were extraordinarily accomplished artisans. When their pieces come on the market today, they are quickly scooped up by collectors at high prices. A number of examples of their works are in the magnificent silver collection of the Charleston Museum.

JOHN FREDERICK FICKEN (1843–1925)

Tillmanite   MAP LOCATION: SOUTHWEST 19

John Ficken was the only Tillmanite to become mayor of Charleston. He was born in Charleston and educated at the College of Charleston. His education was interrupted by his service in the Confederate Army in Georgetown and Charleston. He was allowed by special dispensation to complete his education while performing garrison duty in Charleston, and he graduated from the College of Charleston in 1864. He later served as a clerk for the various commanders of the Department of South Carolina, Georgia, and Florida until the conclusion of the war.

Ficken prepared for a legal career by reading in the office of Col. John Phillips and taking a course in civil law at the University of Berlin in 1869. He received a master's degree from the College of Charleston in 1870, the same year in which he commenced the practice of law. In 1877 he was elected to the state House of Representatives, where he would remain for fourteen years. While in the legislature he became a good friend of Benjamin Ryan Tillman, later the leader of the populist farmers' movement that swept Tillman into office as governor of South Carolina in the Revolution of 1890.

Ficken was the beneficiary of his friend Tillman's attacks on the Bourbons who had ruled Charleston and South Carolina before the Civil War and after Reconstruction. Ficken took advantage of the class antagonisms caused by Tillman's fulminations to defeat incumbent mayor George D. Bryan narrowly and become mayor in 1891 at the head of a "Reform" ticket. But he had won a difficult assignment. Tillman sought to control the liquor trade in South Carolina by means of the dispensary system, under which bars and liquor dealers were outlawed and retail sale of alcohol was restricted to state-operated dispensaries. Charlestonians would have none of it, and illicit saloons known as "blind tigers" proliferated throughout the city. Mayor Ficken's vigorous attempt to suppress the illicit liquor trade led to his rapid decline in popularity and was one of the main reasons he did not offer for reelection in 1895.

Ficken was general counsel and a director of the South Carolina Interstate and West Indian Exposition held in Charleston in 1902. The Exposition was essentially a World's Fair and was championed by the more active of the commercial elite as a way to turn around the city's perennially languishing economy. Though over half a million visitors attended the Exposition (including Mark Twain and President Theodore Roosevelt), it had no real lasting effect on the economy of the city. The only building remaining from the event is the bandstand in Hampton Park, the site of the Exposition.

Ficken continued to serve his city and state on numerous educational and charitable boards and as an attorney until his death in 1925.

ROBERT McCORMICK FIGG, JR. (1901–1991)

Lawyer   MAP LOCATION: SOUTHWEST 20

Robert Figg was arguably the best attorney in the history of the South Carolina bar. Unfortunately, the case with which he is most associated was on the wrong side of history.

Figg was a graduate of Porter Military Academy, the College of Charleston, and the Columbia University School of Law. He was chairman of the Charleston Zoning Board from 1930 to 1932, when that board was establishing landmarks in preservation law. He served one term as a state legislator before his election as solicitor of the Ninth Judicial Circuit for three terms from 1935 to 1947. He wrote the legislation creating the State Ports Authority in 1942 and was one of its first general counsels. His leadership on this issue directly led to Charleston becoming one of the leading container-cargo ports on the east coast.

Figg's brush with history came in *Brown v. Board of Education* (1954), the Supreme Court case that led to the end of legal segregation in the United States. Representing the defendant school boards, Mr. Figg and his co-counsel lost the first round of the case, commonly known as *Brown v. Board I*. In the following year, the Supreme Court issued its decision in *Brown v. Board II* regarding the implementation of *Brown v. Board I*. Legal commentators have suggested that Figg's arguments to the Supreme Court led to the insertion of the phrase "with all deliberate speed" into the opinion of *Brown v. Board II*. With the insertion of that phrase, segregated school districts were long able to delay implementation of *Brown v. Board I*.

In 1959 Figg became dean of the University of South Carolina School of Law. In that position he was widely recognized as the leading figure in South Carolina law. He was a great teacher, practitioner, and example for the rest of the state bar. He served as dean until his retirement in 1970 and remained an active member of the bar until his final illness in 1991. His office was always open to young attorneys to discuss fine points of law or history, for he was acknowledged to be living history.

EDWARD FROST (1801–1868)

Judge and Railroad President   MAP LOCATION: SOUTHWEST 21

Edward Frost was one of the ablest legal minds of antebellum South Carolina. He was born in Charleston, the son of an Episcopal minister and scion of an old Huguenot lineage. He attended Yale College and read law for two years. He achieved almost immediate success as a lawyer and became U.S. attorney in 1832. He served in the South Carolina House until 1843, when he was elevated to "the law bench" (as opposed to the equity court) of South Carolina. Judge Frost was a man of substantial means and could have occupied that position for life with little damage to his finances, but a higher duty called.

The great hope of antebellum Charleston commercial interests was a rail link to the West, or what we now call the Midwest. Capitalists proposed several competing routes, all of which had strong exponents and advantages, mostly political. Judge Frost quit the lifetime sinecure of the bench in the 1850s to head up the Blue Ridge Railway, which he felt was the most logical route. His was an altruistic motive, but he lived in a fickle world. None of the routes were built before the Civil War, when they might have done some economic good. After the war and the destruction wrought by Sherman and his compatriots, the point was moot. Frost resigned the presidency of the uncompleted road at the end of the war and became a member of the state constitutional convention. He was one of two members of the convention to oppose the oppressive "black codes." Despite his tack against the popular will, he was universally esteemed for his good character. The Tiffany window behind the altar in St. Michael's Episcopal Church is dedicated to the memory of Judge Frost.

The memorial to his son **Edward Downes Frost** (1833–1863) is one of the most poignant in the cemetery. It recalls that he "lost his life . . . at Fort Sumter, while in arms for his country, by the explosion of a magazine followed by a conflagration, so that no trace of his remains was left to those who loved him."

SUSAN PRINGLE FROST (1873–1960)

Preservationist and Suffragist   MAP LOCATION: SOUTHWEST 22

Charleston is the most carefully preserved city in America due to the work of a small group of dedicated amateurs. Today, several universities offer degrees in historic preservation, but when it counted, people like Susan Pringle Frost wrote the rules. Miss Frost began her career as a secretary, became one of Charleston's first businesswomen, fought

Alice Ravenel Huger Smith, drawing for *Twenty Drawings of the Pringle House*,
conte crayon and pencil on paperboard, 1914. Courtesy of the Gibbes Museum
of Art / Carolina Art Association

for the vote for women, and emerged as the great voice of historic preservation in Charleston.

Susan Pringle Frost was born in what was then commonly called the Pringle House, also known as the Miles Brewton House, at 27 King Street in 1873. Except for a period from 1889–1919, she always lived in the house. It was one of the main forces in her life. She was educated in the schools of Charleston and at St. Mary's School in Raleigh, North Carolina. She settled into the traditional life of a Charleston spinster until her father's business failed. In an attempt to help her family survive financially, she took up secretarial work and eventually landed employment assisting Bradford Gilbert, designer of the South Carolina Interstate and West Indian Exposition, in 1901. From this position Miss Frost received not only invaluable experience and contacts in architectural history but also skills that would form the basis of her first career. In 1902 she won a competitive examination to become court stenographer to the U.S. District Court, a post she would hold until she entered the field of real estate full-time in 1918.

Long before she gave up her job as court stenographer, Miss Frost began to speculate in local real estate. In 1909 she started quietly buying old Charleston houses, inspired partly by the pluck she had observed in a recent visit to the Chicora Wood rice plantation maintained by her cousin Elizabeth Waties Allston Pringle. By 1912 she had bought several properties on Tradd Street. She focused next on St. Michael's alley before leaving her secretarial position and regaining possession of the Miles Brewton House, along with her sisters, in 1918. The DuPont family substantially aided that effort, as Susan Pringle Frost's sister was a friend and longtime employee of the wife of the corporation president.

Frost now turned her attention to what would become the great work of her life, the preservation of historic Charleston. She had already begun with the purchase of the Tradd Street houses, which she restored and sold (sometimes at great loss) to sympathetic owners. Thus began a pattern that would carry through for the rest of her life. In 1920 she purchased several threatened properties that eventually became known as Rainbow Row. In that same year she became horrified at the possible destruction of the Joseph Manigault House to make way for a filling station for Standard Oil. Along with her cousins Mr. and Mrs. Ernest Pringle, Miss Frost determined that the Manigault House would not be sacrificed for gasoline. She sounded her call to battle on April 12, 1921, sixty years to the day after the firing on Fort Sumter, publishing a proposal in the *News and Courier* for an organization dedicated to preserving the fine historic residences of Charleston. The Manigault House was ultimately saved, due to the incredible financial support and physical labor of the Pringles. The meeting at 20 South Battery proved to be the birth of the Society for the Preservation of Old Dwellings, eventually known as the Preservation Society. Miss Frost was elected the first president of the organization and served in that position until succeeded by Alston Deas in 1927.

For the rest of her life, Miss Frost was the primary proponent of the preservation of Charleston. It was largely due to her efforts that a Board of Architectural Review was established. She personally saved many structures through her strategic purchase of threatened buildings and their sale at less than her cost. In 1944 she wrote *Highlights of the Miles Brewton House.* She lived in the house for the rest of her life and operated it as an inn.

By 1914 Miss Frost was also working actively for women's suffrage. In that year she was elected first president of the Equal Suffrage League of Charleston. By 1917, she became tired of the conservative attitude adopted by the Equal Suffrage League and resigned to become a part of Alice Paul's National Woman's Party. Miss Frost served as South Carolina chairman of the National Woman's Party in 1923 and 1947.

Long after her death, "Miss Sue" is remembered as one of the earliest and most important of the nation's preservationists. It is largely due to her farsightedness and energy that Charleston today has a tremendous number of pre-Revolutionary and antebellum buildings intact. Frost recognized early on that the entirety of Charleston's architectural heritage was important. Ultimately, her strongest appeal was to the pocketbook. One of her most eloquent appeals pointed out that "as each one of these quaint structures is demolished, Charleston becomes a poorer city. We are making less of an appeal to the traveling public and losing the money which these tourists annually leave behind . . . . [I appeal] to the city at large who advertises the historic as an asset, and then destroys the very flavor of the past, thereby vividly recalling the killing of the goose that laid the golden egg."

Sidney R. Bland has written an excellent biography, *Preserving Charleston's Past, Shaping its Future: The Life and Times of Susan Pringle Frost* (1995).

JOHN H. L. FULLER (1835–1871)

Member of the Charge of the Light Brigade   MAP LOCATION: SOUTHEAST 12

> When can their glory fade?
> O the wild charge they made!
> All the world wonder'd.
> Honour the charge they made!
> Honour the Light Brigade,
> Noble six hundred!

One of the most enigmatic stones in Magnolia Cemetery is that of John H. L. Fuller, which states simply Mr. Fuller's death date and the fact that he was "the only member of the gallant 600 that charged at Balaclava, Russia, buried in America." Of the 673 men who made the famous cavalry attack, 278 were killed, wounded, or taken prisoner.

All that is known of Mr. Fuller is that he came here as an officer of the U.S. Revenue Department a few years before his death and that he was married in 1870 to a daughter of Gen. Gilliam of the U.S. Army. He died of yellow fever in Charleston in 1871.

CHRISTOPHER SCHULTZ GADSDEN (1834–1915)

Railroad Executive and Mayor of Charleston   MAP LOCATION: SOUTHWEST 23

Christopher Gadsden was an accomplished railroad surveyor who rose to a high management position. For a short time he was also mayor of Charleston. He was born in Summerville, great-grandson of the Revolutionary War patriot of the same name. He graduated from the South Carolina Military Academy (later the Citadel) in 1852.

He began his work career as a rodman for the New Orleans, Jackson, and Great Northern Railway. In that position he surveyed along the Ohio and Mississippi rivers and points west. He returned to South Carolina in 1854 and worked for both the Charleston and Savannah Railroad and later the Port Royal Railroad. He surveyed for the Port Royal Railroad through the beginning of the Civil War. He enlisted for service with the Confederacy, but was soon mustered out, as it was felt that his service in completing the railroad was more important to the cause of the Confederacy. He remained at his task until General Sherman made further work futile.

After the war Gadsden helped with the reconstruction of the Charleston and Savannah Railroad and was superintendent of the line for thirty-four years. After the line merged with the Atlantic Coast Line, he rose to the position of second vice-president of the consolidated road.

As he rose in his business career, Gadsden followed the tradition of his family in responding to the call of public service. He was a city alderman for twenty years. He was serving as mayor pro tem when Mayor William A. Courtenay unexpectedly resigned in

1877 due to nervous exhaustion. Mayor Gadsden served the remainder of the year until the election of George Dwight Bryan. Gadsden always had a particular fondness for his alma mater, the Citadel, and he served that institution well as chairman of the Board of Visitors from 1898 until his death.

Peter Charles Gaillard (1812–1889)

Mayor of Charleston   MAP LOCATION: SOUTHEAST 14

Peter C. Gaillard was the first mayor of Charleston elected after the Civil War. He was born in Charleston County and educated at West Point, where he graduated in 1835. He was commissioned a second lieutenant and served on the frontier at Fort Crawford, Wisconsin, and Fort Snelling, Minnesota. He saw action in the Seminole War and resigned from the Army in 1839.

Gaillard became a successful cotton factor with the firm of Gaillard and Minot and remained in that trade until the beginning of the Civil War. He had joined the South Carolina Militia in 1852 and had risen to the rank of brigade major. When the war began, he immediately volunteered. He lost an arm in the defense of Battery Wagner and attained the rank of lieutenant colonel.

When Union Maj. Gen. Daniel Sickles allowed civil government to resume in Charleston after the war, Col. Gaillard won the mayoralty by one vote in the Nov. 1865 election. He attempted in his short term to return the city to its pre–Civil War race relations. Bitterness intensified between white and black Charlestonians, and Congress became upset at the slow pace with which African Americans were receiving civil rights. Mayor Gaillard and his council were removed from office in October 1867 by Gen. R. S. Canby shortly after he replaced Gen. Sickles as military commander in Charleston.

Gaillard's grandson, J. Palmer Gaillard, would be elected mayor of Charleston in 1959, almost one hundred years after his grandfather's election.

James Shoolbred Gibbes (1819–1888)

Businessman and Patron of the Arts   MAP LOCATION: SOUTHWEST 24

James S. Gibbes began his career as a cotton factor, a businessman who acted as agent for cotton planters. He lost much of his fortune during the Civil War but was able to recoup and expand his wealth afterward. He was director and president of the People's National Bank and was actively involved in the Home Insurance Company and the South Carolina Railroad, Gas, and Light Company (predecessor to today's South Carolina Electric and Gas Company).

At his death he bequeathed large sums to numerous local charities, most notably the Carolina Art Association. The Gibbes Art Gallery was built through his munificence and named in his memory. His mausoleum is one of the most imposing in the cemetery. The coffins of Gibbes and his family can still be seen reposing behind thick glass in the mausoleum.

The Gibbes Mausoleum. Courtesy of the Magnolia Cemetery Trust

FRANK BUNKER GILBRETH, JR. (1911–2001)

Author   MAP LOCATION: SOUTHWEST 25

Frank Gilbreth, Jr., was known through the nation for his reminiscences of his childhood, but he was most familiar in Charleston for the role he fashioned as a voice of the community. His parents, Frank and Lillian Gilbreth, were famous pioneers in industrial engineering and management consulting, beginning with breakthrough studies of the motions required to perform laboring tasks. They had twelve children, eleven of whom lived to adulthood. Frank Jr. and his sister Ernestine Gilbreth Carey wrote two classic memoirs of the large family headed by efficiency experts, *Cheaper by the Dozen* (1948) and *Belles on Their Toes* (1950), both of which were adapted as movies.

By this point Gilbreth had settled into the newspaper position in Charleston in which he would remain until his retirement. His journalism career had begun in college at the University of Michigan, where he was editor of the *Michigan Daily*. He then worked as a reporter for the *New York Herald Tribune* before moving to Charleston and joining the news staff of the *News and Courier* in 1934. In the same year he married Elizabeth Cauthen of Charleston, with whom he would have one child. Gilbreth left Charleston to work for the Associated Press, first in Raleigh and later in New York. During World War II he was a decorated naval officer in the South Pacific. He returned to the *News and Courier* as an editorial writer in 1947. He stayed with the newspaper for the rest of his career, eventually serving as assistant publisher of the *Post and Courier* and vice-president of the Evening Post Publishing Company. In 1955 he married Mary Pringle Manigault, with whom he would have two children.

In the late 1940s Gilbreth began to write a column of local commentary for the *News and Courier* entitled "Doing the Charleston." The pseudonymous author of the column was a character named Lord Ashley Cooper, a satirical personification of a particular Charleston social type. For those who did not know, Gilbreth annually revealed in the column that he was its true author. "Doing the Charleston" was an important community voice. It provided an outlet for the humorous talents that Gilbreth also demonstrated in other publications, like his popular *Dictionary of Charlestonese* (for example, "flow: what you stand on in a house"). At the same time, the column was also a valuable civic contribution (as was the *Dictionary,* the proceeds of which went to the Good Cheer fund of the newspaper). Ashley Cooper strongly supported historic preservation and the revitalization of downtown; Mayor Joe Riley pointed to the Charleston Place development as an instance in which the influence of the column was crucial in enabling a controversial project to succeed. Gilbreth continued to write "Doing the Charleston" until his retirement in 1993. He also wrote several more works of humorous reminiscence and reflection and a couple of books about Nantucket as well as a novel about college life in the 1920s, *Held's Angels* (1952), and a satirical novel about Charleston society, *Loblolly* (1959).

ROBERT COGDELL GILCHRIST (1829–1902)

Confederate Soldier   MAP LOCATION: NORTHWEST 3

Robert C. Gilchrist was a product of both the North and the South who brought a high level of cultivation into the Confederate ranks. His parents were both Gilchrists, first cousins in fact. Robert Budd Gilchrist would eventually become a U.S. District Court judge, president of the St. Cecilia Society, and captain and commander of the Washington Light Infantry. Mary Gilchrist was from New York, and though her father lost his fortune in the War of 1812, she was heir to a large estate from her mother's side of the family.

Mr. and Mrs. Gilchrist lived in Charleston but traveled frequently to the North, and their children received sympathetic exposure to both cultures.

Educated in the schools of Charleston and by private tutors, young Robert C. Gilchrist showed a precocious talent for art. He no doubt received encouragement from his uncle by marriage, the sculptor John Cogdell, whom his middle name honored. Two of Robert Gilchrist's paintings are in the Gibbes Museum today. Gilchrist graduated from the College of Charleston in 1849. While at the College, he made a lifetime friend of the poet Paul Hamilton Hayne.

After graduation Gilchrist joined the Washington Light Infantry and read law under James Louis Petigru, the outstanding attorney of antebellum Charleston. Like Gilchrist's father and Gilchrist himself, Petigru was a Unionist who believed that South Carolina should not secede. After practicing law for ten years, however, Gilchrist was forced to choose sides. He decided that "when the fatal die is cast I thought it my duty to go with my state right or wrong and by fighting for her endeavor to right her."

Gilchrist was present at Fort Moultrie for the capture of Fort Sumter and served until the close of the war. As lieutenant of Gist's Guard he was posted to Battery Wagner on Morris Island, where some of the bloodiest and most savage fighting of the war took place. The most famous incident was the charge of the Fifty-fourth Massachusetts Regiment, portrayed in the movie *Glory* (1989). Gilchrist later provided a memorable account of the battle in his *Confederate Defence of Morris Island* (1884).

In 1864, Gilchrist was made a judge advocate for the Department of South Carolina, Georgia, and Florida. During that year he authored *The Duties of a Judge Advocate Before a General Court Martial.* After the fall of Charleston, Gilchrist was appointed an artillery major. He fought under Generals Hardee and Johnston until the end of the war.

After the war, Gilchrist moved to New York, where he had inherited extensive lands. He built the first suspension bridge across the Hudson River at Washburn's Eddy. Whether due to a poor site, the failure to persuade the railroad to put in a depot at the bridge, or the antipathy of the locals to a Confederate major, the bridge failed. Gilchrist sold the bridge property at a substantial loss and returned to Charleston to rebuild his law practice. He remained there for the rest of his life, revitalizing and commanding the Washington Light Infantry. One of his last public acts was unveiling the memorial to the Confederate dead of the Washington Light Infantry in Washington Park.

Gilchrist's oldest child, **Emma Susan Gilchrist** (1862–1929), inherited her father's artistic abilities and improved on them. She was a member of the Southern States Art League, the Carolina Art Association, the Associated Artists, and was the founder and first president of the Charleston Sketch Club. Her works were exhibited widely through the South, and she is now represented in local and national collections. She also lectured frequently on "The Story of Early Charleston." She received national recognition for her work when her painting "Up Meeting Street" was reproduced on the cover of *Literary Digest* on December 31, 1927. Her paintings are some of the first in this area to exhibit an awareness of impressionism. She was one of the early influences on the later dean of Charleston artists, William Halsey.

Monument to the Civil War dead of the Washington Light Infantry, dedicated in the cemetery in 1870. Demolished after sustaining damage in the earthquake of 1886, the monument was replaced in 1891 by an obelisk in Washington Park. Courtesy of the South Caroliniana Library, University of South Carolina

Henry Gourdin (1804–1879)
Robert Newman Gourdin (1812–1894)

Merchants   MAP LOCATION: SOUTHEAST 15

The Gourdin brothers were among the most prominent businessmen in antebellum Charleston and played active roles in politics. Both were born on the family plantation, Buck Hall, in St. John's Parish, Berkeley. Henry received most of his education in the Charleston business world, first in the King Street wagon trade and later as a clerk for the merchant Robert Maxwell. He succeeded to Maxwell's business on the latter's retirement and formed the factorage firm of Gourdin, Matthiessen & Co. in 1824. Meanwhile, the Gourdin siblings had sent their orphaned brother Robert for education at the academy at Pendleton, South Carolina. He then attended South Carolina College, from which he was graduated in 1831. Upon his return to Charleston, he studied law and was admitted to practice in 1834. After health concerns caused him to spend a year in Europe, he joined Henry's firm, one of the most successful and respected in antebellum Charleston. For the rest of their lives, the bachelor brothers worked and lived together.

The Gourdins were active in the Nullification movement—Henry was an officer in the state regiment organized to resist federal coercion—and strong supporters of John C. Calhoun. At his death they helped to satisfy the debts of his estate and ensure the future comfort of his family. It was the Gourdin brothers who supervised the midnight disinterment of Calhoun from St. Philip's cemetery after the fall of Morris Island for fear that invading Union soldiers would desecrate the grave.

Elected to the state legislature in 1834 on the States Rights ticket, Henry played a key role in one of the most important business coups in antebellum Charleston, the founding of the Bank of Charleston. Authorized to be far larger than any other bank in the city, this institution filled the void created by the closing of the Charleston branch of the Bank of the United States. Henry would remain a director of the Bank of Charleston from its establishment until his death. He returned to the state legislature for several terms in the 1830s and early 1840s and then again in 1852, when he championed support for the Blue Ridge Railroad. He served during 1853–1856 as president of that attempt to build a rail link from Charleston to the West.

The brothers played an instrumental role in the election of William Porcher Miles as mayor of Charleston, after which Robert Newman Gourdin acceded to Miles's request that one of the brothers run for alderman on the Charleston City Council. He made substantial improvements in the city's finances as chairman of the Committee on Ways and Means.

Robert Newman Gourdin was one of the organizers of the 1860 Association, which published a widely circulated series of disunion pamphlets in anticipation of Lincoln's election. He also contributed to the momentum for secession through his part in the dramatic response of the U.S. District Court to the Republican victory. When news of the election results arrived in Charleston he was serving as foreman of the grand jury for the court, in which capacity he was asked by Judge Andrew G. Magrath if the grand jury wished to make any presentments. Gourdin replied that "the verdict of the Northern section of the Confederacy, solemnly announced to the country by the ballot-box on yesterday, has swept away the last hope for the permanency, the stability of the Federal Government of these sovereign States." The federal grand jury, breaking from the government of which it was an organ, asserted an obligation to "lift itself above consideration of details in the administration of law and justice to the vast and solemn issues which have been forced upon us." Gourdin's bold speech was followed by the immediate resignations of Judge Magrath and U.S. Attorney James Conner. Their actions excited passions that contributed to the atmosphere of the secession convention. Gourdin was a delegate and signed the Ordinance of Secession.

Robert Newman Gourdin was a close friend of Maj. Robert Anderson, the Union commander of Fort Sumter. At Maj. Anderson's behest, and with the concurrence of Gov. Francis Pickens, Gourdin went to Washington, D.C., in an unofficial attempt to avert bloodshed. Gourdin obviously failed in his mission. During the war he served as lieutenant colonel of a reserve regiment organized for home defense.

After the war Robert Newman Gourdin continued to pursue business opportunities but devoted a great deal of his time to the Medical College of South Carolina (of which he was a member of the board of trustees) and to the French Huguenot Church (of which he was president of the corporation). The Huguenot Church could not have survived the nineteenth century without his efforts.

WILLIAM JOHN GRAYSON (1788–1863)

Author   MAP LOCATION: SOUTHWEST 26

W. J. Grayson held a number of responsible positions in his career before becoming one of the South's leading men of letters. He was born in Beaufort and educated there and in private schools in Long Island, New York. He entered South Carolina College as a sophomore in 1807 and graduated in 1809. Grayson taught at Beaufort and at Savannah College after his graduation and in 1814 married Sarah Matilda Somarsall, whose father was a planter and Charleston merchant. Inheritance and marriage produced substantial wealth for Grayson. The census of 1850 recorded that he owned 170 slaves in St. Helena Parish.

Grayson's political career began with a term in the South Carolina House of Representatives from 1813 to 1815. He returned to the state House in 1822 and was reelected twice more before moving to the South Carolina Senate, where he served from 1826 to 1831. While in the legislature Grayson championed education and was pronullification. He entered the U. S. Congress in 1833 as a Whig and was again elected in the following term. He initially declined to run again in 1837, but when he decided to get into the race, it was too little, too late, and he was defeated. Upon the election of the Whig ticket of Harrison and Tyler in 1840, Grayson was appointed collector of the port of Charleston. He kept this plum patronage position through Whig and Democratic administrations until 1853, when his opposition to the 1850–1852 secession movement led to local pressure for his removal. As a result Grayson suffered the unusual experience of losing his federal job because he was too vocally pro-Union.

By 1850 Grayson was publishing the proslavery, antisecessionist writings that were to become his literary legacy. His dismissal as collector resulted primarily from the indignant response to his satirical *The Letters of Curtius* (1851), a Swiftian view of the status of South Carolina's military preparedness for the civil war that he predicted would result from secession. Grayson soon became part of the literary circle that congregated at Russell's Bookstore. This group included William Gilmore Simms, Henry Timrod, Paul Hamilton Hayne, James Louis Petigru, Basil Gildersleeve, and Bishop Patrick Lynch. Grayson, however, eschewed the romantic bent of Timrod and Hayne in favor of the classical forms of Dryden and Pope. His most lasting fame came in reply to Harriet Beecher Stowe's *Uncle Tom's Cabin* (1852). Grayson was infuriated by what he saw as Stowe's ignorant propaganda and replied with a long poem, *The Hireling and the Slave* (1854). This pastoral work compared the lives and status of slaves in the South with those of wage earners in the North. It is as much a polemic in favor of agrarian economy and in opposition to industrialization as it is a defense of slavery. The poem achieved outstanding success in the South. Grayson published two significant collections of verse, *The Hireling and the Slave, Chicora, and Other Poems* (1856) and *The Country* (1858).

Grayson always opposed secession, but he fell in line with his state after the break with the Union was irrevocable. Meanwhile he continued to write. He apparently wrote a biography of William Lowndes that was lost in the Fire of 1861. He wrote a biography of his college roommate and dearest friend, *James Louis Petigru: A Biographical Sketch,* that was published posthumously in 1866. During the war he also wrote an autobiography that was largely neglected until it was finally published in its complete form as *Witness to Sorrow: The Antebellum Autobiography of William J. Grayson,* edited by Richard J. Calhoun (1990). The publication of the autobiography has led to a reevaluation of W. J. Grayson's career as both a statesman and a writer.

WILLIAM GREGG (1800–1867)

Pioneer Industrialist   MAP LOCATION: SOUTHWEST 27

Gregg was the great capitalist of the antebellum South. He rose from humble beginnings to establish the prototypical cotton mill of the old South. In doing so, he proved that concentrated capital could work for the good of the area's economic health, and that industry, particularly the cotton textile industry, could be important to the economic welfare of the South.

Gregg was born near Carmichaels, Monongalia County, in what was then Virginia but is today West Virginia. Though his parents, Elizabeth (Webb) and William Gregg, were Quakers, his father fought in the Revolutionary War. Gregg's mother died when he was four, and he was raised by a kindly neighbor lady until the age of eleven. He received little formal education. At the age of eleven he was apprenticed to his uncle, Jacob Gregg, who had a watchmaking and silversmith business in Alexandria, Virginia. He remained an apprentice in this trade, with a brief period in Georgia as a cotton manufacturer during the War of 1812, and finally was able to go out on his own in 1824.

In that year Gregg moved to Columbia, South Carolina, and established a silver-making concern that made him independently wealthy within a decade. He married an Edgefield District woman, Marina Jones, in 1829 and moved to her home area eight years later to manage the Vaucluse cotton textile factory, in which he had invested. In 1838 he moved to Charleston and became part of the jewelry firm of Hayden, Gregg, and Co., through which he made enough money to enable him to retire to his handsome house on Calhoun Street without any financial worries.

Though Gregg had planned to live the life of a retired gentleman, his life-long habits and curiosities would not allow him to rest. He began to look about at the economic opportunities of the area and became appalled at the waste he saw. He viewed South Carolina's exclusive devotion to an agricultural cotton economy as foolish and saw textile manufacturing as South Carolina's way out of an economic quagmire.

Gregg embarked upon a tour of the New England states and the textile factories there. This trip resulted in a series of articles for the Charleston *Courier* on the textile industry that was published separately as *Essays on Domestic Industry* in 1845. In the *Essays,* Gregg argues that the South's reliance on cotton production alone would eventually sap her capital and render her poor with nothing to show for her former wealth. At a time when South Carolina's politicians were turning most of their energies toward attacking the North and its way of life, Gregg argued that the South should emulate the success of Northern industrial growth rather than attack it.

Gregg decided to practice what he preached. To this end, he assembled a group of Charleston investors for a proposed textile manufacturing plant on Horse Creek near the Vaucluse cotton factory in present-day Aiken County. To convince the legislators that his enterprise was worthy of a corporate charter and the advantages of limited liability, Gregg wrote and published *An Enquiry into the Propriety of Granting Charters of Incorporation for Manufacturing and Other Purposes in South Carolina* (1845). Gregg's petition for a charter won by a single vote when it went before the South Carolina legislative committee on manufactures.

Gregg began construction of the Graniteville Manufacturing Company in 1846. He built his plant of local granite and used the water of Horse Branch Creek to power the mill. In addition, Gregg saw to the construction of a village consisting of over one hundred well-built homes, a school, and two churches. When he opened the mill, poor whites seeking a way out of chronic poverty flooded the village. The mill soon supported over 300 workers and 900 inhabitants. Gregg ruled over it all as a benevolent despot. The community he created, Graniteville, was to be the model for the many textile mills that sprang up all over the South both before and after the Civil War.

Gregg's mill was an enormous success, consistently paying high dividends to his investors after 1851. He was elected to the South Carolina House of Representatives in 1856. During his two terms in the legislature he sought to bring his independent economic thinking to bear on South Carolina's chaotic banking and railroad interests. After he was defeated in a run for the South Carolina Senate, Gregg published a series of articles in *DeBow's Review* in which he urged Southerners to prepare economically for what he saw as the inevitable war with the North. Gregg was elected a delegate from Edgefield District to the secession convention and signed the Ordinance of Secession.

During the Civil War, Gregg continued to operate the Graniteville mill. Despite the serious privations and loss of labor to the military, Gregg was still able to turn a profit. Almost immediately after the Confederate surrender, Gregg went to New England and Europe to purchase equipment to bring the mill up to standards. He died in 1867 as a result of an illness contracted while fighting a break in the mill dam. He was originally buried in Graniteville, but his body and those of his family were brought to Magnolia Cemetery after Gregg's widow resettled in Charleston in the 1870s.

The standard biography of Gregg is Broadus Mitchell's *William Gregg, Factory Master of the Old South* (1928).

ROBERT EMMET GRIBBIN (1887–1976)

Episcopal Bishop   MAP LOCATION: SOUTHWEST 28

Bishop Gribbin was born in Aiken, South Carolina, the son of John and Rebecca (Moore) Gribbin. He was educated in the public schools of Blackville, South Carolina, and received a B.S. degree from the Citadel and a B.A. degree from the College of Charleston. He did graduate work at the General Theological Seminary in New York City and took courses at Harvard and Columbia Universities. He married Emma Manigault Jenkins of Charleston in 1915.

Bishop Gribbin was an Army chaplain in World War I and was for many years the Episcopal bishop of the diocese of Western North Carolina. After his retirement he moved to Charleston, where he supplied numerous churches and was much beloved. He died in 1976 and was buried in his wife's family plot.

GEORGE DANIEL GRICE (1900–1977)

College President   MAP LOCATION: SOUTHWEST 29

George Grice was a long-serving president of the College of Charleston and, after his retirement, one of the first Republican legislators in South Carolina since Reconstruction. He was born in Charleston and graduated from Clemson College in 1923, after which he worked as a schoolteacher for two years until he was made principal of Julian Mitchell School in 1925. He remained in that position until 1932.

Grice arrived at the College of Charleston in 1932 as a professor of mathematics. He was a great favorite of college president Harrison Randolph, as evidenced by his appointments as acting president from 1933 through 1936 and again from 1941 through 1945. He was named president of the College of Charleston in 1945. Grice was instrumental in making the College of Charleston a private institution in 1949, a status it held until 1970 when it became a state college. He retired as president in 1966.

In 1967 Grice won election to the South Carolina House of Representatives. Later that year he resigned his seat to run, successfully, as a Republican for the South Carolina Senate. He served only for the year 1968.

In addition to his work in politics and education, Grice was one of the leaders in the study of marine biology in South Carolina. He helped found the Bears Bluff Laboratory on Wadmalaw Island. Later he obtained a portion of Fort Johnson on James Island for use as College of Charleston biology laboratories. These facilities were later named in his honor.

ELIZABETH BERKELEY GRIMBALL (1875–1953)

Theater Impresario   MAP LOCATION: NORTHEAST 6

Elizabeth Berkeley Grimball left the South to become an important Broadway director, producer, and teacher. She was born in Union, South Carolina, of an old Charleston family. She was educated at Miss Kelly's School and graduated from the Boston School of Expression. She studied stage design and production with the great Broadway designer Norman Bel Geddes. After teaching, producing, and directing in the hinterlands, she moved to Broadway and produced *Shoot, March Hares, Tyrants,* and *Manhaters.*

Miss Grimball founded the experimental theater group at the Drury Lane Theater in New York and the New York School of the Theater. Among her students at the New York School were the young Helen Gahagan Douglas and Lauren Bacall. She wrote *The Snow Queen* (1920), *The Waif* (1924), and co-wrote the textbook *Costuming a Play* (1925). The book went through three editions and was for many years a standard text in theater schools throughout the world.

Miss Grimball was the first woman theatrical teacher included in the international *Who's Who* and the first American woman to head a department at the Mozarteum Academy in Salzburg. She was inducted into Carnegie Hall's Gallery of Famous People. At the close of her life Miss Grimball returned to Charleston, where she founded the Charleston Children's Theater and taught at the Watt School.

JOHN GRIMBALL (1840–1922)

Confederate Naval Officer   MAP LOCATION: SOUTHWEST 30

John Grimball was born in Charleston of mixed heritage. That is, his father John Berkeley Grimball was from an old Edisto Island planter family, and his mother Margaret Ann (Morris) Grimball was the daughter of Declaration of Independence signer Lewis Morris of New York. He entered the U.S. Naval Academy at the age of fourteen and was one of fifteen from an original class of eighty to graduate in 1858. Among his classmates was George Dewey, later admiral of the Navy and hero of Manila.

After graduation Grimball was assigned a Mediterranean posting on the *Macedonian.* When South Carolina seceded from the United States, he tendered his resignation and signed on with the Confederacy. He was commissioned a first lieutenant and saw duty on the *Lady Davis* in various engagements around Port Royal. Following the fall of Port Royal, Grimball was assigned to the ram *Arkansas,* on which he rendered heroic service in the

Stereograph of the cemetery published by George N. Barnard while he was the proprietor of a photography studio in Charleston, 1873–1880. Courtesy of the South Caroliniana Library, University of South Carolina

defense of Vicksburg. After brief service on the *Baltic* in Mobile, Alabama, he was sent to England. There he was assigned to the famous (or infamous) *Shenandoah*.

The *Shenandoah* sailed from Madeira to Australia and then on to the Arctic Ocean, destroying and pillaging United States shipping along the way. The ship's journey decimated the U.S. whaling fleet. She captured thirty-eight ships altogether and crowned her success by burning eight ships near the mouth of the Bering Strait on June 28, 1865. On August 2, 1865, contact with the H.M.S. *Baracouta* en route from San Francisco converted the *Shenandoah*'s glory to worry. The men of the *Shenandoah* learned that the war had been over since April and that they had been destroying ships of their own now forcibly reunited nation. This situation required some fast thinking. Capt. Waddell ordered all guns stowed below decks. The *Shenandoah* then sailed for Liverpool disguised as a merchant vessel. In Liverpool, the colors of the Confederacy were struck for the last time and the ship was surrendered to the English on November 6, 1865.

Not knowing what awaited him in America, Grimball decided to take a much-deserved sojourn at a ranch near Cordova, Mexico, while events sorted themselves out in the United States. Juarez's revolution against Maximilian I made things uncomfortable in Mexico after a time, and Grimball decided to return home.

Once in Charleston, he studied law and was admitted to practice in 1867. The next year, he moved to New York City where he reconstituted his fortunes by practicing law over the next sixteen years. He returned to Charleston for good in 1884.

JOHNSON HAGOOD (1873–1948)

U.S. Army General   MAP LOCATION: SOUTHEAST 16

Johnson Hagood followed the lead of his given name into military service. He was born in Orangeburg, the nephew of Confederate general and South Carolina governor Johnson Hagood. He matriculated at the University of South Carolina until he received an appointment to West Point. He graduated in 1896 and was commissioned a second lieutenant in the artillery.

After serving early in his career in the department of philosophy at the U.S. Military Academy, Hagood advanced to high military position. He was stationed in Washington as assistant to the chief of artillery and a member of the General Staff Corps until his transfer to the Philippines, where he served until 1915. When the United States entered World War I in 1917 he went to France as commander of the Seventh Regiment of the First Expeditionary Brigade, coast artillery. After his elevation to brigadier general in 1918, he distinguished himself as chief of staff of the U.S. Army Services of Supply, in which position he was in charge of supply for the entire wartime U.S. Army. He served in the trenches at Meuse-Argonne and crossed the Rhine into Germany with his men. Hagood was made a major general in 1925 and served as commanding general at a number of posts until his retirement.

Gen. Hagood's retirement came about under extraordinary circumstances. He had always been known for his controversial views and his unabashed way of expressing those views. In 1936, he urged a congressional appropriations committee to take money earmarked for the W. P. A. drama project and spend it on military housing. He declared: "There is a vast flow of silver spreading out all over the country like mud. It will soon dry up without anything to show for it. I shall not be accused of profanity when I say for God's sake put some of it into stone and steel." The outburst was considered a major attack on President Roosevelt's New Deal program, and FDR ordered him relieved of command. After a nasty argument in Congress over the merits of Gen. Hagood's statements, he was transferred to command of the Sixth Corps in Chicago. He took command for one day and retired.

Hagood invented a mortar deflection board, the Hagood tripod mount, and other apparatus for use in coastal defenses. He also wrote several books, including *The Services of Supply: A Memoir of the Great War* (1927) and *We Can Defend America* (1937).

Upon his retirement from the Army, Gen. Hagood became a budgetary consultant for Sears Roebuck in Chicago before retiring to Charleston. Given his views on the arts, it is ironic that his grandson and namesake became an artist and co-owner of Carolina Prints in Charleston.

EDWIN LINDSLEY HALSEY (1838–1903)

Firer of the First Shot?   MAP LOCATION: SOUTHWEST 31

Who fired the first shot of the Civil War? Some would argue for the Citadel cadets who on January 9, 1861, turned away the *Star of the West,* which was attempting to resupply Fort Sumter. There are other claimants where shots were fired in Florida, Mississippi, and Arkansas. Historians and most of the nation have now settled on the Confederates who fired on Fort Sumter early on the morning of April 12, 1861. Edmund Ruffin, a hidebound old Virginia radical, is often given credit for the first shot, but he was probably the third or fourth to fire on Fort Sumter from the Morris Island and Fort Johnson batteries.

Magnolia Cemetery is the final resting place of another candidate. For the long months from the secession of South Carolina and the removal of Maj. Robert Anderson's garrison to Fort Sumter through April 12, 1861, hundreds of fire-breathing Confederates bided their time in the forts and encampments that surrounded the Yankees on Fort Sumter. Except, that is, for E. L. Halsey. His grandson, Ashley Halsey, Jr., recounts the story in his book *Who Fired the First Shot?* (1963):

> It was during the "cold war" between the federal government and the seceding states. Southern artillerymen at Charleston continually tested their guns, usually taking care to aim well clear of the frowning fortress under the Stars and Stripes. To citizen soldiers in the Iron Battery, unaccustomed to heaving about heavy cannon, the toil of endless drills seemed pointless. One night, a twenty-three-year-old private remarked that he was "tired of this nonsense; there will be some fun in the morning."
>
> Shortly after dawn, when the battery went through all the empty motions of firing, an eight-inch columbiad suddenly roared out while aimed at the fort. The solid shot screamed across the water at Sumter. It struck, according to one version, just to the left of the sally port or main gate. The garrison manned its guns (this is a matter of official record) and prepared to reply to further shelling. Instead, the Iron Battery commander rushed over in a small boat under a truce flag to apologize for the "accidental shot."
>
> The shot was no accident. I can say with certainty, for the man who loaded the gun during the night was my grandfather, E. L. Halsey of Charleston. . . .

Halsey rose to the rank of captain during the war, after which he started a successful lumber mill. Halsey Boulevard near the medical complex is named in his honor. He was the grandfather of author Ashley Halsey, Jr., and artist William Halsey.

J. ROSS HANAHAN (1869–1963)

Businessman   MAP LOCATION: NORTHWEST 4

J. Ross Hanahan was one of the great twentieth-century capitalists of the Southeast. He was born in Summerville, the son of a Confederate captain, and attended school in Charleston before graduating *cum laude* from the University of South Carolina in 1890.

After his graduation he began to explore the marl deposits in the rivers around Charleston. His discoveries led to his opening of the Planters Fertilizer and Phosphate Company and numerous cement companies. He was a leading industrialist not only in South Carolina but also in Tennessee, Alabama, and North Carolina.

Hanahan was active in the improvement of Charleston's water quality, and through his efforts, the city of Charleston purchased the Charleston Light and Water Plant in 1917. He became one of the first Commissioners of Public Works. In recognition of his efforts to improve Charleston's water system, Saxon Station's name was changed to Hanahan in his honor. Today the town of Hanahan carries his name.

Wilson Godfrey Harvey (1866–1932)

Governor of South Carolina   MAP LOCATION: SOUTHEAST 17

Wilson Harvey was the first Charlestonian to become governor of South Carolina after the Civil War. Born in the city, he left school at the age of fifteen to work in the business department of the *News and Courier*. At the age of twenty, he became the manager of the *World and Budget* newspaper in Charleston. An organizer of the Enterprise Bank of Charleston in 1894, he became its president in 1904 and held that position until the bank's failure in 1922.

Harvey was an alderman for the city of Charleston from 1903 to 1911 and was instrumental in the extension of the Battery by the construction of a large sea wall. He served as mayor pro tem in 1910. He was elected lieutenant governor of South Carolina in 1920. When Gov. Robert Archer Cooper resigned in May 1922 to accept a position with the federal government, Harvey became governor. In that office he sought to restrict the issuance of pardons and paroles, a system that had led to much corruption in the administration of Gov. Cole Blease. The system was not really reformed until the administration of Gov. J. Strom Thurmond some twenty-five years later. Gov. Harvey attempted enforcement of Prohibition, an effort at which he was largely unsuccessful, for Gov. Harvey was that most unusual political creature, a Charleston "dry."

Gov. Harvey declined to run for a full term, and after a few years on the South Carolina Board of Public Welfare he became an agent and then manager of the Carolina Life Insurance Company. He moved to Tampa, Florida, for the company in 1932 and died there of a heart attack later that year.

Isaac William Hayne (1809–1880)

Secessionist   MAP LOCATION: SOUTHWEST 32

Isaac Hayne was the inheritor of a name prominent in Charleston since the Revolution. His grandfather Isaac Hayne was well known as a patriotic martyr, the American answer to Major André and the South's answer to Nathan Hale. His cousin, Robert Y. Hayne, was the man who answered Webster in the Hayne-Webster debates so forcefully that Southerners never understood that Hayne had lost.

Isaac Hayne was born in Charleston, the son of William Edward and Eloise (Brevard) Hayne. He was a graduate of South Carolina College and a tutor for several years in that college. He was admitted to the bar of South Carolina in 1831 and began his practice in the town of Coosawhatchie, soon after moving to Charleston. Around 1837, he sought his fortune in the West, as did many energetic and ambitious young men of his era, and moved to Alabama, where he practiced law and planted near Montgomery. After he had made his fortune, he returned to Charleston in 1846 and joined the law practice of his cousins Henry William and William Henry Peronneau.

Elected attorney general of the state in 1848, Hayne performed the duties of that office so capably that he was continuously reelected until the overthrow of the old order in 1868. He had been a strident sectionalist ever since he graduated from Thomas Cooper's hotbed of radicalism at South Carolina College at the peak of the Nullification controversy, and he played a central role in disunionist politics. He was a signer of the Ordinance of Secession. At Hayne's death the *News and Courier* called him "pre-eminently a manly man" who was "fearless toward the strong, magnanimous to the weak, tender to those he loved, and unflinchingly true to every trust."

James Calvin Hemphill (1850–1927)

Newspaper Editor   MAP LOCATION: NORTHWEST 5

J. C. Hemphill was a native of the upcountry who became editor of the *News and Courier*. He was one of the leading voices against the rise of Ben Tillman and the agrarian revolution of 1890. He also served as an editor of several other major Southern newspapers, but it was in Charleston that he made his most important mark.

Hemphill was born in Due West, South Carolina, the son of the Reverend Doctor W. R. Hemphill, president of Erskine College. He graduated from Erskine in 1870 and taught for a short time in Kentucky before returning to Abbeville, South Carolina, and taking up a lifelong career in journalism. In Abbeville he and his brother Robert Hemphill published and edited the Abbeville *Medium*. Hemphill participated in the "Redemption" of 1876 as one of Wade Hampton's Red Shirts. It was perhaps from this time that he acquired the courtesy title of "Major," which he used for the remainder of his life.

Capt. Francis Warrington Dawson hired Hemphill in 1880 as the Columbia correspondent of the Charleston *News and Courier*. Hemphill transferred to the Charleston office in 1882 and became city editor in 1885. He assumed Dawson's duties during Dawson's frequent absences from Charleston. Thus it was logical that he was made manager and editor-in-chief of the *News and Courier* upon Dawson's tragic death in 1889. This was a pivotal moment in the history of South Carolina due to the rising influence of Ben Tillman.

Hemphill consistently opposed Tillmanism but without the rancor and vitriol that characterized other "Bourbon" newspapers of the day. His attitude was important, as Hemphill was later able to work with Tillman when Pitchfork Ben consolidated power. In 1895 Hemphill led the forces in opposition to Tillman's call for the convention that ultimately resulted in the South Carolina constitution of 1895. Hemphill, along with Joseph W. Barnwell, W. C. McGowan, and others, worked out a compromise by which the anti-Tillman forces would be represented at the constitutional convention. The compromise was known as the "Tillman-Hemphill" agreement. Tillman repudiated the agreement at the last minute, but its effects were still felt at the convention and in the constitution it produced.

Hemphill was a constant promoter of Charleston and her growth. He ceaselessly touted the advantages of Charleston's harbor and once again "conspired" with Tillman in bringing the Navy base to Charleston in 1902. The base long remained a primary force in Charleston's economy. Hemphill was also a tireless advocate for the rest of the state. He used his considerable political and social connections in the North to "bring the mills to cotton," and he was a proponent of increased tobacco planting in the Pee Dee. Both movements bore fruit, and textiles long dominated the Piedmont just as tobacco did in the Pee Dee.

While at the *News and Courier* Hemphill published a three-volume collection of obituaries and profiles of prominent South Carolinians he had written over the years as *Men of Mark in South Carolina* (1907). It is a valuable historical reference today.

Despite his love of Charleston and his devotion to the *News and Courier,* Hemphill's fondest desire was to obtain an interest in a newspaper and to edit it. When his desires were continually frustrated at the *News and Courier,* he looked elsewhere. His ambition would never be satisfied. In 1910 he became editor of the Richmond *Times-Dispatch.* He left to become editor of the Charlotte *Observer* in 1911, where he mistakenly believed he was to acquire an interest in the paper. He left in 1912 to become an editorial writer for his friend Adolph Ochs on the New York *Times.* Later still, he became the Washington correspondent for the Philadelphia *Public Ledger.* In 1919, he returned to South Carolina and finished out his career by serving as the editor of the Spartanburg *Journal* until his retirement in 1925.

Hemphill retired to Abbeville, where he died shortly after returning from his annual visit to his wife's grave in Magnolia Cemetery.

Isabel Bowen Heyward (1870–1926)

Cofounder of the Poetry Society of South Carolina　　　　MAP LOCATION: SOUTHWEST 33

Belle Heyward was a descendant of the Declaration of Independence signer Thomas Heyward, Jr., and cousin of *Porgy* author DuBose Heyward. She lived at home with her parents at 7 Gibbes Street until a dynamic intellectual entered her life and changed both her and Charleston forever.

Laura Bragg was a confident, self-contained modernist who brought inventive techniques and a world-class mind to the Charleston Museum. Though Bragg neither wrote nor painted, her intelligence, reform-minded judgment, and power as head of the Charleston Museum profoundly affected the direction of the Charleston Renaissance. From her arrival in 1909 until her death in 1978, except for an interval spent in the Berkshires during the 1930s, Bragg was the cultural grande dame of Charleston. She was a leader in the restoration of the Heyward-Washington House, the racial integration of Charleston institutions, and the establishment of the Charleston Free Library.

According to Louise Anderson Allen's *A Bluestocking in Charleston: The Life and Career of Laura Bragg* (2001), Miss Bragg met Heyward soon after her arrival in Charleston in 1909. Bragg moved into the third floor of Heyward's house in 1915. They developed a passionate relationship that contemporaries recognized as a "Boston marriage." As the relationship evolved, Belle became the domestic partner and Miss Bragg the partner who worked. Heyward's connections to Charleston's power structure were ideal for the advancement of Bragg's ideals in her adopted city. The Poetry Society of South Carolina was founded at a meeting in Belle's house, and she and Laura were two of the founders.

As Bragg's work became more all-consuming, the interests of the women diverged. Bragg continued to live at 7 Gibbes Street, but sometime in 1925 she started another romantic attachment with her young protégée Helen McCormack. Belle began a series of trips to Europe. After returning from one of these tours in 1926, Belle had an "accident" with the gas heater in her bathroom at 7 Gibbes and was almost asphyxiated. Nonetheless, she continued on another planned tour of Europe. She returned in early October to find Helen McCormack and Bragg closer than ever. On October 20, 1926, Belle had another "accident" with the gas. This time she died.

Bragg claimed that Heyward had been murdered by a boarder, her cousin Faber Porcher. Josephine Pinckney even started a play about "the murder." Heyward was buried in a family plot in Magnolia. Four years later, cousin Faber Porcher joined her there, just two graves away.

HENRIETTA EMOGENE MARTIN HOAGG (1869–1945)

Bahá'í Missionary   MAP LOCATION: SOUTHWEST 34

Emogene Hoagg was one of the earliest and most devoted followers of the Bahá'í faith in America. Her ardent beliefs led her to travel the world spreading its message and translating the works of the faith's leaders into several languages. She was born in Copperopolis, California, the daughter of a Nashville, Tennessee, doctor who had gone west for the 1848 Gold Rush and never returned east. She was educated at the Irving Institute in San Francisco, where she studied voice and language. In 1892 she married John Ketchie Hoagg, a wealthy engineer and flour mill heir whose fortune later financed his wife's international travels.

On a visit to the home of Phoebe Hearst (William Randolph Hearst's mother) in 1898, Hoagg met Lua and Edward Getsinger, who converted her to the Bahá'í faith. Bahá'ís believe in one God, the unity of all men without regard to race, nationality, or religion, and the essential unity of all revealed religions. Bahá'ís believe that Bahá'u'lláh (1817–1892), who founded the religion in 1863, was the latest prophet in a line that includes Moses, Jesus, and Mohammed. Bahá'u'lláh was succeeded by his son, 'Abdú'l-Bahá (1844–1921) in 1892. Shoghi Effendi (1897–1957) became guardian of the faith in 1921 upon the death of his grandfather, 'Abdú'l-Bahá.

In 1900 Hoagg made a pilgrimage to Haifa in what is now Israel to meet 'Abdú'l-Bahá. He sent her to Port Said, where she received intensive training in the religion. Hoagg's

Late-nineteenth-century view of the cemetery chapel by the New York photography firm
E. & H. T. Anthony. Courtesy of the Magnolia Cemetery Trust

facility with languages was of great help to her and her faith. She eventually spoke and
wrote Italian, French, German, Spanish, and Persian. With her initial training behind her,
Hoagg began to evangelize for her faith first in Paris and then in Italy. She taught in Naples,
Rome, and Florence for a number of years. In 1928 she became manager of the Interna-
tional Bahá'í Bureau in Geneva, which served as the link between Haifa and the West.
She aided Shoghi Effendi in the translation and editing of Nabil-i-A'zam's *The Dawn
Breakers* (1932). She also translated other Bahá'í works into French, German, and Italian.
Shoghi Effendi pronounced her "the most erudite of her generation."

In 1935 Hoagg became a missionary to America, where she traveled throughout the
Middle West, the South, and into Canada. In 1942 she undertook a mission to Cuba.
Following her mission to Cuba, she suffered a heart attack that rendered her essentially
an invalid for the remainder of her life. She traveled about the country staying in the
houses of the devout for months at a time and teaching as her strength allowed. She
lived the last five months of her life in Charleston at the home of Miss Josey Pinson,
where she died.

Frank H. Hogan (1876–1927)

Bootlegger and Murder Victim   MAP LOCATION: NORTHEAST 7

Frank "Rumpty Rattles" Hogan was a locally well-known baseball player, umpire, bar owner, ward boss, labor organizer, and bootlegger, but it took his murder to make him truly memorable. Frank Hogan grew up in the rough and tumble world of Little Mexico, the area just south of Magnolia Cemetery where the trash dump was located. When Hogan was growing up the neighborhood was racially integrated but, then as now, extremely poor and violent. The people who lived there were hard-working but on the bottom of life's ladder. "Rumpty Rattles" Hogan was to become their king.

Hogan began his career on the docks and on the baseball field. His extraordinary size and strength were great assets in both efforts. In both of his chosen fields of endeavor, he was known as a brawler, a successful one.

Charleston experienced prohibition almost twenty-five years before the rest of the country with the advent of Gov. Ben Tillman's dispensary system, which outlawed all saloons. Fortunately for thirsty Charlestonians, there were plenty of entrepreneurs like Hogan who stepped into the gap to provide not only saloons (or "blind tigers") but also bottles of illicit liquor, mostly imported from the swamps of Berkeley County. Hogan ran one of the most notorious "blind tigers" in the city, the Mexico Roost and Robbers Inn.

Despite, or perhaps because of, his reputation Hogan was the political boss of Little Mexico, and his support was actively sought by those in power. He was a major cog in Mayor Grace's machine and for a time was even on the city payroll as a policeman. In a Congressional hearing on the heated race of 1912 between Richard S. Whaley and Edward Hughes, Hogan was called to testify. He estimated that of five hundred votes in his ward, one hundred were for sale. He stated that his first question to voters at the polls was "How much do you want?"

Hogan was, nevertheless, known as someone who took care of his people. There was always a fifty-gallon tin of soup available in his establishment for the benefit of the community. He was known as a soft touch but someone not to be trifled with.

By 1927 Hogan was a moonshine retailer who obtained his product from a former partner named Leon Dunlap. Dunlap's chief source was a John Brown, who with his brother Henry Brown was engaged in moonshine production in nearby Awendaw, South Carolina. When the Browns declared a jump in the price of corn liquor of fifty cents per gallon, they accompanied Dunlap and his associate David Riggs (who happened to be Hogan's son-in-law) to inform Mr. Hogan of the cost escalation.

Hogan was not pleased. As Tom Waring recounted in *Charleston Murders* (1947), "Brown, who must have been accustomed to strong language, said Hogan used words he had never heard before." He told Dunlap and Riggs that he would beat the hell out of them if they got out of the car, but he did not draw the gun in his pocket or threaten any shooting. The visitors drove away, and Dunlap and Riggs retired to a vacant second-story room overlooking the Peking Chop Suey Restaurant on the north side of Market. Hogan was known to have a girlfriend, Myrtle Carter, whom he frequently accompanied home from her job as a waitress at the Peking Chop Suey. When Hogan showed up to pick up Mrs. Carter at approximately one o'clock in the morning, Dunlap shouted something like, "Hogan, if you've got your gun, you'd better get it ready now." Witnesses later differed as to the exact phraseology. In any case, Hogan soon lay in the doorway of the Peking Chop Suey with fourteen buckshot in his body and no life at all.

Leon Dunlap was charged with murder and David Riggs as an accessory. At the trial, Hogan's widow and daughter sat with the defendants. A great deal of evidence was introduced by the defense as to Hogan's violent and generally bad character. After eleven hours of deliberation, the jury returned a unanimous verdict of not guilty by reason of self-defense as to both defendants.

LEON DUNLAP (1894–1945) continued to achieve success in his chosen field. When prohibition ended he was known as the biggest bootlegger in Charleston. His activities attracted the attention of the federal authorities, and in 1936 he was convicted of violation of internal revenue laws and sentenced to five years in the Atlanta penitentiary. After his release he was the proprietor of the Idle Hour Restaurant at 1067 King Street. He died a natural death on October 3, 1945, and is buried a few hundred feet from Frank Hogan in the Greenhill section of Magnolia Cemetery.

JOHN EDWARDS HOLBROOK (1794–1871)

Physician and Naturalist   MAP LOCATION: SOUTHEAST 18

John E. Holbrook was a founder and professor of the Medical College of South Carolina and one of the first American scientists to be recognized in Europe. He was born in Beaufort, where his mother's family lived, but he spent much of his youth near Wrentham, Massachusetts, home of his father's family. He graduated from Brown in 1815 and received his M.D. from the University of Pennsylvania in 1818. He then traveled and studied in Europe for four years and became acquainted with the leading zoologists of his day while studying in Paris.

Holbrook came to Charleston in 1822 and quickly became known for his skill as a doctor. In 1823 he and a group of Charleston physicians organized the Medical College of South Carolina. Holbrook was chosen as the first professor of anatomy. Beloved by his students, he continued to teach at the school for over thirty years. He also maintained an active private medical practice.

In addition to his duties as a teacher and physician, Holbrook took up herpetology, the study of reptiles. It was in this field that he would achieve his most lasting fame. He determined to publish a work on North American reptiles and hired an Italian artist to do the illustrations. After publishing three volumes, Holbrook consolidated his early work together with later studies as the monumental *North American Herpetology; or, a Description of Reptiles Inhabiting the United States* in five quarto volumes in 1842. It was immediately recognized in the United States and Europe as the standard work on the subject.

He began work on a similar study of fishes of the Southern states but soon realized he had chosen a topic too broad in scope. The breadth of the topic and the death of his artist forced Holbrook to narrow his focus to the fishes of South Carolina. He published two numbers of his *Ichthyology of South Carolina* in the 1850s, but a fire at his publisher's in Philadelphia destroyed most of the plates for the work. The coming of the Civil War put an end to the project.

During the war Holbrook served as the chairman of the examining board for South Carolina surgeons. The effects of the war ruined him financially, and the wartime death of his beloved wife, Harriott Pinckney Rutledge, broke his spirit. After the war he spent increasing amounts of time in Massachusetts with family and friends such as Louis Agassiz. When Holbrook died in 1871, Agassiz observed that the pioneering work on North American reptiles "compelled European recognition of American science."

ROBERT LITTLE HOLMES (1830–1861)

First Casualty of the Civil War   MAP LOCATION: SOUTHEAST 19

By all appearances, Robert Little Holmes led an uneventful life. His importance as an historical footnote was due to the manner of his death. For he was, as his tombstone states, "the first sacrifice of life in the service of the State" in the conflict that was to become the Civil War.

Holmes was born in Charleston, the son of Margaret R. and William H. Holmes. The city directory of 1859 lists him as a wood factor residing with his parents on Charlotte Street near Alexander. He was a member of the Charleston Light Infantry and was detailed to Castle Pinckney. In January 1861 he was accidentally shot and killed by a sentinel whom he was approaching. Ironically, the issue of the Charleston *Mercury* that reported his death also reported that Citadel cadets on Morris Island repelling the *Star of the West* had fired the first Southern shots against the flag of the United States.

JOHN H. HONOUR (1802–1885)

Signer of the Ordinance of Secession   MAP LOCATION: SOUTHEAST 20

John H. Honour was an ordained minister, city alderman, and president of the first building and loan association in Charleston. His principal claim to fame is his signature on the Ordinance of Secession.

Honour was born and educated in Charleston. He felt called to the ministry and was ordained a Methodist minister at the rather late age of thirty-four in 1836. Once ordained, however, he did not follow the calling of the ministry. Instead, he joined the Charleston Insurance and Trust Company in 1836 as secretary and cashier. By 1842 he was made president of the company, a position he held until the end of the Civil War. Honour held high positions in many of Charleston's fraternal and benevolent organizations, and he served on numerous city commissions for orphans and the poor.

After the war that he helped to bring about as one of the 169 South Carolinians who signed the Ordinance of Secession, the Reverend Honour served as a director of the

People's Bank, the Bank of the State of South Carolina, and the Charleston Savings Institution. After helping to engineer the Methodist-Lutheran merger that became the Wentworth Street Lutheran Church, he became active in Lutheran affairs. He reported that he had preached in all Protestant pulpits in Charleston except those of the Episcopal church.

Magnolia Cemetery is the final resting place of fourteen signers of the Ordinance of Secession. Courtesy of the Library of Congress

HENRY BUCKINGHAM HORLBECK (1839–1901)

Public Health Officer   MAP LOCATION: SOUTHEAST 21

Henry Horlbeck was a physician who did great service for his native city as its health officer. Born and educated in Charleston, he graduated from the Medical College of South Carolina and studied medicine in Paris and Berlin. He served as a surgeon in the Confederate Army at Fort Sumter, Battery Wagner, and in the field.

Mayor Courtenay appointed Horlbeck health officer of the city of Charleston, a position he held for the remainder of his life. He argued vociferously for the establishment of a modern sewerage system in Charleston but met only partial success. Charleston in the late nineteenth century still relied primarily on privies to take care of its human waste. A survey in the late 1800s found that eighty percent of Charleston's water was contaminated by the privies. Although some neighborhoods south of Broad Street eventually received sewer services in Dr. Horlbeck's lifetime, most of the other areas of the city did not, despite his campaign. Dr. Horlbeck also led a losing battle for the establishment of a system of meat inspection in the city. He always fought for cleanliness in the city, and as a result of his tireless efforts the city suffered no major epidemics during his tenure.

In the 1890s Horlbeck was elected president of the American Public Health Association. He was one of those who pushed hardest for the establishment of the U.S. Quarantine Service. He was an advocate of the research that led to the discovery of the cause of yellow fever. He was also a prolific contributor to medical journals on questions of public health.

When Horlbeck died, he directed that his body be cremated, a most unusual request for that day. It is said that his was only the third recorded cremation in South Carolina history. The reason for this was the botched job at the cremation of South Carolina Revolutionary patriot Henry Laurens, whose head was said to have detached from his body and rolled into the Cooper River. Ever after, South Carolinians had a horror of cremation. Horlbeck's friend Dr. C. W. Kollock took his body to Staten Island, New York, where it was cremated. His ashes lie beneath a very large stone in the Horlbeck family lot.

ALFRED HUGER (1788–1872)

Patrician   MAP LOCATION: SOUTHEAST 22

Alfred Huger was the very model of a gentleman planter. After his Unionist stance sacrificed his bright future in state politics, he became one of the most visible federal officials in Charleston. In that capacity, he demonstrated that local controversies over the value of the Union were disagreements about tactics within an elite solidly united in defense of slavery.

Huger owned a thousand-acre plantation, Longwood, on the Cooper River in the Parish of St. Thomas and St. Dennis in what is now Berkeley County. Like many wealthy planters, he also maintained a town house in Charleston. He was elected to the South Carolina Senate from the Parish of St. Thomas and St. Dennis from 1818 to 1833 and established himself as a leader in that body. His political career foundered, however, when his Lowcountry constituents petitioned him to vote for nullification of the federal tariff of 1832 or resign. He refused to do either. He was chosen as a delegate to the Nullification convention from Unionist Spartanburg District (though he had probably never set foot in that upcountry district) and voted against the Ordinance of Nullification at the convention.

In gratitude for Huger's courageous stand, President Jackson appointed him to the plum job of postmaster of Charleston. Huger waited to accept the appointment until the death of incumbent Thomas Bacot, after which Huger served continuously until the Civil War. He is most famous for the alarm he sounded over abolitionist pamphlets sent to Charleston by followers of William Lloyd Garrison in 1835 and for sanctioning the destruction of that mail. The incident established a government policy drawing an iron curtain across the U.S. postal system to block antislavery agitation. Huger signaled that Unionists might have differed from Nullifiers on the proper response to the tariff issue but would stand shoulder to shoulder with their former adversaries in resisting use of federal resources to end slavery.

Though a reluctant secessionist, Huger followed his state's lead. He closed all the accounts of the Charleston Post Office, deposited the funds with the Bank of Charleston, and notified the postmaster general of his actions. The money was eventually seized by the Confederate government. After the war, the U.S. government sought to collect this money by suing Huger, but he prevailed in the lawsuit. He had by then lost almost everything. Mary Chesnut has a poignant passage in which Huger is described sitting in an armchair in the street, watching his Charleston home burn in the fire of 1861. After the war Huger served as a delegate to the state constitutional convention of 1865.

Huger and his wife, the former Sarah Rutledge, had no children of their own, but they adopted Huger's orphaned nephew Thomas Bee Huger (1820–1862). He served with distinction in the U.S. Navy in the Mexican War and commanded a battery at Morris Island in the bombardment of Fort Sumter. He was mortally wounded in the defense of New Orleans in 1862 while commanding the C.S.S. *McRae*. Thomas Bee Huger had married Marianne Meade, sister of Gen. George Meade of the Union Army. They had several children, who were left in Alfred Huger's care when their parents died. After the war, Gen. Meade, then in command of all the South Atlantic states, offered to take custody of the children from the impoverished Huger. He replied that he would not think of relinquishing them as education of the children in the North would be hostile to the memory of their gallant father.

After Huger's death, fellow Unionist and former governor Benjamin F. Perry said of him:

> Mr. Huger was a Roman in person and character, in heart and intellect. He was tall, slender and courtly in appearance, with a striking face and symmetrical features. His head and face would have adorned a Grecian or Roman medal. In his manners, he was always grave and dignified, yet cordial, frank and simple. For honor, sincerity and probity of character, no one of his illustrious compeers and associates in that proud old school of Carolina gentlemen in which he was brought up, could surpass him. Higher praise no one can bestow or desire. He was a patriot in every thought and feeling of his nature, and moreover, he was a hero by nature, and would have died cheerfully a martyr in defense of his principles.

ALFRED HUGER (1876–1938)

Lawyer   MAP LOCATION: NORTHWEST 6

Born in Charleston, Alfred Huger bore an old name that he burnished further with his literary achievement and greater success as an attorney. He was educated at Porter Military Academy and at Cornell University, from which he received an LL.B in 1903. He became one of the leading maritime lawyers in the country and was instrumental in setting up what became the State Ports Authority. He also served as a major in World War I. He wrote a major chapter of *The Carolina Low-Country* (1931), a work put out by the Society for the Preservation of Spirituals that included submissions from almost all of the important writers and artists of the Charleston Renaissance.

Daniel Elliott Huger (1779–1854)

Planter and Politician   MAP LOCATION: SOUTHEAST 23

Daniel Elliott Huger was prominent in the affairs of South Carolina and the nation throughout the first half of the nineteenth century. He was born at Limerick Plantation, one of his family's estates near Charleston. He received a traditional classical education in Charleston and graduated from the College of New Jersey (now Princeton) in 1798. He entered late into the practice of law, not being admitted to the bar until 1811, after reading law with Chancellor DeSaussure. In any case, his principal income came from the plantations he owned throughout South Carolina. He made his home in Charleston in a magnificent double house at 24 Meeting Street. In his will, he estimated that he owned approximately two hundred slaves.

Huger began his political career in the South Carolina House, where he served from 1803 to 1819. He enjoyed a quick rise to leadership among some of the most famous names of South Carolina politics. His early career in the South Carolina House was coincident with that of William Lowndes, Langdon Cheves, and John C. Calhoun. Gov. B. F. Perry later described him as a virtual dictator in that legislative chamber.

Although a Federalist, Huger was a supporter of the War of 1812. In 1814 he was commissioned a brigadier general in the South Carolina Militia. He was a close fried of Gov. Joseph Alston, who was chief magistrate of the state during the war. In 1819 Huger was elected judge of the Court of General Sessions and Common Pleas. He was widely praised for his judicial knowledge and probity.

Like his cousin and best friend Alfred Huger, Judge Huger was a Unionist. This political stance cost Huger election to the U.S. Senate in 1826, when he was defeated by the radical states' rights candidate, William Smith. By 1830 Huger felt that the issue of Nullification was so important that he resigned his seat on the bench in order to fight against it. He was elected to the South Carolina House again from 1830 to 1831 and served as a delegate to the Nullification Convention for Kingston District. He was leader of the Unionists and voted against the Ordinance of Nullification.

Judge Huger was reconciled with his old friend John C. Calhoun by the late 1830s and drifted closer to the states' rights camp. He was elected to the South Carolina Senate in 1838 and served for three years. In 1842 a coalition of old-line Unionists and states' rights legislators united to elect Huger over the radical states' rights candidate, Robert Barnwell Rhett, to take the U.S. Senate seat of Calhoun, who had resigned to run for president. Huger did not like the intrigues of Washington and was only too happy to give up his seat in 1845 in order that Calhoun might again represent South Carolina in the Senate. Afterward Huger served as a delegate to the states' rights convention of 1852 and did what he could to discourage immediate secession from the Union.

Huger died at his summer home on Sullivan's Island in 1854. Ironically, he is buried only a few feet from his old political opponent, Robert Barnwell Rhett.

Judge Huger acted as mentor to many young men. One of them was the future governor Benjamin F. Perry, who tells many fond anecdotes of Huger in his *Reminiscences of Public Men* (1883).

FRANCIS KINLOCH HUGER (1773–1855)

"Huger of Olmutz"   MAP LOCATION: SOUTHEAST 24

Francis Kinloch Huger was one of the most celebrated and daring heroes of the young republic. The story of his rescue of Lafayette at Olmutz, Austria, and subsequent imprisonment was known by every schoolboy. Today his exciting story is largely forgotten.

F. K. Huger was born in Charleston, the son of Benjamin and Mary Esther (Kinloch) Huger. In 1777, when Lafayette came to America to fight for the American Revolution, he landed north of Charleston to avoid the British blockade. By chance, he landed at the plantation of Benjamin Huger on North Island near Georgetown. Thus began the friendly relations between the Huger family and Lafayette. Benjamin Huger was killed in the cause of the American Revolution when Francis was six years old. Young Francis was sent to England for his education when he was eight. He studied at the University of Edinburgh from 1790 to 1792 and then under the celebrated Dr. John Hunter in London. He joined the medical staff of the British Army in Flanders for a few months in 1794, then went on to Vienna to continue his studies.

There he happened to meet a German doctor named Justus Erich Bollman who was determined to free Lafayette from the prison in Olmutz, Austria, in which the former Marquis was held by the enemies of the revolutionary French army he had deserted when the Terror began. Huger told Bollman of his family's connection to Lafayette and of his wish to help Lafayette if he could. After determining that Huger was sincere, Bollman enlisted him in the effort to rescue Lafayette.

Bollman managed to trade encoded notes with Lafayette to plan an escape. Lafayette was customarily given a carriage ride and a walk in a field near Olmutz for exercise and air. On the chosen day, Huger and Bollman waited for him in the field with an extra horse and a large sum of money to aid in his escape. They also had a carriage waiting for him in the nearby border village. Lafayette took his walk across the field with one guard. After a bitter struggle, Huger, Bollman, and Lafayette were able to render the guard unconscious, but in the confusion, one of the horses galloped away. Huger and Bollman pressed the money on Lafayette and put him on his horse. As the Marquis rode away, Huger yelled to him in English, "Get to Hof." Lafayette did not know that a village named Hof was nearby and thought that Huger was crying, "Get off."

Huger insisted that Bollman, who was injured, take the remaining horse. Proceeding on foot, Huger was captured within an hour. Lafayette was recaptured in a local village that night. Bollman rode around northern Austria for a week looking for Lafayette until he, too, was captured. Huger and Bollman were held in chains for three months before they were brought before a military court. Neither Huger nor Bollman would implicate anyone else. They were both sentenced to hard labor at Olmutz.

The escape plot captured international attention. Huger and Bollman were lionized in the United States, where Lafayette was regarded as a great hero. After a few months both Huger and Bollman were released from prison and expelled from Austria.

Huger returned to America and entered the University of Pennsylvania. He received his M.D. in 1797. He was commissioned a captain in the Second Artillery of the U.S. Army in 1798 and held that post until his resignation in 1801. He become a planter and owned plantations near Georgetown and a summer residence near Stateburg. Early in the War of 1812 he rejoined the Second Artillery as a lieutenant colonel and was honorably discharged as a full colonel in 1815. He served a term in the South Carolina Senate in 1816–1817.

When Lafayette made his triumphal return to America in 1825, the U.S. Congress voted the Marquis a tribute of $200,000. When Lafayette came to Columbia, he was greeted by Huger, who accompanied him to Charleston. Lafayette offered Huger half of the $200,000, but Huger answered that he had provided for his daughters and that his sons were well educated enough to be able to take care of themselves.

Huger removed to Pendleton in the 1820s and represented that district briefly in the South Carolina House of Representatives. He remained in Pendleton for most of the rest of his life. When he came back to Charleston at the end of his life he was spoken of in the awed whispers befitting a living legend. He died on February 14, 1855, though his stone in Magnolia Cemetery misprints the year of his death as 1835. His son Benjamin Huger became a major general in the Confederate States Army. His son Cleland Kinloch Huger was an extremely successful planter and merchant.

WILLIAM HARLESTON HUGER (1826–1906)

Physician   MAP LOCATION: SOUTHEAST 25

William H. Huger was deservedly one of the most beloved Charlestonians of his time. He was born in the city and received his secondary education at the schools of Christopher Cotes and J. P. Allen. He graduated from South Carolina College in 1846 and from the Medical College of South Carolina in 1849. He did postgraduate work in Paris and Dublin.

When Dr. Huger returned to Charleston in 1852, the city was in the throes of a yellow fever epidemic. He opened a ward in the uncompleted Roper Hospital, as the city hospital was already full, and determined to move into the hospital to remain among his patients. Though we now know that yellow fever is caught from mosquitoes, it was thought then that yellow fever was contagious, particularly to people who had not been "acclimated." Thus it was an extraordinarily brave young doctor who willingly exposed himself to the disease.

In 1854 Dr. Huger accepted the position of physician to the Charleston Orphan House. He was annually reelected to the post by City Council and served until his dying day. The Orphan House was one of the great symbols of civic pride in Charleston in the nineteenth century. Prominent visitors were always taken there so that they might see this expression of the "benevolence of slaveholders," as historian Barbara Bellows has so aptly put it.

During the war Dr. Huger served tirelessly as a surgeon, first on James Island and then in charge of the army hospital in Charleston. He served in the yellow fever epidemic in Wilmington in 1864. He was back in Charleston at the surrender of the city in time to organize the evacuation of some six hundred wounded soldiers by rail from the hospitals of Charleston to temporary hospitals in Cheraw, South Carolina.

Dr. Huger was a devotee of the track in Charleston, which in its time was as important to horse racing as Churchill Downs is today. Indeed, the gates of Belmont are the gates from the old Washington Race Course in Charleston. Dr. Huger was for many years steward of the now-defunct Jockey Club.

Mary Vereen Huguenin (1909–1994)

Co-Editor of Charleston Receipts   MAP LOCATION: SOUTHWEST 35

Mary Vereen Huguenin was a Georgia native who married into an old Charleston family and enriched the lives of Charlestonians with her work for charities. She was born and raised in Moultrie, Georgia, and was sent to Mt. Vernon Seminary in Washington, D.C., for her education. While at Mt. Vernon she befriended Lavinia Huguenin of Charleston. She visited her friend in Charleston and there fell in love with Lavinia's brother, Thomas A. Huguenin. They were married in 1932. Together they restored the Andrew Hassell House at 64 Meeting Street and Halidon Hill, which they had moved from Quinby Plantation in Berkeley County.

She and her friend Anne Montague Stoney co-edited the cookbook *Charleston Receipts* in 1950 as a fundraiser for the Junior League of Charleston. They collected recipes from members and produced a local classic. Mrs. Huguenin's savvy marketing skills were crucial to the book's early success. The book has been continuously in print for over forty years and has sold over 600,000 copies.

Mrs. Huguenin was also involved in founding what is now the Charleston Speech and Hearing Clinic and the Trident United Way.

Horace Lawson Hunley (1823–1863) and Crew Members of the *H. L. Hunley*

Confederate Submariners   MAP LOCATION: SOUTHEAST 26

The saga of the submersible vessel *H. L. Hunley* is one of the most famous incidents of the Civil War in Charleston. Dubbed in its time "a peripatetic coffin," the submarine has often been reported in legend to have claimed the lives of even more crews than it actually did before bringing a Union vessel and five Yankee sailors with it in going down for the last time. The lasting allure of this story shares with the cemetery a mesmerizing, horrifying source of fascination. Wandering around the graves of Magnolia naturally invites visitors to indulge in the classic claustrophobic fantasy of imagining burial alive. The *Hunley* provided almost every man who entered it the experience of that terror.

The stepson of a wealthy plantation owner in Louisiana, H. L. Hunley graduated from law school at the University of Louisiana (now Tulane) and served a term in the state legislature in 1848–1849. His ties to the plantation economy strengthened with the 1850 marriage of his sister to sugar tycoon Robert Ruffin Barrow. Hunley evidently became involved in the export trade, and from 1857 until secession he also held a position in the office of the collector of the port of New Orleans. When the war came, his business interests as well as his Confederate loyalties quickly prompted him to focus on local efforts to resist the Union blockade of Southern ports.

As elsewhere in the Confederacy, this impulse led to attempts to advance the technology for submersible vessels so as to enable them to attack blockading ships. Hunley, Barrow, and other investors formed a syndicate to fund tinkering toward this end by the owner of a machine shop, James McClintock. The men had to scuttle their first prototype, the *Pioneer,* on the fall of New Orleans in April 1862. McClintock and Hunley shifted base to Mobile, where they added the aid of William Alexander, an engineer in the Confederate Army detailed to help with the experiments, and a Confederate soldier wounded at Shiloh, Lt. George Dixon. Hunley personally financed the experiments that produced the *American Diver,* which sank without loss of life while being towed in February 1863. Hunley then lined up investors for a third venture, which in honor of his contributions was named for him.

Adapted from a cylindrical iron boiler, the *Hunley* was about forty feet long, four feet high, and three-and-a-half feet across the middle. It was propelled by a central crank turned by seven crew members seated along a long bench while the commander of the vessel stood to pilot it. The only light inside came from a candle that also served to warn the crew when they would soon run out of oxygen. Partly because local topography made use of the *Hunley* more practical in Charleston than in Mobile and also because the Union blockade and overall military situation were more urgent there, the owners sent the submarine by rail to Charleston in August 1863. They keenly noted the offer of a $100,000 reward for sinking either the *New Ironsides* or the *Wabash,* two of the most formidable ships in the South Atlantic blocking squadron.

In the next six months, the *Hunley* sank three times and experienced several terrifying near disasters. Placed by the Confederate Navy in command of a crew of volunteers, Lt. John Payne evidently stepped on a lever that caused the vessel to dive with its hatches open on August 29, 1863, drowning five men. When the ship was recovered, arms and legs had to be sawed off the bloated bodies in order to pull the dead men through the small hatches of the submarine. Hunley then recruited a new crew of civilian volunteers from the machine shop in Mobile. He was in personal command of his namesake when it sank for the second time on October 15, 1863. Divers found its nose stuck in the mud at a 30° angle, almost sixty feet under water. Upon the raising and opening of the ship, even Gen. P. G. T. Beauregard thought the eight contorted figures frozen in their desperate struggle to pump water and find air were "indescribably ghastly." This second crew was buried at Magnolia in early November 1863. Lt. Dixon next stepped forward to request permission to command the *Hunley.* Gen. Beauregard reluctantly permitted him to recruit a third crew, which posed remarkably little difficulty. But Lt. Dixon was under orders not to submerge the vessel when it set out from Sullivan's Island on February 17, 1864. The *Hunley*

The interment of the third and final crew of the *Hunley*, April 2004.
Courtesy of the *Post and Courier*

carried beneath it a fifteen-foot-long spar fixed with an explosive device that the crew intended to embed in the hull of the U.S.S. *Housatonic* before reversing course and unwinding a cord that would detonate the charge. The plan worked and the blockading ship sank with a loss of five Union lives. It was the first recorded instance of a successful attack by a submersible vessel. The eight-man crew did not live to celebrate this accomplishment, however, for the *Hunley* soon joined the *Housatonic* on the bottom of the sea.

The reasons for the third sinking of the *Hunley* have not been conclusively determined, in part because so many calamities are plausible possibilities. Perhaps because tides and currents overwhelmed the men cranking the propeller, perhaps because the ship took on enough water to lose buoyancy, perhaps because the rudder broke off in a collision, perhaps for some other reason, the *Hunley* made little progress home before everyone aboard suffocated to death.

The discovery of the *Hunley* wreck in May 1995 prompted a massive effort to restore the vessel and inter the bodies that had been entombed in the harbor for more than a century. Coincidentally, the bodies from the first crew joined those of the second crew at Magnolia not long before the burial of those from the third crew. The five initial casualties had been buried in a seamen's graveyard that was somehow lost beneath concrete and asphalt when the Citadel built Johnson Hagood Stadium in 1948. They were recovered when the stadium was renovated in 1999. A group of Confederate reenactors organized ceremonies for these men on March 25, 2000, that featured a 4.5-mile long procession of the caskets on horse-drawn caissons. With public interest heightened by the impending raising of the *Hunley* wreck from the water, which would take place within five months, about 2,500 people were at Magnolia for the interment of the first crew alongside the second crew. Burial of the third crew on April 17, 2004, began with a similar procession from White Point Garden to Magnolia Cemetery. This occasion generated massive publicity; approximately three hundred reporters from seventy news organizations attended the eight-hour-long ceremony. Organizers estimated that the procession featured 9,000 men and women in period costume, watched on their route and at the cemetery by as many as 20,000 onlookers. The event was described as the last Confederate funeral and was surely one of the most spectacular.

TRISTRAM TUPPER HYDE (1862–1931)

Mayor of Charleston   MAP LOCATION: NORTHWEST 7

T. T. Hyde was a rather colorless banker, real estate developer, and insurance agent who became the standardbearer for the "aristocrats" of Charleston in the mayoral campaigns of 1911, 1915, and 1919 against the Irish Catholic insurgent John P. Grace. The races were some of the most violent and corrupt in Charleston history. It is ironic that T. T. Hyde, a Baptist Sunday School superintendent, was one of the major actors in the drama.

Hyde was born of a respectable Charleston family (some of his Tupper cousins developed Tupperware) and was educated at the High School of Charleston. He started a real estate and insurance firm, Tristram T. Hyde and Sons, which developed much of what is now known as North Charleston. At one time he was president of the Commercial National Bank. He rose to the rank of major in the Sumter Guards. He was for thirty years superintendent of the Sunday School for Citadel Square Baptist Church. Hyde was altogether respectable: a sober, industrious businessman. When he became the handpicked candidate of retiring mayor Robert Goodwyn Rhett and the "Broad Street Ring," there was every reason to think that he would be easily elected.

Only one person stood in Hyde's way, John P. Grace. Grace was the candidate of the working man. He was a booster who was remarkably progressive yet shunned by the Progressives. He was an Irish nationalist who was both loved and hated in Charleston with an intense passion. In the mayoral election of 1911 Grace caught Hyde and the Broad Street Ring flat-footed. Hyde was a poor speaker at best. Grace was never less than eloquent. As in the election of 1891, long-simmering resentments came to the surface against the Broad Street Ring's high-handed ways. In the Democratic primary (which was tantamount to election), Grace defeated Hyde by a substantial majority.

Grace's term was marked by many progressive steps. He pretty much let the liquor interests have their way. Grace would fine the "blind tigers" of Charleston on such a regular basis that the fines in reality became a tax or license fee. When election time neared and reform-minded governor Richard I. Manning threatened to send in state constables to enforce the liquor regulations, Grace stepped up raids, but it was understood these raids were primarily for show.

In the election of 1915 the Broad Street Ring was determined not to be caught off guard again. They captured control of the Charleston Democratic Executive Committee, which would rule in the case of any election disputes or challenged ballots. In addition, Governor Manning ordered state militia troops to Charleston to ensure an "orderly" election. Governor Manning also authorized anti-Grace county sheriff J. Elmore Martin to swear in additional deputies as necessary.

Despite or perhaps because of the heavy police presence, the election proceeded very smoothly. The first returns gave Hyde a lead of nineteen votes, a lead which grew to 109 votes the next day. Grace claimed that his votes had been short-counted and demanded a recount. The ballot boxes were sealed and taken to a second-floor room at the southeast corner of King and George Streets, where they were watched by Grace and Hyde lieutenants. The votes were to be recounted at noon on October 15.

At the appointed hour, a fight broke out in the next room and pistols were shot off in both rooms. People in the corner rooms sprang for the windows and at least two ballot boxes were thrown into the street and their ballots irretrievably scattered. When the dust had settled, five people were shot. An *Evening Post* reporter, Sidney Cohen, lay dead. The city was ready to explode.

Charges and countercharges were slung back and forth, but the confusion was such and the witnesses so partisan that no facts were ever definitively established. The executive committee, controlled by Hyde's forces, certified his election by a twenty-eight vote margin. Grace squawked but ultimately stepped aside in the interests of peace.

After the election, Grace seemed bent on political suicide. He and his newspaper, the Charleston *American,* fervently embraced the Irish nationalist cause to a degree that walked right up to the point of treason and sometimes beyond. His pro-German editorials caused the federal government to revoke the paper's second-class mailing privileges. Some of Grace's newspapermen were indicted as complicitous in the scuttling of the German steamer *Liebenfels* in Charleston harbor channel in February 1917. Grace narrowly escaped imprisonment himself. Hyde, on the other hand, strongly backed the war effort and successfully sought expansion of Charleston's Navy Yard. Moreover, he had arranged for city control of the waterworks as a wartime measure and thus solved a chronic water shortage that had long plagued Charleston. In addition, he had put the city budget in the black and had overseen a reduction in municipal taxes. Hyde would have seemed to be a sure thing for reelection in 1919.

But Hyde was not without critics, and not only from the Grace side. Hyde's tight administration of the city during World War I and his extreme fiscal conservatism to achieve a tax reduction resulted in such draconian law enforcement and reduction of city services that he became vulnerable. Baptist that he was, Hyde ruthlessly enforced prohibition, often ignoring constitutional niceties such as search warrants. In his administration the city police conducted over two thousand raids on liquor establishments, sixty percent without warrants. Hyde also closed down the red-light district that had been tolerated but regulated in past administrations. The trade simply dispersed throughout the city and concentrated in areas outside the city limits. In addition, a wartime shortage of labor prompted a Hyde-sponsored "work or jail" law that required all able-bodied men to carry employment certification. This law resulted in much harassment of ordinary citizens. Taken together, these measures engendered a great deal of anti-Hyde feeling. When added to the economic dislocations resulting from the abrupt shift to peacetime, Hyde was in trouble.

Hyde's spokesman harped on Grace's seditious wartime record, but Grace countered that the navy base was expanded on land owned by Hyde and Robert Goodwyn Rhett, which Hyde and Rhett sold to the government at greatly inflated prices. The Charleston *American* labelled Hyde a "paytriot," and the charge stuck. Grace's machine was indeed a machine and well-oiled. Hyde's campaign sputtered along with no momentum, always on the defensive. Grace and his main lieutenant, W. Turner Logan, were able to gain narrow control of the city executive committee and thus ensure that in a close election Grace would triumph.

The election could not have been closer. The first returns showed Hyde ahead by one vote of over 5000 cast. After ballot challenges before the Grace-controlled executive committee, Hyde lost by twenty-five votes. Like Grace four years earlier, Hyde raged at the unfairness but ultimately withdrew in the interests of peace and lived the rest of his life as a real estate and insurance broker.

HELEN VON KOLNITZ HYER (1896–1983)

Poet   MAP LOCATION: NORTHEAST 8

Helen von Kolnitz Hyer was a prolific and long-lived poet. She was born in Charleston and educated at Ashley Hall and Simmons College in Boston. While at Ashley Hall she helped found the literary magazine and wrote the school song.

During World War I, Miss von Kolnitz sold war bonds and worked at the Charleston Museum under its director, Paul Rea. At the museum she was in charge of public instruction and started the museum collection of Charleston-made objects, today the finest such collection in existence. She met her husband, Edward Hyer, at the museum and followed him in museum work, first to Nashville, Tennessee, and later to Grand Rapids then Lansing, Michigan. There she raised her five children and helped her husband start a weekly newspaper, *The Michigan Conservationist,* which ran for six months and then died off, along with the banks, in 1934. After the closing of the *Conservationist,* Mrs. Hyer held a number of jobs with the state of Michigan until her return to South Carolina.

All her life she wrote in leisure hours as her world filled up with children, grandchildren, and great-grandchildren. Not surprisingly, she wrote much of her work for juveniles, including *Hurricane Harbor* (1927), *The Magnificent Squeak* (1929), and *The Wings and the Woodle and Other Stories* (1935). She also published two nature studies, *On Shiny Wings* (1926) and *Stories by Seasons* (1930).

Hyer is most remembered for her poetry. She was a founder of the Poetry Society of South Carolina and published four volumes: *Santee Songs* (1923), *Wine Dark Sea* (1930), *Danger Never Sleeps* (1970), and *What the Wind Forgets: A Woman's Heart Remembers* (1975). In recognition of her career, she was named South Carolina's second poet laureate in 1974. Mrs. Hyer was a beloved figure throughout the state, especially to the young.

DUNCAN NATHANIEL INGRAHAM (1802–1891)

Naval Officer   MAP LOCATION: SOUTHEAST 27

Duncan Nathaniel Ingraham followed many family precedents into his career as a naval commander. His grandfather, father, and uncle were all sea captains, as were several prominent relatives by marriage. His father served with John Paul Jones on board the *Bonhomme Richard* in its famous Revolutionary War engagement with the *Serapis*. Born in Charleston, Ingraham became a midshipman in the United States Navy by the age of ten and served throughout the War of 1812. He continued to rise in rank afterward and served in the Mexican War. His greatest fame came while he was commanding a sloop in the Mediterranean in 1853. Martin Koszta, a follower of Kossuth, had come to the United States and declared his intention of applying for American citizenship but had returned for a time to Turkey, where he was captured and imprisoned on an Austrian vessel. Ingraham determined that Koszta was entitled to American protection and secured his release by threat of force. His conduct was widely applauded and earned him a Congressional medal.

After a tour of duty as chief of the Bureau of Ordnance, Ingraham was again commanding in the Mediterranean when South Carolina seceded. He resigned his commission in January 1861 and entered the Confederate Navy. He served as chief of ordnance until November 1861, when he was placed in command of naval forces on the South Carolina coast. He supervised construction of the ironclads *Chicora* and *Palmetto State* in Charleston and commanded the two ships in a surprise attack on the Union blockade on the night of Jan. 30–31, 1863. After disabling two Union ships and scattering the others in the area, he joined Gen. P. G.T. Beauregard in announcing that the blockade had been raised, which would by international law have required the federal government to notify neutral nations of its intent to reinstitute the blockade. That slow procedure would have opened the port of Charleston for months. But Union ships had quickly returned to their positions, and England declined to treat the blockade as broken. Ingraham gave up his shipboard position as flag officer in March 1863, three months after his sixtieth birthday, but retained shore command of naval forces in South Carolina.

Ingraham was married in 1827 to Harriott Horry Laurens, whose grandfathers were Henry Laurens and John Rutledge. He was a friend of Mary Chesnut and appears often in her chronicle of the Civil War.

LOUIE BOYD JENKINS (1921–1991)
MARGARET QUANTE JENKINS (1923–2002)

Physicians   MAP LOCATION: NORTHEAST 9

The Jenkinses were two of the outstanding doctors in Charleston for most of the second half of the twentieth century. Dr. Louie Jenkins rose from life as a poor boy in Florence County to become one of the preeminent surgeons and clinical professors in the country.

He was born in Florence, South Carolina, and graduated from Florence High School in 1938. He graduated with honors from the College of Charleston in 1941 and again with honors from what is now the Medical University of South Carolina in 1945. He served in the U.S. Navy from 1944 to 1949. He became widely recognized for his extraordinary skills as a surgeon. He served as chief of staff of Roper, Baker, and St. Francis Hospitals and as president of the Medical Society of South Carolina. Under his tutelage, literally scores of physicians received their training. He was a demanding but fair teacher.

Dr. Margaret Q. Jenkins attended Newberry College and then the Medical College of Georgia, where she was one of two women in her class. After her graduation in 1949 she met and married Dr. Louie Jenkins while on an internship at Roper Hospital. Dr. Margaret Jenkins went on to complete a residency in pediatrics at Roper and joined the faculty of MUSC in 1953 as its first female professor. Earlier in her career she established the MUSC Cystic Fibrosis Clinic, which she headed until her retirement in 1989. In addition she served for many years as director of the Rheumatic Fever Clinic and the Pediatric Ambulatory Division. She took the lead in numerous initiatives that were important to the community. For example, she founded the Charleston Poison Control Center, for which she was honored by the U.S. Public Health Service, and started a well-baby clinic on Edisto Island. She was also the first woman to chair a board of the Greater Charleston YMCA. In 1966 she was elected a fellow of the American Academy of Pediatrics.

Amazingly, the Drs. Jenkins combined these busy careers with raising five daughters.

Micah Jenkins (1835–1864)

Confederate General   MAP LOCATION: SOUTHEAST 28

Micah Jenkins was one of South Carolina's most precocious and outstanding warriors during the Civil War. He was born on Edisto Island and entered the South Carolina Military Academy (later the Citadel) in 1851. He graduated first in his class at the age of nineteen. In 1855 he helped to establish the King's Mountain Military Academy, which continued to operate until the outbreak of the Civil War. At the beginning of the war, Jenkins helped to organize the Fifth South Carolina Regiment and was elected colonel.

Jenkins fought valiantly at First Manassas and in battles around Richmond. He commanded a brigade at Seven Pines and was commended by Gen. D. H. Hill for bravery and competence. Promoted to brigadier general in July 1862, Jenkins was severely wounded at Second Manassas. There Robert E. Lee rode up to him and reportedly said, "I hope yet to see you one of my lieutenant generals."

Ordered in 1863 to Tennessee, where he fought at Chickamauga and in Longstreet's Knoxville campaign, Jenkins returned to Virginia in time for the second day of the Battle of the Wilderness. As he was riding into battle at Longstreet's side, he said, "I am happy; I have felt despair of the cause for some months, but am relieved, and feel that we will put the enemy back across the Rapidan before night." He was almost immediately killed by what we now term "friendly fire" from his own troops.

At his death, Gen. Jenkins left four sons. Maj. Micah Jenkins became a hero of the Battle of San Juan Hill. Another son, John Jenkins, became a major general in the U.S. Army.

EDWARD IREDELL RENWICK JENNINGS (1898–1929)

Artist   MAP LOCATION: SOUTHWEST 36

Edward I. R. "Ned" Jennings was perhaps the most unusual artist in Charleston history. He experimented with a wide range of artistic media and looked back to classical models and forward to abstraction. His short life ended with a self-inflicted gunshot wound in his studio in the Confederate Home.

The son of the Charleston postmaster, Jennings attended Porter Military Academy. He became the youngest member of the Charleston Light Dragoons to go to the Mexican border in 1916 and was a field hospital worker in World War I. While working near the front, Jennings was gassed and for a few weeks blinded. Briefly enrolled at the College of

Ned Jennings, *Dracula*, watercolor, ca. 1927. Courtesy of Harlan Greene

Charleston, he went on to study art at Teacher's College of Columbia University and theater design at Carnegie Tech.

Upon his return to Charleston in 1924 Jennings became affiliated with a number of local cultural organizations. He staged, designed, and wrote shows and pageants for those groups. He was most closely associated with the Charleston Museum and its director, Laura Bragg. He designed a number of dioramas for the museum in a "Drama of Civilization" series. At the time of his death, he was also curator of art at the museum and an instructor at the Carolina Art Association.

Jennings was particularly noted for his work with masks. The masks were often called "weird" by contemporary observers, and they remain strange and fascinating today. Jennings was afflicted with a severe cleft palate, and he often wore the masks and performed with them in social situations. John Bennett said of Jennings that he had "closed in upon himself a queer emotional defense, and outlet, in his macabre dances. These were remarkable . . . strange things."

Jennings left Charleston to spend the greater part of 1927 studying art in Paris. Upon his return, he experimented with abstract and surrealist art.

Jennings continues to have an influence in Charleston sixty years after his death. In 1979 a retrospective of his work was held at the Gibbes Art Gallery during the Spoleto festival. The character Ned Grimke in Harlan Greene's important novel *Why We Never Danced the Charleston* (1984) is loosely based on Ned Jennings.

Caroline Howard Gilman Glover Jervey (1823–1877)

Novelist   MAP LOCATION: SOUTHEAST 29

Caroline Jervey was the second daughter of Caroline (Howard) and the Rev. Samuel Gilman. Her parents were born in Massachusetts, but both played an important role in the literary and cultural life of South Carolina and the nation in the years before the Civil War. Caroline Gilman was a prolific writer of poetry and prose whose books included *Recollections of a Housekeeper* (1834), *Recollections of a Southern Matron* (1837), and *The Poetry of Travelling in the United States* (1838). In addition, she edited and largely wrote one of the first children's magazines in the country, *The Rose-Bud* (later *The Southern Rose Bud* and then *The Southern Rose*) from 1832 to 1839. The Rev. Samuel Gilman was the pastor of the Unitarian Church at Charleston from 1819 until his death in 1858. Although he wrote a number of books, he is best remembered today as the author of Harvard's alma mater, "Fair Harvard."

Their daughter Caroline was born in Charleston and received the typical education of a Southern girl of her day, broadened of course by her parents' wide knowledge. She was married at the age of seventeen to John Wilson Glover, a young planter from near Walterboro, South Carolina. Six years later, her husband was drowned off the Charleston Bar and she was left a widow with three young children. She moved back to her parents' home at 11 Orange Street and began her own writing career. Most often she wrote anonymously, but when she took a pseudonym it was her mother's maiden name, Caroline Howard.

She wrote two novels in addition to assorted works for children and short stories. *Vernon Grove; or, Hearts as They Are* (1858) was originally serialized in the *Southern Literary Messenger*. The publication excited much favorable comment and something of a rave review from the *Atlantic Monthly*, which declared that the work "will give its author high rank among the lady novelists of our day and country." *Helen Courtenay's Promise* appeared in 1866. She also joined with Caroline Howard Gilman on *Poems and Stories by a Mother and Daughter* (1872) and *The Young Fortune Teller* (1874).

In 1864 Mrs. Glover married Charleston physician Lewis Jervey. The only child of this marriage was a daughter, Clare Jervey (1864–1933). Clare Jervey was, with Susan Pringle Frost, one of the first independent businesswomen in Charleston. Like Miss Frost, Miss Jervey was a stenographer, and had a business listed in her name as early as 1906 in the Charleston city directory. In addition to her business career, Miss Jervey preserved and organized the papers of her grandmother, Mrs. Gilman. They are on deposit at the South Carolina Historical Society. She also compiled the extremely valuable book, *Inscriptions on the Tablets and Gravestones in St. Michael's Church and Churchyard* (1906).

THEODORE DEHON JERVEY (1859–1947)

Lawyer and Author   MAP LOCATION: SOUTHEAST 30

Theodore D. Jervey was a lawyer who made a bad career choice. He earned his living as an attorney but satisfied himself as a writer. He was born in 1859, the son of Theodore Dehon Jervey, Sr., and Anne Hume Simons. In an autobiographical fragment, Jervey described himself in boyhood as "especially interested in books, though otherwise he was of an indolent disposition." He graduated from the Virginia Military Institute in 1879 and soon after embarked upon a career in law.

Jervey was an extraordinarily prolific author for a man who maintained an active legal practice and who served as city recorder (judge) for a number of years. Among the books he published are: *Migration of the Negroes: A Study of the U.S. Census Tables* (1895); *The Negro Problem* (1902); *The Elder Brother: A Novel* (1905); *Robert Y. Hayne and His Times* (1909); *The Railroad, the Conqueror* (1913); *The Great War: The Causes and the Waging of It* (1917); and *The Slave Trade: Slavery and Color* (1925). Jervey was also for many years president of the South Carolina Historical Society.

FANNY MAHON KING (1865–1952)

Artist   MAP LOCATION: NORTHWEST 8

Fanny Mahon King remains a quiet presence among the better twentieth-century Charleston artists. She was born in Aiken, the daughter of Minna (Legaré) and Charles Mahon. She was married to Thomas Gadsden King. She was educated in Washington, D.C., but received most of her instruction in art in Charleston, albeit from out-of-town artists. King studied with a number of nationally prominent artists: William Posey Silva, Frank

Swift Chase, Harry Leith-Ross, Alfred Hutty, Emile Gruppe, Ivan F. Summers, and G. Howard Hilder.

With Emma Gilchrist, she was in the group of artists who slightly preceded the Charleston Renaissance. Her medium of choice was oils. The great majority of Charleston artists expressed themselves in watercolors to better interpret the extraordinary local light. King's Lowcountry scenes and still-lifes hold up quite well today and exude a haunted quality that is no small part of their appeal. She was an early prizewinner in the competitions of the Southern States Art League. Her works are in the permanent collections of the Nashville Museum of Art, the High Museum in Atlanta, and the Gibbes Museum of Art in Charleston.

King lived out her life at Point Pleasant Plantation near Meggett, South Carolina. Though she painted prolifically, most of her work is tied up in private collections and commands high prices when it comes on the market. She lies in an unmarked grave near Emma Gilchrist.

KING OF THE CLOUDS (1882–1883)

Confirmed Rumor   MAP LOCATION: SOUTHEAST 31

For many years a legend has been passed amongst the groundskeepers of Magnolia Cemetery that an Indian chief buried in Magnolia Cemetery directs the birds of the area to congregate in the area of the next interment. The birds seem to have some prescience, at least according to the groundskeepers, though it may be the same foreknowledge that allows a seer to predict with absolute certainty that a Democrat will encounter strong opposition from a Republican.

The truth of the King of the Clouds is both less grandiose and more poignant than his legend. All that is known of King of the Clouds is from the interment record of Magnolia: a one-year-old infant was buried on December 17, 1883; he died of "cerebro spinal meningitis" at the Indian camp on Ashley Street, attended by Dr. E. E. Jenkins; his place of nativity is listed as "Dakota"; the expenses of his lot and burial were $7.50.

He lies in the Strangers' Ground, section 1, row 14, lot 14. He is listed in the interment records as "Clouds, King of the."

SAMUEL LAPHAM (1892–1972)

Architect   MAP LOCATION: SOUTHWEST 37

A partner in the most important architectural firm in twentieth-century Charleston, Samuel Lapham, Jr., made substantial contributions to the landscape of his native city. After preparatory education at the University School of Charleston, he earned a bachelor's degree at the College of Charleston. He then went to the Massachusetts Institute of Technology for training in architecture, graduating in 1916. He worked briefly in Boston and Akron before entering the Army. His unit reached France in the final months of World War I. Lapham then returned to Ohio, but in 1920 Albert Simons invited him to come home to form an architectural firm.

Simons & Lapham designed or restored scores of buildings in Charleston and the Lowcountry. During the 1920s their practice centered on wealthy Northerners purchasing Charleston vacation homes or plantations for shooting parties. This work included many of the private residences on the grounds of Yeamans Hall, where they were also involved in the design of the main club house. The nature of this market is illustrated by the fact that the dog kennels they designed in 1929 for E. F. Hutton's plantation at Prospect Hill cost $12,000, considerably more than the $9,800 that Albert Simons had spent on his own house at 84 South Bay Street six years earlier. During the Great Depression the firm received numerous public commissions, including the WPA-funded Dock Street Theatre restoration and extensive undertakings at the Charleston Navy Yard and Parris Island. Apart from his work for the firm, Lapham also served during the late 1930s as an architect for several public housing projects in Charleston. Lapham returned to active military duty in World War II, based in Atlanta. Notable commissions after the war included the Municipal Airport Terminal (1947) and Petigru College at the University of South Carolina (1948).

In addition to their design partnership, Lapham collaborated with Simons on *Early Architecture of Charleston* (1927), and the two joined with Samuel Gaillard Stoney to produce *Plantations of the Carolina Low Country* (1938). Lapham was active in the College of Charleston alumni association and served for a time as its president. He was also a member of St. Cecilia Society, the Carolina Yacht Club, the South Carolina Society, the Charleston Club, and other groups. As his tombstone indicates, he was made a Fellow of the American Institute of Architects in 1937.

MARY WILKERSON MIDDLETON PINCKNEY LEE (1874–1959)

Grande Dame   MAP LOCATION: SOUTHWEST 38

Mrs. Robert E. Lee III, as she was known at her death, was born Mary Wilkerson Middleton in Charleston in 1874. She was the daughter of Ralph Izard Middleton and Virginia Memminger Middleton. On her mother's side she was the granddaughter of Christopher Gustavus Memminger, first secretary of the treasury of the Confederacy. On her father's side she was a direct descendant of Declaration of Independence signer Arthur Middleton and of Senator Ralph Izard, the first U. S. senator from South Carolina. Her great-grandfather Lt. Ralph Izard was a naval hero of Tripoli. Mrs. Lee christened the destroyer *U.S.S. Izard,* which was named in honor of him in 1942.

Mrs. Lee was first married to prominent attorney and author Gustavus M. Pinckney, her first cousin. Mr. Pinckney died in 1912, and seven years later the widow Pinckney married Col. Robert E. Lee III, a member of the Washington, D.C. bar. Mrs. Lee quickly became one of the leading lights of Washington society and so remained to the end of her life.

After the death of Col. Lee, Mrs. Lee fell in love with Frederich August Richard, Count von Strensch L'Estrange de Blackmere. A mischievous Charleston cousin of Mrs. Lee coined a couplet that was forever associated with her:

> Mary Middleton Pinckney Lee
> On the prowl for number three.

Mrs. Lee never married a third time, but she assembled her late husbands and boy-friend in a plot in Magnolia Cemetery, where she joined them in 1959.

ROBERT E. LEE III (1869–1922)

Lawyer   MAP LOCATION: SOUTHWEST 38

Col. Robert Edward Lee III was born in Petersburg, Virginia, on February 11, 1869. He was the son of Gen. Robert E. Lee's nephew, Confederate cavalry general William Henry Fitzhugh "Rooney" Lee, who is best remembered for prompting his Harvard classmate Henry Adams to observe that "the Southerner had no mind; he had temperament." Col. Lee received a law degree from, appropriately enough, Washington and Lee University and became a member of the bar of the District of Columbia. He served as an aide-de-camp and colonel on the staff of Virginia governor A. J. Montague. In 1919 he married Mrs. Gustavus Pinckney of Charleston, née Mary Middleton.

Col. Lee died of heart complications in Roanoke in September 1922. He was not destined to rest in peace for a few years. Originally he was entombed with his family at Lee Chapel on the campus of Washington and Lee University. Mrs. Lee instituted suit to bring his body to Charleston, and the board of trustees of Washington and Lee finally acceded to her wishes in 1938.

GEORGE SWINTON LEGARÉ (1869–1913)

Lawyer and Member of Congress   MAP LOCATION: NORTHWEST 10

George S. Legaré used his extraordinary charisma to gain election to the U.S. House of Representatives at the age of thirty-three. He was born in Rockville, South Carolina, a sleepy fishing village and local resort some twenty-five miles from Charleston. He put himself through Porter Academy by working in a dairy. He studied for two years at the University of South Carolina before he obtained a clerkship in Washington, D.C., which allowed him to study at Georgetown University. He received his law degree in 1893.

Legaré was a bulldog in the courtroom. His eloquence and passion in prosecuting his cases marked him early on as one of the great trial lawyers of the Charleston bar. In 1898 he became corporation counsel for the city of Charleston. In 1903 he won a hard-fought battle to become a member of Congress. He was well known in Congress for his gregarious good nature and affability. He contracted tuberculosis and battled it throughout his last years in Congress. He finally succumbed to its effects in 1913.

Legaré's son, **William Storen Legaré** (1901–1930), who was only twelve years old when his father died, showed evidence of his father's precocity in politics. He was elected to the South Carolina Senate at the age of twenty-six and was talked of as a candidate for governor when his life was cut short in a car accident. He is buried beside his father. George

Legaré's granddaughter, Nancy Stevenson, became the first elected female state-wide office-holder in South Carolina history when she was sworn in as lieutenant governor of South Carolina in 1979.

HUGH SWINTON LEGARÉ (1797–1843)

Scholar and Statesman MAP LOCATION: SOUTHEAST 32

Hugh Legaré is a prominent figure in the history of American intellectuals engaged in public affairs. His essays and letters explored central ideas of his era and set a standard of erudition and rigor in Charleston literature unsurpassed in the antebellum United States. At the same time, he yearned for political power as well as literary recognition. His frustrations in that quest seemed to himself and other observers a cautionary parable, though his successes would carry him into Congress and the Cabinet.

Legaré was a celebrated prodigy in his youth. For years he devoted fifteen hours each day to reading. Some of his iron determination may have reflected his self-consciousness about his appearance. Infection from a smallpox vaccination as a child on St. John's Island

The 1857 monument to Hugh Swinton Legaré after Hurricane Hugo in 1989.
The monument was later reconstructed. Courtesy of the Magnolia Cemetery Trust

distorted his growth and left him with a fine head and torso but badly shriveled and misshapen arms and legs. He received his early education at the College of Charleston and at Moses Waddel's famous Willington Academy. He graduated first in the South Carolina College class of 1814. He then traveled in Europe, settling at the University of Edinburgh to study the Scottish amalgamation of the civil law system descended from Rome and the common law tradition of England.

A promising and competitive young man of substantial though not spectacular wealth, Legaré won a seat in the state legislature upon his return to South Carolina in 1820. Defeated for reelection, he began to practice law in Charleston. The city sent him back to the state legislature from 1824 until 1830, when his colleagues elected him to succeed James L. Petigru as attorney general. Meanwhile, he played a leading role in the 1828 launching of the *Southern Review,* a quarterly that sought to provide Charleston with a counterpart to Boston's respected *North American Review.* As its title suggested, the new journal reflected deepening sectional tensions. The publication provided a forum for writers of different political views, however, and hardly limited itself to current affairs. Legaré contributed more than two dozen essays over the four years that the *Southern Review* lasted, addressing such topics as "Classical Learning," "Codification," and "Early Spanish Ballads." In these and later writings, Legaré showed conflicted passions for both the classical inheritance he had mastered so well and the contemporary appeal of Romanticism.

Legaré's opposition to Nullification limited his longterm prospects in state politics, and the tariff controversy also introduced to South Carolina a popular political culture for which he was ill-suited. Although eager to be a statesman, he would not immerse himself in the day-to-day business of politics among either voters or party leaders. He wisely accepted an appointment as *chargé d'affaires* in the Brussels legation from 1832 to 1836, a plum offered for his Unionism and because Secretary of State Edward Livingston shared his interest in civil law. On his return serendipity handed him a seat in Congress, as John C. Calhoun used the election of Legaré to punish incumbent Henry Laurens Pinckney for his course in the Gag Rule controversy. Legaré promptly lost the seat by declining to follow Calhoun's lead on federal financial policy. Politically homeless, he found a patron in the equally isolated President John Tyler, who named Legaré attorney general after most of the Cabinet inherited from William Henry Harrison resigned in protest in September 1841. Legaré served ably in the position, and when Daniel Webster finally followed his Whig colleagues out of the administration in 1843 Tyler also made Legaré interim secretary of state. Legaré had been holding the two posts for about six weeks when he joined the president in Boston for the dedication of the Bunker Hill Monument. Long troubled by digestive maladies, he suffered a severe attack on the day of the ceremonies. He died shortly afterward in the Beacon Hill home of scholar George Ticknor, one of the many admiring friends Legaré had won both through his talents and the sociability of a lifelong disappointed bachelor.

Michael O'Brien's *A Character of Hugh Legaré* (1985) is one of the great works of Charleston biography.

An advertisement for the Sea Grass Basket Company. Courtesy of the Folklife Resource Center, McKissick Museum, University of South Carolina

CLARENCE WILLIAM LEGERTON (1882–1958)

Merchant   MAP LOCATION: NORTHEAST 10

C. W. Legerton was the owner of Charleston's most popular bookstore and helped see to the survival of the African American sea grass basket craft by his marketing skills. The son of Charles William and Jennie (Adams) Legerton, he graduated from Clemson in 1903 with a degree in textile engineering. He worked in management positions in the mills around the Southeast until he returned to Charleston to help run his family's company.

In that capacity, Legerton was able to begin marketing sweetgrass baskets bought from local artists. Sweetgrass baskets are one of the most striking survivals of African culture in the present-day United States. Legerton formed a company called the Sea Grass Basket Company, later Seagrassco, that operated as a subsidiary of Legerton's bookstore and helped to popularize the baskets. His motives were more economic than altruistic, but the infusion of money into the African American communities which produced the baskets contributed to the survival of those communities as well as the art form.

Today, sweetgrass baskets are celebrated for their beauty and cultural significance. Readers seeking a better understanding of the craft and surrounding culture should read Dale Rosengarten's *Row Upon Row: Sea Grass Baskets of the South Carolina Lowcountry* (1986).

HARRIETTE DuBOSE KERSHAW LEIDING (1878–1948)

Civic Leader and Writer   MAP LOCATION: SOUTHWEST 29

Harriette Kershaw Leiding was active in the civic life of Charleston for most of her life. Her books are her legacy to future generations.

She was born at Sewanee, Tennessee, the daughter of the Rev. Dr. John Kershaw and Susan DeSaussure Kershaw. Her father was for many years rector of St. Michael's Episcopal Church in Charleston. Her paternal grandfather was Maj. Gen. Joseph Kershaw,

C.S.A., of Camden. She was educated at Sumter High School and at the Peabody Normal Institute in Nashville, Tennessee.

Miss Kershaw was married to Herman Gustavus Leiding. Early in life she became involved in numerous civic organizations, including the Civic Club, Tuesday Club, Pen Club, Sketch Club, and the United Daughters of the Confederacy. She was a leader in World War I benefit activities. She was a director of the Gibbes Art Gallery.

Mrs. Leiding published four books in her lifetime: *Street Cries of an Old Southern City* (1910), *A Walk Around Ye Olde Historic Charleston* (1911), *Historic Houses of South Carolina* (1921), and *Charleston, Historic and Romantic* (1931). As with the works of Alice and D. E. H. Smith and Harriott Horry Rutledge Ravenel, her works went a great distance in making more widely known the history of Charleston and the Lowcountry. They were a great impetus to early preservation efforts.

Mrs. Leiding lies in an unmarked grave beside her husband's marked grave.

Timothy Willard Lewis (1825–1871)

Reconstruction Missionary   MAP LOCATION: SOUTHEAST 33

Given its context, the tombstone of T. Willard Lewis is one of the most shocking in the cemetery. Upon the gothic marble are engraved the words "The Freedman's Champion, Counsellor, and Friend." Why is such a man buried in the ground that has one of the highest concentrations of slave traders and slave owners in the western hemisphere?

T. Willard Lewis was born in South Royalton, Massachusetts, the fifth child of a pious Methodist family. He was originally thought to be a pleasure-seeker. By 1842 the good Lord had grabbed him up to do His work. Lewis attended Union College for three years but quit to join the ministry. He served churches all over Massachusetts, but it was at Hopkinton that he apparently met the Claflin family, an association that would stand him well in later life.

Lewis was the first Methodist clergyman sent to minister to the emancipated slaves in Beaufort, South Carolina, after the Union capture of Port Royal early in the Civil War. After Charleston fell in February 1865, Lewis was in charge of reorganizing the Methodist Episcopal Church (North) in South Carolina. In that position, he was in conflict with both the old Methodist Episcopal Church (South) and the insurgent African Methodist Episcopal Church as they bickered over congregants, funds, and church buildings. Lewis and a group of freedmen founded Centenary Methodist Church and soon bought the old Wentworth Street Baptist Church to worship in. The church is still active almost 150 years later.

Lewis was instrumental in important initiatives for the education of freedpeople and preparation of African-American ministers. In 1886 he helped to found the Baker Bible Institute on East Bay Street, which trained almost thirty ministers in its short life. A few years later he was at the center of the group that purchased the former Orangeburg Female Institute for the use of Claflin University, which the legislature chartered in December 1869. Lewis was the first chairman of the board for the new school. He oversaw the merger of the Baker Bible Institute into Claflin and raised vital early funding from the Freedmen's

Aid Society. He was not able to see his work to full fruition, however, for he was swept away in a yellow fever epidemic. He was not yet fifty years old.

HENRY WHILDEN LOCKWOOD (1891–1944)

Mayor of Charleston   MAP LOCATION: SOUTHWEST 40

A son of the waterfront and grandson of a Civil War blockade runner, Henry W. "Tunker" Lockwood was one of Charleston's most beloved mayors. The boulevard that runs along the Ashley River bears his name today.

Lockwood was an alderman when Mayor Burnet Maybank was elected governor of South Carolina in 1938. Lockwood was selected by City Council to serve out the remaining year of Maybank's term. So able and popular was his administration that he was re-elected without opposition in 1939 and in 1943.

Mayor Lockwood kept the city on a strict "pay-as-you-go" policy and was able to reduce considerably the debt that almost bankrupted the city of Charleston during the Depression. During the early years of World War II, he cleaned out the old red-light district of Charleston and formed an advisory committee to work for the elimination of venereal disease, a real concern in a wartime Navy town like Charleston. As the *News and Courier* said at Mayor Lockwood's death, "a thorough realist, Mayor Lockwood was no puritan. He believed it was better to control evil than to attempt to create an impression that it did not exist."

Mayor Lockwood died, too young, of a heart attack in 1944.

ROBERT WHILDEN LOCKWOOD (1835–1890)
THOMAS J. LOCKWOOD (1831–1877)

Blockade Runners   MAP LOCATION: SOUTHEAST 34

The Lockwoods were among the best known of the seamen who took ships through the Union blockade during the Civil War. They came to Charleston from Smithville, North Carolina, in the mid-1850s and worked as steamboat captains. Thomas J. Lockwood was affiliated throughout the war with John Fraser & Company; his brother Robert began with that firm before moving to the Chicora Importing and Exporting Company.

Thomas J. Lockwood was such a successful blockade runner that he was known as "the father of the trade." At the outset of the war he outfitted the steamer *Gordon* as a privateer. It was on this vessel, renamed the *Theodora* but still commanded by Lockwood, that Confederate diplomats James Mason and John Slidell slipped through the blockade in October 1861 and reached Cuba. There they embarked for England on the *Trent,* from which their arrest by the Union Navy would be one of the major diplomatic incidents of the war. Meanwhile Lockwood brought the *Theodora* back to Charleston with a cargo of arms, coffee, and 200,000 Cuban cigars. After the Confederate Navy bought the speedy *Theodora,* Lockwood returned to his antebellum packet the *Carolina,* now refitted and renamed the *Kate.* This sidewheeler became one of the most famous blockade runners of the war, eluding Union defenses about twenty times in 1862. Lockwood is reported to have received $2000 in gold for one trip. He mostly worked through Charleston, but he also did business in the Cape Fear River region. Unfortunately, the *Kate* delivered a pestilential cargo of yellow fever there in summer 1862. The resulting epidemic took over seven hundred lives in Wilmington, or more than fifteen percent of the town population. Wilmington took its revenge in November 1862 when the ship sank after hitting a snag. Lockwood moved on to the *Elizabeth* and later traveled to England to supervise construction of the deluxe blockade runner *Colonel Lamb,* which he operated at the end of the war.

Robert Lockwood commanded the *Ella Warley* early in the war, and after its capture in April 1862 he was imprisoned in Fort Lafayette. Upon his release he was entrusted with the fast steamship *Margaret and Jessie,* said to be able to make the trip from Charleston to Nassau in forty-four hours. He took the vessel on several trips into the Confederacy before the Union Navy trapped the steamer on its way into Wilmington in October 1863. Lockwood led the blockaders on a dramatic overnight chase that involved at least five Union vessels. He was eventually captured, however, and spent most of the rest of the war back at Fort Lafayette. The *Margaret and Jessie* went into the service of the U.S. Navy, which rechristened it the *Gettysburg.*

WILLIAM TURNER LOGAN (1874–1941)

Member of Congress   MAP LOCATION: SOUTHEAST 35

A law partner and political ally of John P. Grace and J. C. Long, William Turner Logan was a Congressman from Charleston for two terms. He was educated in the public schools and at the College of Charleston, from which he received a B.A. in 1895. He studied law at the University of Virginia and was admitted to the bar.

Logan was corporation counsel for the city of Charleston from 1914 to 1918, when his law partner John P. Grace was mayor. He was elected to the U.S. House of Representatives and served from 1921 to 1925. He was unsuccessful in his bid for renomination in 1924 but continued to wield political influence until his death shortly before the onset of World War II.

SARAH BUCHANAN PRESTON LOWNDES (1842–1880)

Southern Belle   MAP LOCATION: SOUTHEAST 36

Sally "Buck" Preston was the very paradigm of a Southern belle. There has been a great deal of speculation that Buck was the basis for Margaret Mitchell's Scarlett O'Hara. Nonsense. Buck would not have considered Scarlett a social equal. Buck's true life was a little too large to come credibly from the pen of a mere novelist. Fortunately for history, she was the pet of the childless Mary Boykin Chesnut, who made Buck the central character of her own Civil War narrative (originally published as *Diary from Dixie,* though now known in the C. Vann Woodward edition as *Mary Chesnut's Civil War*).

Portrait bust of Sally "Buck" Preston by Hiram Powers, probably made during an 1858 visit to Europe or on the occasion of her marriage to Rawlins Lowndes in 1868. Courtesy of the Historic Columbia Foundation

Buck was the daughter of John Preston, a Virginia aristocrat who followed family to Columbia, South Carolina, and later became a Confederate general. Though Buck was born in America, she spent much of her adolescence in Paris. There her beauty and grace as a horsewoman attracted the admiration of Napoleon III and the well-known envy of Empress Eugenie. Her family returned to Columbia before Fort Sumter. In Columbia, Miss Preston made friends with Mary Boykin (Miller) Chesnut, wife of South Carolina's U.S. senator James Chesnut.

During the war, Buck was involved in a prolonged romantic attachment to Gen. John Bell Hood. The tragic crescendo and decrescendo of their love is the story upon which Mrs. Chesnut hangs her narrative. Chesnut attempts to use the trajectory of the romance as an allegory to trace the rise and fall of the Confederacy.

After her break with Gen. Hood, Preston exiled to France with her family. Upon her return to South Carolina, she became engaged to the dashing Col. Rawlins Lowndes, whose grandfather had been a Revolutionary leader and South Carolina's first U.S. senator. Buck died from complications after an operation to remove a gynecological cancer.

Originally a bust of Mrs. Lowndes by Hiram Powers graced the temple-like structure which marks her grave. After the bust was vandalized, it was removed to the Hampton-Preston Mansion in Columbia.

Caroline Lowndes Mullally was Mrs. Lowndes's only child to survive to adulthood. She achieved great success as one of Charleston's first female real estate dealers and preservationists.

Andrew Gordon Magrath (1813–1893)

Politician   MAP LOCATION: SOUTHWEST 41

A. G. Magrath combined the solidity of a successful law practice with an alertness to the direction in which the winds were blowing in mid-nineteenth-century South Carolina politics. He was born in Charleston, where his father had established himself as a merchant after escaping from detention in Ireland for his participation in the rebellion of 1798. Magrath received his early education at Bishop England's school and graduated from South Carolina College in 1831. He inevitably read law with James Louis Petigru, after which he studied under Justice Joseph Story at Harvard Law School. He was admitted to the South Carolina bar in 1835.

Magrath began to make a mark in politics when elected to the state legislature in 1840 and 1842. He opposed the Bluffton movement in 1844 and played a prominent role in the defeat of separate secession in 1850–1852, including service in the state convention. In 1856 Franklin Pierce appointed him U.S. district court judge for the District of South Carolina. When William Aiken announced soon afterward that he would not seek reelection to Congress, Magrath made himself available for the nomination without resigning from the bench. Edmund Rhett sharply criticized him in the Charleston *Mercury* as an opportunist and a nationalist. In a famous duel at the Washington Race Course, Magrath's brother Edward killed *Mercury* co-owner William Taber, whom he held responsible for publication of the editorials. Magrath gave up his candidacy for Congress and remained on the bench. His most notable decision was in the prosecution of William Corrie for importation of African slaves on the *Wanderer.* Building on a recent rise in local hostility to the federal prohibition of the Atlantic slave trade, Magrath ruled that the African slave trade was not piracy despite an 1820 Congressional statute that explicitly defined it as such and imposed the death penalty for participation in it. White Charlestonians enthusiastically applauded Magrath's ruling that the purchase and sale of slaves, whether on the African coast or the South Carolina coast, was a legitimate business.

On the day after Lincoln received enough votes to win the presidency in 1860, Magrath dramatically resigned from the federal bench, ripping off his judicial robes and treading on them. This immediate, electrifying response from a formerly moderate cooperationist showed how different the situation was from what it had been a decade earlier and perhaps illustrated some of the opportunism that Edmund Rhett had assailed. Magrath headed the Charleston slate elected to the secession convention and was a signer of the Ordinance of Secession. He then became head of the Department of State in the Executive Council, which gave him a lead role in the negotiations with the federal government over Charleston harbor. Soon after the Confederate government organized, he returned to the district court bench. His early decisions upheld conscription and sequestration policies, but he eventually became a leader for opponents of the Davis administration. In 1864 he was elected governor, the last to be chosen by the state legislature, with the expectation that he would emulate the states' rights strategies of Zebulon Vance in North Carolina and Joseph Brown in Georgia. He promised to do so in a passionate inaugural address, but the Confederacy abandoned South Carolina before South Carolina could abandon the Confederacy. Magrath forlornly protested the evacuation of Charleston, and he fled Columbia the night before Sherman's army occupied the city. The United States Army arrested Magrath on May 25, 1865, and held him in Fort Pulaski until December.

While in prison, the widower Magrath struck up a correspondence with Mary Eliza McCord of Columbia, whom he married soon after his release. He resumed the practice of law and reclaimed a place in the top rank of the profession. The South Carolina Bar Association elected him its first president in 1884.

ARTHUR MIDDLETON MANIGAULT (1824–1886)

Confederate General   MAP LOCATION: SOUTHEAST 37

Scion of some of South Carolina's wealthiest and most distinguished families, Arthur Middleton Manigault was a brigadier general in the Civil War and adjutant general of South Carolina after the war. He was educated in secondary schools of Charleston but eschewed a college education in order to learn the export trade, the basis of his family's large fortune.

Manigault served as a lieutenant in the famous Palmetto Regiment during the Mexican War. After his return he married Mary Proctor Huger, granddaughter of U. S. senator Daniel Elliott Huger, in 1851. In 1856 he became a rice planter on his extensive inherited estates in Georgetown County.

At the commencement of the Civil War, Manigault was elected captain of the North Santee Mounted Rifles. After serving for a time on Gen. Beauregard's staff, he was elected a colonel of the 10th South Carolina Volunteers in May 1861 and was soon sent to Corinth, Mississippi, with his regiment. He was promoted to brigadier general in April 1863. He received a severe head wound at the Battle of Franklin and was disabled for the rest of the war.

After the war Manigault resumed rice planting until his election as adjutant general of South Carolina in 1880. He remained in that office until his death at one of his Georgetown plantations on August 16, 1886.

His memoirs were edited by R. Lockwood Tower and published in 1983 as *A Carolinian Goes to War: The Civil War Narrative of Arthur Middleton Manigault*.

LOUIS MANIGAULT (1828–1899)

Founder of Alpha Sigma Phi Fraternity and Adventurer   MAP LOCATION: SOUTHWEST 42

Louis Manigault was born to travel in high style. He was born in Paris, the son of Charles Izard Manigault and Elizabeth Manigault (Heyward) Manigault. The Manigaults were extremely wealthy and cultivated rice planters. Louis grew up with every advantage as to education and travel and studied at Mr. Cotes's School before his admission to Yale in 1845.

At Yale Louis applied himself to his studies and behaved as a Southern gentleman of his time and station. While in his first year he founded the Alpha Sigma Phi Fraternity with two classmates. The fraternity now has numerous chapters around the country and is still quite active. Louis withdrew from Yale at the close of his second year at the request of his father, who felt that travel was the best education for a young man. He and his family traveled throughout Europe and the Middle East. Upon the family's return to America, young Louis embarked upon the great adventure of his life: a two-year sojourn in the Far East, where he was engaged as a clerk by Robert Bennett Forbes, an opium trader.

Manigault kept a meticulous journal that chronicled his adventures in China, Java, and the Philippines. At one point Manigault and a companion were set upon by bandits outside the city of Canton. The two attempted to fight off the bandits with the only weapons at hand, their umbrellas. Their comic defense had serious consequences, as both young men suffered for life from the effects of saber wounds inflicted by the bandits.

Upon his return to America, Louis took up rice planting at his father's plantations along the Savannah River. His intelligence and attention to detail brought him early success. He married a Savannah belle, Fannie Habersham, and led the life of a young squire at Gowrie Plantation. At the coming of the Civil War, Louis was exempt from conscription due to his China wounds, but he volunteered as an assistant to Dr. Joseph Jones, a surgeon and scientist who compiled extensive epidemiological reports on conditions of the fighting men of the Confederacy.

The war shattered the world of the Manigaults, and the early death of Fannie shattered Louis as well. For the rest of his life, he lived with his brother Dr. Gabriel Manigault, director of the Charleston Museum, at the family home at 6 Gibbes Street. Louis is listed as a "collector" in the Charleston city directories of 1884–1898. He died at the home of his daughter in Pinopolis in 1899.

Louis Manigault's extensive surviving diaries have proven a boon to historians of the antebellum South. A book of his correspondence with his father was edited by James M. Clifton and published as *Life and Labor on Argyle Island: Letters and Documents of a Savannah Rice Plantation 1833–1867* in 1978. A biography by his descendant Annie Jenkins Batson, *Louis Manigault, Gentleman from South Carolina,* was published in 1995.

To celebrate the one-hundred-fiftieth anniversary of the founding of Alpha Sigma Phi Fraternity, a throng of loyal brothers and alumni met at Louis Manigault's tomb in August of 1995 and dedicated a small marble tablet commemorating the fraternity's founding and Manigault's memory.

J. ELMORE MARTIN (1859–1921)

Politico   MAP LOCATION: SOUTHWEST 43

J. Elmore Martin was the leading Charleston lieutenant of his close friend Ben Tillman. Martin came to the city from Barnwell in 1881 and was elected alderman ten years later. He played an instrumental role in the election of the Tillmanite mayor John Ficken, who in turn appointed Martin chief of the city police. In this position Martin directed efforts to induce Charlestonians to comply with the dispensary system introduced in 1893, through which Tillman sought to turn the liquor trade into a state-controlled monopoly. After J. Adger Smith won election as mayor in 1895 on the strength of local opposition to the dispensary system, he promptly fired Martin. But John Gary Evans, Tillman's handpicked successor as governor, countered by placing Charleston under a state-directed metropolitan police. This maneuver restored Martin to his position as chief on the same day that the city council narrowly approved the replacement nominated by Smith. Martin continued to serve as chief, winning support from conservative Protestants for his enforcement policies, until local resentment led Gov. William H. Ellerbe to terminate the state takeover in 1897 and return control of law enforcement to city government. Shortly afterward the governor appointed Martin to fill a vacancy as the sheriff of Charleston County. Martin entrenched himself in that office for the next twenty-four years, winning five straight elections, and played a dominant role in county politics until his death.

Burnet Rhett Maybank (1899–1954)

Mayor of Charleston, Governor of South Carolina,   MAP LOCATION: SOUTHWEST 44
United States Senator

Burnet Maybank was always a smart, affable young man in a hurry. His charisma and ability made him useful to his city, state, and nation until his untimely death at the age of fifty-five. He was the first Charlestonian to be elected governor by popular vote. He never lost an election.

Burnet Maybank was born in Charleston of a distinguished old family. He was the direct descendant of five antebellum South Carolina governors. He graduated from Porter Military Academy and from the College of Charleston and went to work as a cotton broker, a field in which he quickly achieved enormous success. He ran for and was elected alderman of city council in 1927 and was made mayor pro tem in 1930. Mayor Stoney and a number of city business leaders decided that year to unite behind a compromise candidate in order to avoid the vicious sort of municipal election that had plagued Charleston for most of the twentieth century. They united behind thirty-two-year-old Burnet Maybank. Former mayor John P. Grace even gave his endorsement, but only temporarily. Despite Grace's eventual backing of another candidate, Maybank won by a landslide.

Maybank could not have inherited a more discouraging situation. Charleston's debt had multiplied, and almost twenty percent of the city's revenue was going to pay interest on the city's bonded indebtedness. To make matters much worse, the People's National Bank failed in January 1932 and Charleston lost its payroll. Charleston was a town in trouble, on the edge of bankruptcy. Maybank arrived on the scene like a white knight.

Maybank slashed salaries and the budget; he was forced to use scrip to pay city workers. He was able to refinance the city debt. The election of Franklin Roosevelt proved to be most fortuitous for Maybank's administration. Maybank was a longtime friend of South Carolina's junior U.S. senator, James F. Byrnes, who became an ally and floor leader for Roosevelt. In addition, Harry Hopkins, head of the Federal Emergency Relief Administration

(FERA) and later the Works Progress Administration (WPA), was a close friend of Maybank's. With the help of Maybank's friends, the federal government pumped over forty million dollars into the Charleston economy during Roosevelt's first term alone.

Maybank's first term was magic. Charleston's budget was balanced. Taxes were reduced twenty-five percent. After years of bitter factional disputes in Charleston elections, Maybank ran unopposed in 1935. His machine became extremely powerful. Maybank's candidates crushed the remnants of both Grace's and Stoney's organizations and delivered Maybank ninety percent majorities in the Charleston area.

Maybank's administrations were marked by vigorous action, not just talk. The mayor put tremendous energy into creating affordable housing for both whites and blacks (albeit segregated) throughout the city. He started the Azalea Festival, which annually brought in thousands of tourists and tourist dollars for the local economy. In a further move to entice tourists, Maybank oversaw Charleston's "transition" away from prohibition by essentially declaring legal what was actually illegal; in fact he merely refused to meddle with the status quo. The most public demonstration of Harry Hopkins's friendship came with the renovation of the derelict Planter's Hotel into the Dock Street Theatre by the WPA. The theater remains one of the centers of Charleston's culture.

Maybank became chairman of the South Carolina Public Service Authority in 1934 in addition to his duties as mayor. In his position as chairman, Maybank was influential in the creation of the Santee Cooper Authority and Lakes Moultrie and Marion. Though later generations might question the eventual economic and ecological costs of the project, it went far towards revitalizing the Charleston economy.

In 1938 Maybank ran for governor of South Carolina. No Charlestonian had ever been elected governor since the 1868 state constitution had taken the power to choose the governor from the legislature and given it to the people. As a rule, upcountry citizens hated Charlestonians at that time. (Things have not improved tremendously.) With his thick Charleston accent, Maybank was a virtual poster boy for Charleston. His chief opponent in the all-important Democratic primary was Col. Wyndham Manning, the aristocratic son of popular former Gov. Richard I. Manning. After a hard-fought campaign and a long, *long* night waiting for the Charleston returns to come in, Maybank was the victor. Manning's family still claims that most of the votes cast for Manning in Charleston County were cast into the Ashley River.

Governor Maybank was a faithful, if conservative, adherent of the New Deal. He continued to push for hydro-electric projects, rural electrification, and affordable housing. He also used his intimate knowledge of cotton to fight for the interests of farmers and textile manufacturers. His reputation among the people of the state only grew as Maybank demonstrated his capable, competent leadership style as governor.

When President Roosevelt appointed Maybank's long-time political ally James F. Byrnes to the U.S. Supreme Court in 1941, Governor Maybank jumped into the heated contest to succeed Byrnes in the U.S. Senate. After a bitter battle against former governor Olin Johnston, Maybank won the interim election and in 1942 won election to a full term. In the Senate, Maybank was known as an extremely hard worker and a shrewd soldier in legislative battles. He served on the Armed Services Committee, became a high-ranking member of the all-important Appropriations Committee, and was chairman of the Banking and Currency Committee from 1949 to 1952. On most matters, he followed the lead of the Democrats, though he parted ways with the national party on civil rights initiatives and voted for the Taft-Hartley Act. He always fought for a strong national defense (not a hard position to take in World War II) and supported the formation of the United Nations. He continued to fight for housing for all groups after World War II. He wrote the Defense Production Act, which established economic controls and a watchdog committee (of which Maybank was chairman) during the Korean War.

Maybank faced attacks in the election of 1948 due to his part in the appointment of his former political crony J. Waties Waring to the federal bench. Despite these attacks and some strong opponents, Maybank won the Democratic primary without a runoff. In the 1954 Democratic primary, Maybank was unopposed, the first time a U.S. senator from South Carolina had run unopposed in the Democratic primary since popular election of senators was instituted in 1913.

Maybank would not live to enjoy his triumph, however. He died of a heart attack at his summer home at Flat Rock, North Carolina, on September 1, 1954. His death set off a political war when the South Carolina Democratic Executive Committee nominated powerful state senator Edgar Brown for Maybank's seat without a primary. Outraged South Carolina voters turned out by the tens of thousands to write in the name of former governor J. Strom Thurmond. Thurmond became the only successful write-in candidate in the history of the U.S. Senate.

Maybank was genuinely mourned by his constituents and colleagues. Sen. Lyndon B. Johnson of Texas revealed as much about himself as about the late senator when he said admiringly of Maybank, "We knew him as one with an uncanny eye for the weakness of an opposing position and with the skill and ability to exploit that weakness to the fullest advantage." Sen. Paul Douglas of Illinois was not the only eulogist to mention Maybank's virtually unintelligible Charleston brogue:

> One of Burnie's most endearing, if often puzzling characteristics, was his rapid and frequently unintelligible speech when he was stirred up on a matter of great importance. Northerners find the Charleston accent difficult enough to understand at best, but to this Burnie joined his training as a cotton broker where speech and action has to be rapid. The result was that his sentences would pour out in a perfect Niagara of speech. I, at least, could barely understand a word, but I could guess how much he cared about the topic by the tones of his voice and by the frequency with which he would raise and wave his forefinger. It was, therefore, always very endearing, exciting, and stimulating to hear him speak.

MARY VARDRINE McBEE (1879–1965)

Founder and Principal of Ashley Hall School   MAP LOCATION: NORTHEAST 11

Born in Lincolnton, North Carolina, Mary Vardrine McBee sought and received an education at the best schools available to a woman of her day and spent the rest of her life giving a superior education to the women of Charleston and the nation. She received her

B.A. from Smith College, an M.A. from Columbia University, and the D. Litt. from Converse. She also did work at the University of Jena in Germany.

Miss McBee founded Ashley Hall School in 1909 and was its principal until her retirement in 1949. Since its founding, Ashley Hall has been one of the finest girls' schools in the country. Among its graduates have been Josephine Pinckney, Madeleine L'Engle, Josephine Humphreys, and Alexandra Ripley.

Miss McBee is buried in a plot surrounded by several other teachers and administrators of Ashley Hall.

LOUISA SUSANNAH CHEVES McCORD (1810–1880)

Planter and Intellectual   MAP LOCATION: SOUTHEAST 8

Louisa McCord was one of the most remarkable representatives of the Old South. She managed her own plantation, was fluent in several languages, ran a hospital during the Civil War, raised thirteen children and step-children, wrote poetry, and was a distinguished political economist. Mary Chesnut, no idle flatterer, was in awe of her and wrote that "Mrs. McCord is the clearest-headed, strongest-minded woman I know, and the best and the truest."

Louisa S. Cheves was the daughter of Mary (Dulles) and Langdon Cheves, Sr. Born in Charleston, she traveled with her parents throughout the early republic and received an astonishingly comprehensive education for a woman of her time. She studied not only at Grimshaw's School in Philadelphia and under the tutelage of M. and Mme. Picot, but also from her brothers' tutors. She benefited from quiet observation of the distinguished guests in her father's house.

Louisa got the reputation of a bluestocking and was presumed destined to be a spinster when at the age of twenty-nine she married David J. McCord, the first mayor of Columbia. McCord was also father-in-law to Louisa's older brother, Langdon Jr., and the father of ten children by his first wife. This sister/mother-in-law, brother/son-in-law relationship along with frequent intermarriage among the Cheves, Smythe, Haskell, and McCord families has led to an extraordinarily complex lineage. It is the sort of situation which gives rise to the old Charleston witticism, "What others call incest, we call genealogy." Louisa bore three children of her own: Langdon Cheves McCord (1841), Hannah Cheves McCord (1843), Louisa Rebecca Hayne McCord (1845). Much of the large conjoined family lived at Lang Syne Plantation, which Louisa had received when Langdon Cheves divided his property among his children in 1841.

Louisa McCord was a prolific writer. She published a five-act classical tragedy, *Caius Gracchus* (1841), and articles on political economy in American and European journals in addition to her translations of Bastiat's *Sophismes économiques* (1848). Her husband published a volume of her poetry, *My Dreams* (1848), without his wife's knowledge or permission. She hated it. After her husband's death in 1855 she devoted herself to the raising of her only son, Langdon Cheves McCord. He died of Civil War wounds in Virginia in 1862. Of his death, Mrs. McCord wrote to Mary Chesnut:

Louisa S. McCord. Courtesy of
the Georgia Historical Society

The light of my life is gone, my hope fled, and my pride laid low. God pity my poor
girls. I can scarcely rouse myself to take care of them. My helpless daughters. And his
poor young wife, who daily expects her confinement. . . . It is all over now, and it
is right perhaps that the country will never know how much it has lost in my glori-
ous boy.

Louisa sought solace by raising provisions instead of cotton at Lang Syne and through
her wartime hospital work in Columbia. She was the head nurse at the hospital set up on
the grounds of the South Carolina College.

After the burning of Columbia and the end of the war, Mrs. McCord removed to
Canada for two years. Afterwards, she came to live with her daughter Louisa, Mrs. A. T.
Smythe, in Charleston. There she lived the life of the stoic that she was and worked on a
biography of her father which was unfinished at her death. She is buried at the side of her
father's huge obelisk.

Louisa McCord has lately become a darling of historical scholarship. Her life and works
are extensively considered in Elizabeth Fox-Genovese's landmark study *Within the Plantation Household: Black and White Women of the Old South* (1988) and Catherine Clinton's
Tara Revisited (1995). Her essays on political economy, which fully display her antifemi-
nist, proslavery, and free trade ideas, have been republished in a volume edited by Richard
Lounsbury, *Louisa S. McCord: Political and Social Essays* (1995). A companion volume,
Louisa S. McCord: Poems, Drama, Biography, Letters (1996), contains the remainder of her
writings discovered to date.

Helen Gardner McCormack (1903–1974)

Museum Director   MAP LOCATION: SOUTHWEST 45

Helen McCormack was an interesting and interested woman whose love of Southern culture made her an important figure in the preservation of the history of Richmond, Virginia, and of her native Charleston. She was educated at Memminger School in Charleston and received her A.B. degree in English from the College of Charleston in 1925. She soon started working at the Charleston Museum, where Laura Bragg put her in charge of the South Carolina Culture department. She brought modern archival and museum management techniques to what had been at best a haphazardly organized collection.

In 1928 she moved to Richmond to help reorganize the collection of the Valentine Museum. She became director in 1930. During her ten years at the Valentine, her signal accomplishment was the restoration of the Wickham-Valentine House, which had been designed by Charleston native Robert Mills and built in 1812. In 1936, she received a Rockefeller Foundation grant to continue her studies of modern museum methods in New York and Europe.

McCormack returned to Charleston in 1941 to become assistant director of the Gibbes Art Gallery. Coincident with her duties at the Gibbes, she received the first fellowship from the Charleston Scientific and Cultural Educational Fund to reorganize the collections of the South Carolina Historical Society. She served as secretary of the Carolina Art Association Civic Arts Committee, which published the seminal *This Is Charleston* in 1944. *This Is Charleston* was a documentary survey and evaluation of Charleston's architectural heritage. It has been and is the single most important guide and tool for the preservation of Charleston.

McCormack was named director of the Gibbes in 1953, a position she held until 1966 when she cut back her work by taking the post of curator. She lived out her last years in an apartment at the Confederate Home just steps away from the South Carolina Historical Society and the Gibbes Art Gallery.

Thomas Ballard McDow (1853–1904)

Killer   MAP LOCATION: SOUTHEAST 38

Thomas McDow was an extremely intelligent young Charleston doctor. Francis Warrington Dawson was the nationally recognized editor of the Charleston *News and Courier*. Dr. McDow shot Capt. Dawson dead and attempted to conceal his body. The killing led to the most sensational trial in nineteenth-century South Carolina.

McDow was born in Camden, South Carolina, the son of a doctor. He was graduated from Cumberland University in Tennessee with first honors in 1874. He was valedictorian of the class of 1879 at the Medical College of South Carolina. He quickly established a large practice and, by his own admission, married Kate Ahrens for her money. McDow had a home and office at 75 Rutledge Avenue.

Around the corner from McDow at 43 Bull Street was the residence of Francis War-rington Dawson, one of the most respected men of the city. He was a native of England and had come to America to fight for the Confederacy. He had acquitted himself well and had risen to the rank of captain. After the war, Capt. Dawson was a successful crusading editor. He had become part owner of the Charleston *News,* which he merged with the Charleston *Daily Courier* in 1873 to form the Charleston *News and Courier.*

Dawson employed a young Swiss woman, Hélène Marie Burdayron, as a governess for his children. He considered her under the protection of his household. Dawson became suspicious of Miss Burdayron's extracurricular activities and had her followed by a police detective to discover if she was keeping "disreputable company." She was. Her disreputable company was a married man, Thomas McDow.

On March 12, 1889, at sometime between 3:00 and 4:00 in the afternoon, Dawson went to the basement office of Dr. McDow to confront him about the relationship. What happened next is in dispute. What is not in dispute is that at some point McDow shot Dawson in the back, causing Dawson's nearly immediate death. McDow admitted that he then attempted to bury Capt. Dawson's body under the floor of a basement closet but was prevented from doing so by bricks and debris a few inches under the floorboards.

Some passersby had heard the shot and informed a Private Gordon of the City Police of the disturbance. Private Gordon rang the bell at Dr. McDow's office door and saw Dr. McDow peek out. Gordon thought he heard something being moved in the office, and Dr. McDow shortly came out, looking disheveled. McDow assured the policeman that nothing was wrong and then walked to a corner grocery, where he bought an apple and two candles. He calmly ate the apple on the return trip to his office.

Upon his return, McDow rested a while and reflected upon his options. He moved the body back to its original location and turned himself in to a policeman at around 6 pm. McDow was first taken for a consultation with former judge and governor Andrew G. Magrath. Afterwards, he was lodged in the jail, where he remained until his trial in June.

At the trial, the prosecution team consisted of Solicitor William St. Julien Jervey and Henry Augustus Middleton Smith, a member of the board of the *News and Courier* and later a federal judge. McDow was represented by Magrath and Asher D. Cohen. McDow's plea was not guilty by reason of self-defense.

The trial attracted excited attention from the national press not only because of the prominence of the victim but also because of the underlying illicit relationship of the young doctor and the Swiss governess.

The trial was sensational. Miss Burdayron testified as to just what she and Dr. McDow did and did not do and why. She analyzed his motives, her own motives, and Dr. McDow's offer to divorce his wife and run away to France with her. The Swiss governess testified to all of this in a halting accent that exasperated the lawyers and further titillated observers.

Dr. McDow testified that Capt. Dawson came to his office, spoke to him in a rude and arrogant manner, and threatened to publish details of McDow's liaison if he did not agree to stop communicating with Miss Burdayron. McDow testified that Dawson then began to beat him with a cane. McDow admitted that he then pulled his pistol from his back pocket and shot Dawson. He ascribed his attempted burial of Dawson and his delay in contacting the police to panic.

McDow's testimony was somewhat corroborated by an African-American coachman who testified that he saw Dawson enter McDow's office, heard a struggle, and then heard a voice that said, "You would take my life and now I have taken yours."

Magrath and Cohen were extremely effective in cross-examining the state's witnesses. The prosecution's summation was merely adequate. The defense's summations were brilliant. McDow was acquitted two hours after the jury retired. It was widely speculated that the jury, a majority of whom were African Americans, sympathized with Dawson's killer in retaliation for the racist views of the *News and Courier.*

McDow lived another fifteen years at 75 Rutledge Avenue and died of an apparent heart attack, alone, in his own bed. He is buried in his wife's family plot. Capt. Dawson is buried a few hundred feet away, just across the Magnolia Cemetery line in St. Lawrence Cemetery.

Clelia Peronneau Mathewes McGowan (1865–1956)

Pioneer of Women's Rights and Civil Rights   MAP LOCATION: SOUTHWEST 46

Clelia McGowan led a dramatic life almost from birth. She was a pioneer in the women's rights and the civil rights movements and was the first woman to hold public office in South Carolina.

Clelia Peronneau Mathewes was born in Columbia on January 30, 1865, shortly before Gen. Sherman came to visit the town in his march. She literally made the history books before she was a month old, as Mrs. Chesnut recorded that during the destruction of Columbia the new mother in confinement "had to get out [of] bed or be burned in it" and sat with her baby in the woods through the night.

Young Miss Mathewes was obviously marked and saved for history. She stayed with her family as they moved to North Georgia at the close of the war, but came to Charleston to study at Miss Kelly's School. She spent some time at the Confederate Home College and at the age of nineteen sailed to Sweden to study with Madame Rosalie Roos Olivecrona. Madame Olivecrona had been Miss Mathewes's mother's tutor for a number of years before the Civil War. She was a noted feminist and antislavery authority. Her letters from the United States were published in 1982 as *Travels in America, 1851–1855.* Madame Olivecrona's profound effect on her Charleston student was reflected not only in Miss Matthewes's political stances and work but also in the name of her only daughter, Rosalie Olivecrona McGowan.

Clelia Mathewes married William C. McGowan of Abbeville, South Carolina, who was the son of Confederate general Samuel McGowan. They had three children together. After her husband's death in 1898, Mrs. McGowan moved back to Charleston.

In Charleston Mrs. McGowan became an activist on behalf of women's rights. She sought suffrage to a degree almost improper for a young widow of her time. When women achieved the vote, Mrs. McGowan quickly made history, as Gov. Roper Cooper appointed her to a seat on the South Carolina Board of Education in 1919. She was the first female to hold a state office, elective or appointed. In 1923 McGowan ran for city council of Charleston and won, leading the slate. She was the first female alderman in

South Carolina and perhaps the first elected female officeholder in the state. In the same year she published a book of poetry, *Plantation Memories, and Other Poems.* In 1930 Mrs. McGowan was the guiding force behind the founding of the Charleston Free Library (today the Charleston County Public Library).

Her most important legacy was her involvement in various interracial committees which she formed, chaired, or spearheaded. Her commitment to racial justice was a significant step toward amelioration of the oppressive conditions under which African Americans lived.

CLARA GOODING MCMILLAN (1894–1976)

Member of Congress   MAP LOCATION: SOUTHWEST 47

Clara G. McMillan was the second congresswoman from South Carolina. She was born in Brunson in Hampton County and educated at the Confederate Home College in Charleston and at Flora MacDonald College in Red Springs, North Carolina. She was married to Thomas Sanders McMillan, the congressman from Charleston from 1925 until his death in 1939. After his death Mrs. McMillan was elected to serve out his term. She declined to offer for reelection and was succeeded by L. Mendel Rivers, later one of the most powerful members of Congress.

After her retirement from Congress, Mrs. McMillan was appointed an information liaison officer for the Department of State in Washington. She served in that position until 1957, when she retired to Ulmers, South Carolina.

THOMAS SANDERS MCMILLAN (1888–1939)

Member of Congress   MAP LOCATION: SOUTHWEST 47

Thomas S. McMillan was a poor boy from the country who rose through hard work to serve his constituents and the country as one of the most powerful congressmen in Washington. He was born in Ulmers in what is now Allendale County and was educated in the local public schools. He graduated from the Collegiate Institute in Orangeburg in 1907. After teaching school for two years in Aiken County, he won a competitive scholarship to the University of South Carolina in 1908. He graduated from the University of South Carolina in 1912 and completed its law course in 1913. He was admitted to the bar in that year and began his practice in Charleston.

McMillan's intelligence, perseverance, and work ethic gained him rapid success in his adopted home. He was elected in 1917 to the South Carolina House of Representatives, where he served until 1924. He was elected speaker pro tem in 1921 and 1922 and speaker of the House in 1923 and 1924. In 1924 he ran for U.S. Congress against the popular incumbent, William Turner Logan, and won. He achieved distinction and became chairman of the House Agriculture Committee, an exceedingly important position for a state so dependent on agriculture. He died in office on September 29, 1939.

Robert Withers Memminger (1867–1925)

Judge R. W. Memminger was a man of forceful opinions, one of which has gained him immortality. He was born in Charleston, the grandson of Christopher Gustavus Memminger and the first cousin of Gustavus M. Pinckney and Mary Middleton Pinckney Lee. He was educated in the schools of Charleston and at the University of Virginia, after which he read law with Charles H. Simonton.

He embarked upon a career with his admission to the bar in 1891. In 1899 he was elected judge of the civil and criminal courts of Charleston. In 1905 he was elected to the position of circuit judge for the Ninth Judicial Circuit, a position he held until 1925, when God retired him. He was the trial judge in the lurid murder case of *State v. Bigham,* which was the basis of Katharine Boling's *A Piece of the Fox's Hide* (1972).

In assessing his judicial demeanor upon Judge Memminger's death, the *News and Courier* opined that he "acquired a reputation for conducting his courts in the interest of the law rather than of the lawbreakers. He was ready to go to any lengths in protecting a defendant against what appeared to him to be injustice, but he believed that the guilty should be punished and that the court's duty was to effect their punishment. He was not a negative or colorless judge but felt it to be a part of his duty to exert his power and influence from the bench to shape the administration of justice in the courts over which he presided. His charges and his rulings were characterized by boldness and vigor. He was insistent that jurors and grand jurors and witnesses should understand their obligations and pointed these out in the clearest and strongest terms."

No case gives more meaning to the *News and Courier*'s assessment than that of *State v. Schiaderessi* (1915). Charleston in the early twentieth century notoriously flouted laws regarding liquor. Juries regularly brought "not guilty" verdicts for bootleggers and bar owners in cases in which there was clear and convincing evidence against the defendants. Judge Memminger feared just such a result in the Schiaderessi case. In a long, weary, almost resigned charge, he instructed the jury thus:

> I cannot . . . admit to you that we, the people of Charleston, are law-bidding [*sic*]. I cannot say that. I don't think there is any particular class or particular people to blame, but as long as I have lived here and as much as I think of and love the people of Charleston, I think that they are the most lawless set there ever was. It matters not who they are, or what they are, they seem to do pretty much exactly as they want to. The hunter shoots the deer without the least regard for the law. Another man will pay another to vote for him, and another, if he has the necessary nerve and ferocity, will keep another from the polls if he doesn't vote as he wants. There is nothing they will not do. I have charged you that we are not law-abiding.

Much to the amazement of everyone, especially the hapless Mr. Schiaderessi, the jury convicted. Mr. Schiaderessi appealed to the South Carolina Supreme Court, which declined to reverse Judge Memminger's charge. It is still good law today.

Margaret Simons Middleton (1891–1980)

Author   MAP LOCATION: NORTHWEST 11

Margaret Simons Middleton was primarily a family person, but in her spare time she brought attention to several important Charlestonians who had been otherwise forgotten by history. She was the author of *Jeremiah Theus: Colonial Artist of Charles Town* (1953); *Henrietta Johnston of Charles Town, South Carolina: America's First Pastellist* (1966); *David and Martha Laurens Ramsay* (1971); and *Affra Harleston and Old Charles-Towne in South Carolina* (1971).

Her only son, Charles F. Middleton, Jr., gave his life for this country in World War II. Her daughters have been quiet leaders in Charleston throughout their lives. Her son-in-law, Congressman L. Mendel Rivers, Sr., was one of the most important people in the history of Charleston.

Nathaniel Russell Middleton (1810–1890)

President of the College of Charleston   MAP LOCATION: SOUTHEAST 39

Nathaniel Russell Middleton was the grandson of Nathaniel Russell, a Rhode Island-born magnate, and the great-nephew of Arthur Middleton, a signer of the Declaration of Independence. His distinguished ancestry was no doubt a factor in Middleton's obtaining the position of president of the College of Charleston, for he had little if any experience in education at that time. Middleton was born in Charleston in 1810 and educated at Mr. Southworth's Church School and Geneva College in New York. He graduated from the College of Charleston in 1830. Two years later he married his cousin Margaret Emma Middleton.

Middleton became a planter after his graduation from the college but met with little success. He sold his lands in 1852 and became treasurer of the Northeastern Railroad Company. He had been a trustee of the College of Charleston from 1848 and served in the South Carolina House of Representatives from 1850 to 1852. A few years later he was named treasurer of the city of Charleston.

In 1857 Middleton was made president of the College of Charleston. Early in his career as president, Middleton was successful in reforming the disciplinary system at the college. Before Middleton could accomplish any lasting reforms, however, war fever was upon Charleston. After the firing on Fort Sumter, young men had better things to do than attend college. After the war, the college was continually beset with extreme financial difficulties. Middleton labored mightily to boost enrollment and ameliorate the financial condition of the college, but to little avail. Finally, the college came under a financial crisis in 1880 that prompted Middleton's resignation. He stayed on at the college for most of the rest of his life as a professor emeritus.

MINNIE ROBERTSON MIKELL (1891–1987)

Artist   MAP LOCATION: SOUTHWEST 48

Minnie Mikell was an experimental artist in a town not noted for its experimentation. A Charleston native, she was educated in the schools of Charleston and was married to Alexander Mikell.

Minnie Mikell was one of the nine founders of the Charleston Etchers' Club, probably the most important group of Charleston artists. She was a student of Alfred Hutty, a locally and nationally important etcher and painter, and experimented with a variety of media and artistic fashions including cubism and fauvism. She illustrated a number of local publications. She is portrayed painting a watercolor in a photograph by Eudora Welty titled *A Charleston Courtyard* in Miss Welty's book *In Black and White: Photographs of the '30s and '40s* (1985). Mrs. Mikell's works are in the permanent collections of the Gibbes Museum of Art, the Columbia Museum, and the State Museum.

MARGUERITE CUTTINO MILLER (1895–1956)

Artist   MAP LOCATION: SOUTHWEST 49

Marguerite Cuttino Miller was born in Charleston, the daughter of William Capers and Georgie (Gordon) Miller. She was educated at the Misses Sass's School and Ashley Hall and received further artistic training at the Pennsylvania School of Fine Arts in Philadelphia. She taught art at Ashley Hall from 1918 through 1926 and was the director of the school of the Carolina Art Association in 1927 and from 1930 to 1933. She was a member of the Southern States Art League.

Miss Miller was an important teacher and artist of the Charleston Renaissance. Her watercolors and pastels show an extraordinary grace and sophistication for her time and place. One of her most devoted students would become Charleston's most important portrait painter of her era, Alicia Rhett.

JOHN C. MITCHEL, JR. (1838–1864)

Irish and Southern Nationalist   MAP LOCATION: SOUTHEAST 40

John C. Mitchel, Jr., was mourned as a Confederate martyr not only because he died in command of the symbolically important Fort Sumter but also because his family linked the Southern bid for independence and the Irish struggle against England. His father was a famous Irish nationalist convicted by a packed jury of high treason against the Crown in 1848. He was transported first to Bermuda and later to Tasmania. His oldest son John Jr., voluntarily joined him in exile. The younger Mitchel's favorite pastime in Australia was hunting kangaroos, though on one occasion he was nearly killed by a cornered kangaroo that leapt onto him.

MOSS OAKS & LAKE.   CONFEDERATE MONUMENT.
MAGNOLIA CEMETERY.

A souvenir card for cemetery visitors, published in 1883. Courtesy of the Historic Charleston Foundation

The Mitchels escaped from Australia in 1853 and fled to the United States, where the rest of the family joined them. The elder Mitchel edited newspapers, first in San Francisco and then in New York. His ardent antiabolitionist sentiments prompted him to found the *Southern Citizen* in Knoxville in 1856 and continue it from Washington, D.C., the next year. John Jr. was educated in New York at Columbia College and became a civil engineer. He was chief engineer for a railroad in Alabama during the secession crisis, and along with his two brothers he promptly went to Montgomery and volunteered his services to the Confederacy. His younger brother would die in Pickett's Charge, and the other brother would lose an arm in the army. Their father, who had moved to France, returned in 1862 and became a prominent Confederate editor in Richmond. At the end of the war the federal government held him prisoner for several months in Fortress Monroe along with Jefferson Davis, whose policies he had often criticized during the war.

John Jr. headed to Charleston in 1861 and was commissioned a second lieutenant in the 1st South Carolina Artillery. He was said to be the first foreign-born supporter of the Confederacy to receive a military commission in South Carolina and perhaps anywhere in the South. He served in the first bombardment of Fort Sumter on April 12–13, 1861, and was part of its initial Confederate garrison. He remained in the area through the war, serving at times on Morris Island and James Island, and earned promotion to captain. In 1864 he succeeded Maj. Stephen Elliott as commander at Fort Sumter, where the beleaguered force was standing guard against invasion while enduring bombardments that came to number 300–500 shells per day.

The fort was under such a bombardment on July 20, 1864, when, according to one later account, a sentinel on the parapet sent down a request for permission to take shelter. Mitchel supposedly refused and later refused a second request, which he decided to investigate personally. He had only been standing on the parapet a brief time when he saw a 300-pound shell heading straight toward him. He never flinched, demonstrating the courage he expected from men under his command, and was struck by a fragment when the shell exploded near him. Capt. John Johnson reported that the wounded Mitchel's immediate response was to lament, "They have killed me, captain, but I ought to have been a major." He lingered for four hours, at the end of which he delivered nobler last words that recalled the famous farewell of Patrick Sarsfield at the battle of Landen in 1693: "I willingly die for South Carolina, but would that I could have died for Ireland."

Mitchel was buried at Magnolia, where his grave was marked only by the flowers brought every Memorial Day by the Ladies Memorial Association until the women installed a marker in 1878. On the semicentennial anniversary of Mitchel's death a group of Irish-Americans in Charleston replaced that tombstone with the present monument, a replica of the parapet at Fort Sumter on which Mitchel last stood. Softening Mitchel's loyalty to Ireland, this monument records his last words as "I wish to show my garrison how it becomes a patriot and soldier to die for his country."

JOHN S. MITCHELL (1815–1887)

Physician   MAP LOCATION: SOUTHWEST 50

Dr. Mitchell was one of the most beloved physicians of nineteenth-century Charleston. He was born in Charleston in November 1815. He attended the school of Christopher Cotes and graduated from the College of Charleston. He was graduated from the Medical College of South Carolina in 1837. He was for many years the physician of the Shirras Dispensary until he became a surgeon in the Confederate Army at the commencement of the Civil War.

Dr. Mitchell was senior warden of St. Paul's Episcopal Church and carried over his Christian spirit into his medical practice, which was to a large extent provided without charge to the sick of Charleston. Yet despite his pious devotion to the people of Charleston, he was no prude, for as the *News and Courier* noted at his death, he was "a capital raconteur and his genial good humor and bonhomie made him a great favorite, either when lightening the sorrows of the suffering or heightening the good fellowship of a hunting party, for up to recent years he was an earnest devotee of the chase."

After Dr. Mitchell's death, his patients erected an imposing monument over his grave in gratitude for his skill and benevolence.

NELSON MITCHELL (1812–1864)

Lawyer   MAP LOCATION: SOUTHWEST 51

Nelson Mitchell was a quiet hero who has only recently attracted public notice. It was due to his courageous work that the captured African American soldiers of the Fifty-Fourth Massachusetts Volunteer Infantry Regiment (immortalized in the 1989 movie *Glory*) were held as prisoners rather than executed.

Mitchell was born in Charleston. He was educated at South Carolina College, from which he graduated second in the class of 1832. He took up the practice of law soon after graduation from college and was elected to the South Carolina House of Representatives from 1846 to 1858. There he served, despite his well-known Unionist sympathies, as chairman of the Committee on Federal Relations from 1850 to 1854 and chairman of the Judiciary Committee from 1854 to 1858.

During the war Mitchell was called upon to serve as a lawyer for one of the most despised groups of defendants in the wartime South. President Jefferson Davis and the Confederate Congress had declared that all captured African Americans fighting as soldiers for the Union were to be treated as slaves in insurrection and executed as such. The first test of this policy came when six African American soldiers of the Massachusetts Fifty-Fourth were captured at Battery Wagner. When South Carolina attorney general Isaac W. Hayne determined to prosecute the captured black soldiers, Mitchell took up their cause despite the feeling of the community. One of the defendants, Daniel States, described Mitchell's efforts:

> A lawyer named Mitchell came to jail and offered to defend us before the court. He did a good deal for us, and talked with Sergeant Jeffries and Corporal Hardy, who went to trial as the two test cases. Mitchell did this without pay, and was very kind to us at all times. He worked hard and won the case, coming to us at midnight and calling up to Jeffries, "All of you can now rejoice. You are recognized as United States soldiers."

Mitchell died a year later. At his death even the rabidly Confederate Charleston *Mercury* acknowledged that his legal career had earned him widespread "respect for his acumen and learning, and uncorruptedness." Over one hundred thirty years after Mitchell's death Robert Rosen dedicated his book *Confederate Charleston* (1994) in part "to the memory of Nelson Mitchell, Esquire, the most admirable of the Confederate-era Charleston lawyers."

Nelson Mitchell lies in an unmarked grave, ironically near to the Confederate defender and historian of Battery Wagner, Robert Gilchrist.

SYED AHMED ALLEY (1869–1898)

SHAIK ABDUL HOCK (1861–1907)

SHAIK MOTEAR RAHMUN (1880–1905)

KHORSHED ALLY SHEIK (1844–1909)

Mohammedans (Muslims)   MAP LOCATION: SOUTHEAST 41

Between the office of Magnolia Cemetery and the Confederate Cemetery, there are four graves positioned perpendicularly to the other graves in the section. The graves are pointed towards Mecca. The occupants are Muslims, or as their stones designate them, Mohammedans. Instead of crosses, their stones bear the symbol of the star and crescent. What were Muslims doing in late-nineteenth- and early-twentieth-century Charleston? How did they get here? What can we know of them?

Very little.

Syed Ahmed Alley, "a Mohammedan of Calcutta, India," died April 29, 1898, of meningitis at 33 State Street. He may be the person still listed in the 1900 city directory as Ahmed Alli, peddler, with a wife, Dela, at 177 Smith Street. Kanaith and Sahhe Alli, likely his children, are listed at the same address, which was the residence of John Rudden.

Shaik Motear Rahmun is not listed in any city directory. He died of acute nephritis at 7 Horlbeck Alley. His stone identifies him as a native of Calcutta, East India.

Shaik Abdul Hock is listed in the Charleston city directory of 1900 and of 1906 as a peddler residing on Philadelphia Alley. According to cemetery records, he was born in Calcutta and died of typhoid at St. Francis Hospital. His name is spelled alternatively as Huck and Huch.

Khorshed Ally Sheik was born in the village of Barnum, District of Hooghly, East India. He is listed in the 1900 directory as a peddler at 274 Ashley Avenue and listed in the 1906 directory as Koshnod Ali, living with the aforementioned Abdul Huck (Hock). Khorshed Ally Sheik died of Bright's Disease at St. Francis Hospital. His is the only of the four with an epitaph: "His courteousness, high character, and integrity won for him the respect and confidence of all with whom he came in contact."

FRANK WITHERS MUNNERLYN, JR. (1911–1990)

Mayor of Church Street   MAP LOCATION: NORTHWEST 12

Frank "Gie" Munnerlyn was a beloved figure in Charleston's business and social life, so much so that even the mayor of Charleston recognized him as "the Mayor of Church Street." He was born in his parents' house at 95 Church Street and, except for his years at the Citadel and as an Army officer in World War II, he lived there all his life.

Munnerlyn's father died when Frank was seven. His mother took a job at South Carolina National Bank, and Frank and his older brother, Barron, took jobs as office boys on Broad Street. He attended Crafts School, Porter Military Academy, and the Citadel.

Munnerlyn was an insurance agent with Penn Mutual Life Insurance Agency for over fifty years. He was a member of virtually every social organization in the city from the St. Cecilia, Hibernian, and South Carolina Societies on down. He was president of the St. Andrew's Society and commodore of the Carolina Yacht Club. He remained a bachelor all his life and was said to be the oldest man on the "stag list" for Charleston debutante balls in the history of the city. Though he never married, he always sought out the companionship of young people. He became a second father to the noted physicist James Robert Goodgame.

When he died he left a substantial bequest to his alma mater, the Citadel. The canteen there is named in his memory.

Andrew Buist Murray (1844–1928)

Businessman and Philanthropist   MAP LOCATION: SOUTHEAST 2

Andrew Buist Murray was Charleston's personification of a Horatio Alger character. He was an orphan raised in the Charleston Orphan House who by dint of hard work and good marriage raised himself and left his name to grace Charleston's priciest thoroughfare. He was the son of Scottish immigrants, James and Isabella (Buist) Murray. His mother

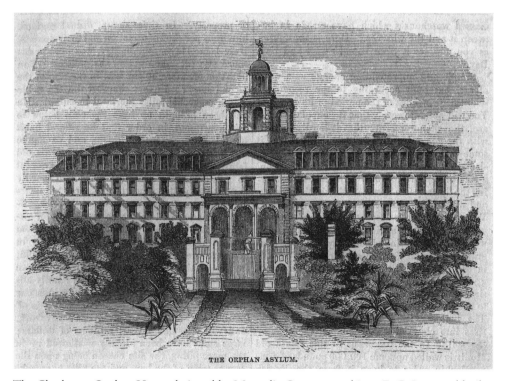

The Charleston Orphan House designed by Magnolia Cemetery architect E. C. Jones and built in 1853–1855. Courtesy of the Thomas Cooper Library, University of South Carolina

died when he was three, and his father ten years later. Thereafter he was reared and educated at the Charleston Orphan House on Calhoun Street. In 1860 he was taken in by Washington Jefferson Bennett, owner of the Bennett Rice Mill. Murray served in the defense of Charleston during the Civil War.

After the war he went to work at his patron's rice and lumber mills on the Cooper River. He became a partner in the business in 1874 upon the death of Mr. Bennett and in 1876 married Mr. Bennett's daughter, Mary Hayes Bennett. In 1894 after the death of his brother-in-law and the retirement of the other partner, Murray took over the business himself.

Mr. and Mrs. Murray had no children but devoted themselves throughout their lives to judicious philanthropy. Mr. Murray gave the money to build the drive around Hampton Park and the infirmary at the Citadel, both of which bear the name of his wife. In addition, he gave over half the funds to extend the Battery wall and build a drive along Charleston harbor. That drive was named Murray Boulevard in his honor.

Murray made an incredible fortune in his lifetime but gave away over one million dollars before his death in 1928. He was Charleston's great philanthropist.

FRANK KERCHNER MYERS (1874–1940)

Jurist   MAP LOCATION: NORTHWEST 13

Frank Myers was born in Wilmington, North Carolina. He read law in Florence, South Carolina, under P. A. Wilcox and was admitted to the bar in 1896. He became a clerk and court reporter in the office of Mordecai and Cohen in Charleston. One of his fellow employees in that firm was a young Irish-Catholic orphan, James F. Byrnes, who with the benefit of a formal sixth-grade education had risen from the status of runner to secretary to clerk to lawyer and court reporter at Mordecai and Cohen. Byrnes moved away to Aiken and advanced in his career, but he never forgot his old friend and fellow employee. Myers practiced law and continued to serve as a court reporter until the death of Master-in-Equity G. H. Sass, when Gov. Martin Ansel named Myers as Sass's replacement. Myers was never opposed for reelection in twenty-six years on the bench.

When U.S. District Court Judge Ernest Cochran died in 1934, it was widely assumed that the choice of South Carolina's senior U.S. senator, Ellison D. Smith, would be J. Waties Waring. But Sen. Smith was not in favor with the president, and the junior U.S. senator, James F. Byrnes, was. Thus Roosevelt appointed Byrnes's choice, Judge Myers, to the U.S. District Court bench. Judge Myers acquitted himself admirably on the federal bench until his unexpected death, when he was at last succeeded by J. Waties Waring.

Judge Myers' son-in-law was mayor of Charleston, governor, and U.S. senator Burnet R. Maybank, Sr. His grandson is former lieutenant governor Burnet R. Maybank, Jr.

John Sanders O'Hear (1806–1875)

Signer of the Ordinance of Secession   MAP LOCATION: SOUTHEAST 43

John S. O'Hear was a wealthy physician and planter. He was born in Charleston and received his early education in her schools. He graduated from the Philadelphia Medical College in 1824 and commenced the practice of medicine in St. Andrew's Parish, the center of his family's plantation wealth. In 1847, Dr. O'Hear bought land in St. Thomas and St. Dennis Parish, where he achieved success as a planter. Due to a shotgun accident in 1850, Dr. O'Hear lost the use of one hand. His disability effectively ended his medical practice and precluded his participation in the war.

Dr. O'Hear was active, however, in the secessionist movement leading up to the war. He was a delegate to the states' rights convention of 1852 and the secession convention. He invested his entire fortune in slaves and Confederate bonds. His magnificent house on the Wando River was burned by Union troops who learned that he had signed the Ordinance of Secession.

Leonard Talbert Owens (1910–1985)

Salesman   MAP LOCATION: SOUTHEAST 44

Leonard Talbert Owens was a salesman whose best product was himself. He was born in Pinopolis and raised and educated in Charleston. He attended Mitchell Elementary School and Porter Military Academy until he developed a talent for truancy and a fondness for horse racing on the Charleston Neck. He went to work early in life and for most of his career was a salesman for Palmetto Fixtures and Notion Company on North Market Street. At the end of his career he worked as a salesman for Charleston Paper Company.

A successful salesman, he had an innate fondness for people and a natural ability to make them like him. But Owens was also a cautious and protective man, always mindful of the safety of others. He used a particular farewell to anyone who crossed his path. This leave-taking phrase is his only epitaph and, given its context, is one of the most startling and strangely humorous in the cemetery: "BE CAREFUL."

Belle Percival (d. 1914)

Madam   MAP LOCATION: NORTHWEST 14

Belle Percival ran a well-known brothel in Charleston at 61 Beaufain Street. The establishment must have been one of the most elegant places of its kind in town, to judge from the silver, jewelry, and other finery Miss Percival left behind when she died in November

1914. The cause of death was a fractured skull resulting from what the coroner ruled was an accidental fall down the stairs at the Beaufain Street home.

A man named Isaac Schumpsky, who identified himself as an occupant of Miss Percival's house and a longtime acquaintance familiar with her wishes for her burial, arranged for a procession of nineteen carriages to carry her mourners to Magnolia for the interment. Miss Percival was buried in a silk plush royal purple red cedar casket with solid copper lining and brass corners and trimming.

When the state moved to escheat Miss Percival's property because she had no known heirs, a woman from Ontario materialized to claim that Miss Percival was her daughter and had been born in Canada as Anna Louise Purcell. She said that she would be able to identify the body from a mole and a scar left by a dog bite. The state opposed the exhumation. The state Supreme Court observed that the remains of the deceased should not be disturbed without serious consideration, "whether it be the body of one called saint or called sinner, if we dare to pretend to a knowledge of that character." But it concluded that Bridgett Purcell had made a sufficient showing that she was the mother to be entitled to the exhumation. Examination of Miss Percival's body revealed both the mole and the dog-bite scar that Mrs. Purcell had described, and she and her family inherited the proceeds of Miss Percival's business.

PI KAPPA PHI FOUNDERS

Pi Kappa Phi is an international student fraternity founded at the home of Simon Fogarty at 90 Broad Street on December 10, 1904. The founders, Simon Fogarty, Andrew Kroeg, and L. Harry Mixson are all buried at Magnolia Cemetery. The fraternity is today one of the largest student fraternities in the world, with chapters at colleges throughout the United States and the world.

ANDREW A. KROEG (1885–1922) died an untimely death after a short, uneventful life. He was a Mason, a member of the South Carolina Society, and a communicant of Grace Episcopal Church. He was a past Grand President of the Pi Kappa Phi Order. MAP LOCATION: NORTHWEST 9

LAWRENCE HARRY MIXSON (1887–1962) inherited his father's business, William H. Mixson Seed Company, and went on to found the South Carolina Seedmen's Association. He was a Mason and a member of the St. Andrew's Society, the Agricultural Society of South Carolina, and First (Scots) Presbyterian Church. MAP LOCATION: SOUTHWEST 52

SIMON FOGARTY (1887–1966) is regarded as the true founder of the Pi Kappa Phi Order. He was born in Charleston, a son of Simon Fogarty and Catherine (Wall) Fogarty. After his graduation from the College of Charleston in 1906, Fogarty studied at the University of Tennessee and the University of Michigan and obtained a master's degree in education from New York University in 1920. In his early life he served as principal at a number of Charleston elementary schools, including Simonton, Mitchell, and Krafts. He became a federal probation officer in 1943 and retired as chief probation officer for the Eastern District of South Carolina in 1958. MAP LOCATION: NORTHEAST 5

Fogarty lived to see the fraternity he founded in his home with two other members grow to fifty-three chapters and over twenty thousand members. He died revered around the world for his actions as a seventeen-year-old.

Princess Henrietta Pignatelli (d. 1948)

Jewish-American Princess   MAP LOCATION: SOUTHEAST 45

Princess Henrietta Pignatelli was born Henrietta Pollitzer in Bluffton, South Carolina. On her mother's side, she was descended from the Guerard family, an old Lowcountry name. Her father was a member of one of the Lowcountry's most distinguished Jewish families. The Pollitzers numbered among their kinsmen an extraordinary number of important intellectuals, including Anita Pollitzer, who introduced Georgia O'Keefe to Alfred Steiglitz and who was O'Keefe's earliest biographer, champion, and great friend.

Henrietta Pollitzer first married Edward V. Hartford, vice-president of the Atlantic and Pacific Tea Company (A&P) and one of the heirs to the great A&P fortune. Upon Hartford's death in 1922, his young widow became one of the wealthiest women in the world. In 1937, she married the much younger Prince Guido Pignatelli of Italy.

In the late 1920s, the then Mrs. Hartford bought a large plantation, Wando, upon which she built an enormous colonial revival plantation house in 1931. There she entertained friends from Charleston and international society. The house burned in 1942 in a spectacular fire.

Princess Pignatelli did not publicize her age. When she died in 1948, *Time* magazine reported that she was "sixtyish." Tragically, her only son, Huntington Hartford, dissipated his enormous inheritance and died destitute.

After Princess Pignatelli's death the Preservation Society of Charleston revealed that it was her anonymous gift that had purchased the Joseph Manigault House and saved it from demolition.

Gustavus M. Pinckney (1872–1912)

Lawyer and Author   MAP LOCATION: SOUTHWEST 38

Gustavus Pinckney was born in Charleston, the son of C. C. and Lucy (Memminger) Pinckney. His maternal grandfather was the first Confederate secretary of the treasury, Christopher Memminger. Pinckney was educated in the law and became a distinguished member of the Charleston bar. He also published several books, including *Life of John C. Calhoun* (1903), *The Coming Crisis* (1905), and *Fruits and Specimens from My Acre* (1907).

In 1909 Pinckney married Miss Mary Middleton, his first cousin on the maternal side. He died in 1912 and was buried in his parents' lot in Magnolia Cemetery. His body was moved later to a lot in Magnolia that his widow bought for the repose of her husbands, her boyfriend, and herself.

Josephine Pinckney at the Dock Street Theatre in 1950 with (left to right) Albert Simons, Harold A. Mouzon, and George C. Rogers, Sr. Courtesy of the South Carolina Historical Society

JOSEPHINE LYONS SCOTT PINCKNEY (1895–1957)

Author   MAP LOCATION: SOUTHWEST 53

Josephine Pinckney was in her day one of Charleston's most commercially and artistically successful novelists. Today her works are sadly and undeservedly neglected. Miss Pinckney was born in Charleston, daughter of a wealthy Confederate captain. She graduated from Ashley Hall and studied at the College of Charleston, Radcliffe College, and Columbia University. Miss Pinckney was one of the founders of the South Carolina Poetry Society in 1920, and she published a book of poems, *Sea-Drinking Cities,* in 1927.

Pinckney's poetry was distinguished, but her best and best-known work was her fiction. Her first novel, *Hilton Head* (1941), was an historical romance based on the life of Henry Woodward, the first South Carolinian of English descent. *Three O'Clock Dinner* (1945) was Pinckney's most commercially successful novel; the movie rights alone brought $125,000. It is a study of Charleston society and manners that contrasts an old Charleston family, the Redcliffs, with the newer, rawer Hessenwinkle family. *Great Mischief* (1948) is a fascinating and bizarre retelling of the Faust legend set in Charleston and hell. The devil is said to have the appearance of an old Charleston gentleman, and the entrance to hell is through the floor of a Charleston pharmacy. *My Son and Foe* (1952), like *Three O'Clock Dinner,* is again concerned with family conflicts, this time set on the fictional island of

St. Finbar. Miss Pinckney's last novel, the posthumously published *Splendid in Ashes* (1958), concerns the shifting fortunes of a charismatic Charleston businessman, John A. Grimshawe. The novel opens at Grimshawe's funeral and seems to be narrated by the city of Charleston itself.

In addition to her literary endeavors, Miss Pinckney was also involved in the founding of the Society for the Preservation of Spirituals and of the Historic Charleston Foundation. She died on a visit to New York in 1957.

Barbara L. Bellows's *A Talent for Living: Josephine Pinckney and the Charleston Literary Tradition* (2006) is an excellent biography.

LOUISA BOUKNIGHT POPPENHEIM (1868–1957)
MARY BARNETT POPPENHEIM (1866–1936)

Clubwomen   MAP LOCATION: NORTHWEST 15

The Poppenheim sisters were among the foremost Southern representatives of what Americans in the late nineteenth and early twentieth centuries called the New Woman. Their education and civic activism propelled them into innovative positions of independence and leadership, though they also held closely to many traditional values.

The Misses Poppenheim were the elder of the four daughters of Christopher Pritchard Poppenheim and Mary Elinor (Bouknight) Poppenheim, first cousins who married in 1864. Christopher, who grew up on a rice plantation in Goose Creek, served in Hampton's Legion during the war. Mary helped to found a soldiers' aid association in her native Edgefield County. After the war they settled in Charleston, where the young husband opened a dry goods store. His wife determined to educate all four of their daughters at Vassar College, founded in 1865 and recognized as the most rigorous and prestigious American institution of higher education for women. As Southerners, they were decided rarities at Vassar and sometimes felt out of place but admirably immersed themselves in the experience. Louisa served as president of the student association and Mary as its vice-president, and both were active in many other organizations.

Upon graduation, both Misses Poppenheim returned to the family home at 31 Meeting Street, where they lived with their mother until her death in 1915 and afterward together until Mary's death in 1936. Their younger sisters married, Christie to a fertilizer manufacturer from Richmond and Ida to Daniel Ravenel of Charleston, but the overall family pattern typifies the late-nineteenth-century decline in the marriage rate among college-educated women. Louisa and Mary centered their lives not on marriage and child-raising but on the rapidly growing social and political world of women's clubs. They were founding members of the Century Club, the Civic Club, and the Intercollegiate Club and also members of the Ladies Benevolent Society, the Ladies Memorial Association, the Rebecca Motte chapter of the Daughters of the American Revolution, the United Daughters of the Confederacy, the Women's Exchange, and the YWCA. From 1899 to 1913 they published and edited the *Keystone,* one of the most important voices in the women's club movement. The magazine became the official organ for five Southern state federations of women's clubs and three state divisions of the United Daughters of the Confederacy.

The more vivacious of the sisters, Louisa was the most influential South Carolina club-woman of her era. She was the second president of the South Carolina Federation of Women's Clubs and an officer in the national General Federation of Women's Clubs. She worked for the establishment of kindergartens, playgrounds, parks, and Parent-Teacher Associations; for representation of women on local boards of education and the state board of charities; and for reforms in the criminal justice system like the creation of juvenile courts and the appointment of prison matrons. She was a conservative force on many of the controversial issues of the period, which in part reflected her commitment to a distinctive Southern identity. She was instrumental in maintaining a policy of racial segregation in the General Federation of Women's Clubs. She did not support the women's suffrage movement and sought to ensure that South Carolina remained the only state in the country that did not permit divorce, though she did promote the admission of women to the College of Charleston.

Quieter and more scholarly, Mary devoted her greatest efforts to the United Daughters of the Confederacy. She was a charter member of the Charleston chapter, which was the third to join the national organization, and she found in the UDC an excellent vehicle for building on her historical studies at Vassar. She was the first historian of the state division and longtime chair of the national committee on education. She rose to president of the state division and, for the 1917–1919 term, president-general of the UDC. Her leadership of the national organization during World War I involved her in a number of overseas initiatives. She was one of the first women elected to the South Carolina Historical Society as well as one of the first women to serve on the South Carolina Historical Commission. Demonstrating a particular interest in women's experiences during the Civil War and afterward, she was one of the editors of *South Carolina Women in the Confederacy* (2 vols.; 1903–1907) and a member of the committee that prepared *The History of the United Daughters of the Confederacy* (1938).

Joan Johnson has edited the Poppenheims' college correspondence in *Southern Women at Vassar* (2002) and discussed them at length in *Southern Ladies, New Women: Race, Region, and Clubwomen in South Carolina, 1890–1930* (2004).

William Dennison Porter (1810–1883)

Secessionist Legislator and Cofounder   MAP LOCATION: SOUTHEAST 46
of Magnolia Cemetery

W. D. Porter was an influential insider in nineteenth-century South Carolina and played an important role in the decision for secession. He was born in Charleston and educated at the academy of Christopher Cotes and then at the College of Charleston, from which he graduated with second honors in 1829. He read law under James Louis Petigru and entered the bar in 1833. Porter established a reputation as an excellent lawyer and advocate. He practiced successively with some of Charleston's most distinguished attorneys: Alexander H. Brown, James Conner, and eventually his own son-in-law, William H. Brawley.

Porter served in the South Carolina House of Representatives from 1840 to 1847. In 1848 he was elevated to the state Senate, where he served continuously through the end of the Civil War. He was elected president of the Senate in 1858 and retained that office until elected lieutenant governor in 1865. He was removed from that office when the federal forces took control of South Carolina government.

Porter is a prime example of a moderate for most of the 1850s who took a leading role in the final drive for secession. He was president of the 1860 Association, a group formed specifically to promote disunion. He published a widely circulated tract entitled *State Sovereignty and the Doctrine of Coercion* (1860), in which he recast the ideas of Turnbull and Calhoun on the rights of the states.

Porter was an incorporator and director of Magnolia Cemetery and was active in numerous other educational and charitable causes. He was also captain of the Washington Light Infantry. He served as master-in-equity for Charleston County from 1880 to 1882.

ELIZABETH WATIES ALLSTON PRINGLE (1845–1921)

Planter and Author   MAP LOCATION: SOUTHWEST 54

Elizabeth Waties Allston Pringle was a child of the rice culture of South Carolina. She grew up in the culture and tried to sustain it long past the time when it was economically practical. Her experiences eventually formed the basis for two classic books.

Elizabeth Allston was raised amid great wealth as the daughter of Adèle Petigru (sister of James L. Petigru) and Robert F. W. Allston. Her father was one of the most successful antebellum rice planters and wrote a fine book on rice cultivation. He served as governor of South Carolina and owned seven plantations near Georgetown, South Carolina, comprising some four thousand acres. In 1856 he bought the magnificent Nathaniel Russell House in Charleston. "Bessie" Allston was educated by an English governess until she reached the age of nine, when she was sent to Madame Togno's School in Charleston.

The Civil War shattered the Allston family. Governor Allston died in 1864 and left an estate laden with debt. The only real property the family retained was Chicora Wood Plantation and the Nathaniel Russell House in Charleston. His widow set up a boarding school in their Charleston home, where Bessie helped as a teacher. Though the school was somewhat successful, the Allston family moved back to Chicora Wood in 1868.

Elizabeth Allston married John Julius Pringle, of neighboring White House Plantation, in 1870. Their time together was precious but short. They lost an infant son, and Pringle died suddenly from malaria in 1876.

Mrs. Pringle returned to Chicora Wood, where she helped out with the myriad duties of a plantation. She bought out her husband's other heirs in White House and began to manage it herself in 1885. She assumed control and management of Chicora Wood as well after her mother's death. Pringle was innovative in her agricultural techniques and usually managed to show a small profit, but rice production was dying a slow death in South Carolina as the competition of cheap rice from Arkansas, Texas, and Louisiana slowly took its toll.

Partly to satisfy her literary leanings and partly to make money, Mrs. Pringle began to submit excerpts from her diary to the New York *Sun* in 1903 under the pen name Patience Pennington. She continued to write these diary entries for a number of years.

She developed, polished, and telescoped the diary entries and published them as *A Woman Rice Planter* (1913). Alice Ravenel Huger Smith's drawings provide magnificent illustration of the text. *A Woman Rice Planter* tells the story of the transition away from the rice culture with charm, humor, and sadness. It is a beautiful elegy for a lost way of life.

Mrs. Pringle finally had to abandon rice planting altogether. She sold White House Plantation after the main house burned. During two visits to California, her friend Phoebe Apperson Hearst urged her to set down her recollection of growing up in the rice culture. This she did in *Chronicles of Chicora Wood,* the story of the Allston family. She finished the book shortly before her death. It was published posthumously in 1922.

Mrs. Pringle had published a series of stories in the *Atlantic Monthly* in 1914 and 1915 about two black orphans she attempted to raise. These stories were published in 1984 as *Rab and Dab.*

Harrison Randolph (1871–1954)

College President   MAP LOCATION: SOUTHWEST 55

Harrison Randolph was the youngest president in the history of the College of Charleston and served the longest, for forty-five years. He was born in New Orleans but raised in Virginia, the home of his illustrious ancestors. He studied at Pantops Academy in Charlottesville and at the University of Virginia, from which he graduated with an M.A. in 1892.

From 1890 to 1895 he studied and taught mathematics at the University of Virginia. Afterwards he was a professor of mathematics at the University of Arkansas for two years. In 1897, at the age of twenty-six, he became professor of mathematics and president of the College of Charleston. He presided over some of the College's hardest but most productive years. His work was recognized with honorary doctorates from Washington and Lee University in 1897 and the University of South Carolina in 1905. He retired as president of the College of Charleston in 1942.

Beatrice St. Julien Ravenel (1904–1990)

Author   MAP LOCATION: SOUTHWEST 56

Born in Charleston in 1904, Miss Ravenel was the daughter of Charleston's great twentieth-century poet Beatrice Witte Ravenel and the granddaughter of Charleston historian Mrs. St. Julien Ravenel. It is hardly any wonder that she became a very fine writer herself.

Miss Ravenel was educated in Charleston schools and was a graduate of the College of Charleston. She was for many years the book editor and a reporter for the *News and Courier.* She also regularly published articles in *Antiques* magazine. Her most important work was *Architects of Charleston* (1945), a meticulously researched and beautifully written book. In 1947, she edited *Charleston Murders,* to which she contributed a chapter. *Charleston Murders* was a very racy book for its day and is still one of the most entertaining and sought-after works of Charleston literature.

Beatrice Witte Ravenel and her daughter, Beatrice St. Julien Ravenel.
Courtesy of the South Carolina Historical Society

Though she never married, Miss Ravenel was the devoted companion of Dr. Richard Whitaker. When friends would question her relationship with this younger man, she would answer, "He's too young to marry and too old to adopt." Miss Ravenel remained interested and interesting to the end of her life. She divided the great bulk of her substantial estate between the Huguenot Society and the Charleston Library Society.

BEATRICE WITTE RAVENEL (1870–1956)

Poet   MAP LOCATION: SOUTHWEST 56

Beatrice W. Ravenel was one of the group that founded the Poetry Society of South Carolina in 1920 and was the finest poet to emerge from the Society. She was born in

Charleston, third of the six Witte sisters. According to her sister Laura W. Waring's memoir, she was "the brain" of the family. She attended Miss Kelly's School and in 1889 was enrolled in the women's division of Harvard College (later named Radcliffe College). She wrote for the *Harvard Advocate* and the *Harvard Monthly*, student literary magazines, and attained a fine reputation among literary circles of her time.

She returned home and married Francis Gualdo Ravenel, son of Dr. and Mrs. St. Julien Ravenel, in 1900. She gave birth to their only child, Beatrice St. Julien Ravenel, in 1904. Mrs. Ravenel was left a small fortune upon her father's death in 1908, but poor management by her husband virtually dissipated the inheritance in the 1910s. Her husband died in 1920.

To help support herself, Mrs. Ravenel again took up writing fiction for national magazines and articles for local newspapers. By the time of the founding of the Poetry Society, Mrs. Ravenel was experimenting with imagist poetry. As the critic Louis Rubin has written, "Almost overnight she put aside the sentimental abstractions of the waning genteel tradition and began producing free verse of a notable economy of diction, precision of language, and vivid imagery."

The only book of Mrs. Ravenel's published in her lifetime was *The Arrow of Lightning* (1925). It received high praise but limited distribution. In 1926 she married her first husband's cousin, Samuel Prioleau Ravenel, and stopped publishing her writings. But she did continue writing. After the poet's death in 1956 her daughter discovered a batch of manuscripts hidden in her desk. These poems, startlingly sexual in their content, constitute some of her best work. A posthumous selection of her later works together with poems from *The Arrow of Lightning* was compiled and edited by Louis Rubin in 1969 as *The Yemassee Lands.*

Harriott Horry Rutledge Ravenel (1832–1912)

Author   MAP LOCATION: SOUTHEAST 47

Harriott Horry Rutledge Ravenel was one of Charleston's most important women of letters and was greatly responsible for the twentieth-century revival of interest in Charleston history. She was born in Charleston, the daughter of Edward Cotesworth and Rebecca Motte (Lowndes) Rutledge of Hampton Plantation. She was educated at Madame Talvande's School, the same school that produced the Southern diarist Mary Boykin Chesnut. She married Dr. St. Julien Ravenel in 1851 and lived in Charleston until the outbreak of the Civil War, when she and her family removed to Columbia. Through great effort, she saved her family home there during the burning of the city at the end of the war. After her husband died in 1882, she spent much of the next years at the family plantation Acton, near Stateburg.

Her literary career began with the novel *Ashurst*, first published serially in 1879 in the *Weekly News* of Charleston under the pseudonym Mrs. H. Hilton Broom. It was considered by many of her admirers her finest work. In 1896 she published *Eliza Pinckney*, a biography of one of her famous ancestors. In 1901 she published *The Life and Times of William Lowndes of South Carolina, 1782–1822*, a biography of her grandfather.

Mrs. Ravenel's most important work was *Charleston, the Place and the People* (1906), a romantic mix of history, legends, and memories. Whatever its value as history, this charming and remarkable book sold very well and excited much interest in Charleston and in its history throughout the country. Its most important legacy, however, was that the book served as a catalyst to the preservation of Charleston's historic treasures that were substantially intact but sadly neglected by the first decade of the twentieth century.

Three of Mrs. Ravenel's descendants, Herbert Ravenel Sass, St. Julien R. Childs, and Beatrice St. Julien Ravenel, later wrote important histories of Charleston.

MARY MACK MARTIN RAVENEL (1869–1933)

Matron and Murder Victim   MAP LOCATION: SOUTHEAST 48

Sweet white South of Broad widows simply aren't murdered. It is unseemly. But Mrs. John Ravenel was murdered on a public street in the heart of downtown Charleston. To this day no one has any inkling of who might have killed her, or why.

Mrs. Ravenel was a native of Detroit. She was first married to William Martin, a wealthy plantation owner from Savannah. Her second husband was John Ravenel, son of Dr. and Mrs. St. Julien Ravenel. He died a number of years before Mrs. Ravenel's ghastly end. To all appearances Mrs. Ravenel lived a quiet, blameless life at her home on Tradd Street.

On the night of November 20, 1933, she dined with a friend at the Fort Sumter Hotel (now the Fort Sumter House Condominiums), adjacent to White Point Gardens. She left the hotel at about 9:30 p.m. and was found at about 10:00 pm lying on the sidewalk near the corner of Meeting and Water Streets. She still had her pocketbook and jewelry. The people who found her thought she had been hit by a car and took her to Roper Hospital. At Roper she told an attendant, "A man hit me." Shortly afterwards she died.

Charleston police worked on the case for years. It is said that Chief of Detectives John J. Healy conducted ballistics tests on every .38 caliber weapon brought to the police station but to no avail. Mary Ravenel's mysterious death will remain a mystery.

ST. JULIEN RAVENEL (1819–1882)

Chemist and Inventor   MAP LOCATION: SOUTHEAST 47

Dr. St. Julien Ravenel was a medical doctor, scientist, and inventor whose brilliance was of enormous aid to his state before, during, and after the Civil War. He was born in Charleston and received his elementary education here. He studied for a time in the schools of New Jersey. He completed his studies at the Medical College in Charleston, from which he received his degree in 1840. He did further study in Philadelphia and Paris before returning home to practice and teach medicine.

Dr. Ravenel's main interests, however, were in natural history and chemistry, particularly agricultural chemistry. He established the first stone lime works at his plantation, Stony Landing, on the Cooper River in 1857. It was at Stony Landing that he also invented the *Little David,* a low-set, cigar-shaped boat fitted with an iron spar that would deliver an explosive charge, or torpedo. This vessel and its descendants saw action in the defense of Charleston Harbor during the Civil War.

During the war, Dr. Ravenel also saw service in Columbia as the surgeon in charge of a Confederate hospital and as the chemist in charge of the laboratory where much of the medicine for the Confederacy was made.

Charleston and its economy were completely devastated at the end of the Civil War. Dr. Ravenel's experiments did much to help South Carolina's recovery. He turned his attentions to the tremendous deposits of phosphates in the lands and river beds around Charleston and invented a process by which phosphate rock could be made soluble. This process made phosphates available for use as fertilizer and led to the creation of one of the few profitable industries in postwar Charleston. Dr. Ravenel continued to refine various processes by which raw materials found in the lowcountry could be used as fertilizer. He also devised the system of artesian wells from which Charleston was able to receive clean fresh water.

Dr. Ravenel was married to Harriott Horry Rutledge in 1851. The achievements of their descendants honor the memories of Dr. and Mrs. Ravenel.

MOTTE ALSTON READ (1872–1920)

Scholar   MAP LOCATION: SOUTHWEST 57

Motte Alston Read was an extraordinarily learned man whose life was unfortunately cut short by rheumatoid arthritis. He was born in Augusta, Georgia, the son of a Virginian, William Melvin Read, and a Charlestonian, Jane Ladson Alston. The memoirs of his grandfather, J. Motte Alston, were written at Read's behest and later published as *Rice Planter and Sportsman, the Recollections of J. Motte Alston, 1821–1909.*

Read studied geology at Harvard from 1889 to 1893 before spending three years on a Texas cattle ranch for his health, which he always maintained was no less educational than his time in Cambridge. He then studied in Munich. While in Europe he conducted paleontological research for his major publication on gastropods in the Seisser Alp during the Triassic period. He became an instructor in geology at Harvard, where he received a degree in 1902 as a member of the class of 1893. He taught briefly at the Massachusetts Institute of Technology but had to resign his professorship as his rheumatoid arthritis became more severe.

After trying Washington, D.C., for a time, Read moved back to Charleston, where he was elected professor of biology and geology at the College of Charleston, but his declining health prevented him from taking up the academic appointment. He tried the dry climate of the Texas family ranch one more time, with unsatisfactory results. He finally returned to Charleston, where he died of the lingering effects of rheumatoid arthritis at his home at 8 Atlantic Street.

Read served as curator of the South Carolina Historical Society and was also a member of numerous academic societies. His most significant cultural contribution to Charleston was his extensive collection of Japanese woodblock prints. The prints were key to the artistic development of Read's best friend and love, Alice Ravenel Huger Smith. Read's print collection is today housed in its own gallery at the Gibbes Museum of Art.

ANTOINETTE ROSE GUERARD RHETT (1884–1964)

Artist   MAP LOCATION: SOUTHWEST 58

Antoinette Rhett was one of the finest etchers and watercolor artists of the Charleston Renaissance. She was born in Baltimore, Maryland, of an old Charleston family. She was educated at Converse College and married to Arthur Rose Rhett, brother of Robert Goodwyn Rhett. She was one of the favorite pupils of Alfred Hutty, a nationally important artist of Charleston and Woodstock, New York.

Mrs. Rhett was one of the founders with Hutty and others of the Charleston Etchers' Club. Her etchings were generally small and delicate depictions of natural subjects, though she also etched and painted Charleston scenes. She was one of the only Charleston artists to experiment with colored etchings. She exhibited with the Printmakers of California, the Brooklyn Society of Etchers, the Print Club of Philadelphia, the New Orleans Art Association, the Mississippi Art Association, and the Southern States Art League. Her paintings are in the collection of the Gibbes Museum and the South Carolina State Museum.

In addition to her artistic interests Mrs. Rhett was for many years on the board of the Footlight Players, Charleston's primary dramatic organization. Mrs. Rhett and her husband also raised prize cocker spaniels. After her husband's death, Mrs. Rhett lived in the Confederate Home. She is buried in an unmarked grave beside her husband.

ROBERT BARNWELL RHETT (1800–1876)

Fire-eater   MAP LOCATION: SOUTHEAST 49

Often called "the Father of Secession," Robert Barnwell Rhett was perhaps more conspicuous than influential in the movement for Southern independence. His biographer William Davis summarizes a common scholarly judgment in reporting that South Carolina seceded "not because of Rhett but in spite of him." But Rhett called for disunion loudest and longest, and it is not unreasonable to conclude that he significantly helped to shape the radical political climate of the state. Thanks to Rhett Butler in *Gone With the Wind*, the name Rhett is now synonymous with the Lowcountry aristocracy of the Old South. Fittingly, Robert Barnwell Rhett's family was represented in the cast of the movie, as his great-granddaughter Alicia Rhett played the role of India Wilkes.

When he was born in Beaufort in 1800, his name was not Rhett but Smith. His ancestors included such notables as Sir John Yeamans, one of the Barbadians who established Charles Town, and the landgrave and governor Thomas Smith. In 1837 he and his brothers changed their surname to Rhett, explaining that they sought to honor their distinguished maternal ancestor William Rhett, captor of the pirate Stede Bonnet and a key figure in Charleston in the early eighteenth century, who had no male descendants. They

HON. ROBERT BARNWELL RHETT, OF SOUTH CAROLINA.—PHOTOGRAPHED BY COOK, CHARLESTON, S. C.

Robert Barnwell Rhett, engraving after a January 1861 portrait by Charleston photographer George S. Cook. Courtesy of the Library of Congress

also sought a more distinctive and impressive name because several of the brothers had become active in public life.

Robert Barnwell Smith, or Rhett, was already well launched on the career that would encompass much of South Carolina political history from the Nullification controversy through the Civil War. He represented the Colleton District in the state legislature from 1826 through 1832, when he became state attorney general. He held that office until 1837, resigning when the Beaufort and Colleton congressional district elected him to the U.S. House of Representatives. He remained in Congress until 1849. Throughout these years he maintained a complicated relationship with John C. Calhoun, sometimes working in partnership but sometimes charting a separate course. The most notable of these independent initiatives was the so-called Bluffton Movement, in which Rhett called for South Carolina to secede in response to the tariff of 1842. The legislature elected Rhett to take Calhoun's old seat in the U.S. Senate in late 1850, when Rhett was at the center of the movement for secession in response to the Compromise of 1850. He resigned from the Senate in 1852 after a state convention rejected that step.

Rhett's electoral success demonstrated the complicated workings of Jacksonian democracy in South Carolina. He had little confidence in the wisdom of majorities and considered himself entitled to govern by virtue of inheritance and social position. He settled into the congenial role of a planter in the mid-1830s by buying, at an advantageous price, the lands and slaves of a British citizen required to divest himself of slaves by the emancipation policy of the Empire. Rhett also took himself seriously as a patriarch. He and his first wife, Elizabeth Washington Burnet, had twelve children during their marriage from 1827 to 1852. A little over a year later, he married Catherine Herbert Dent, with whom he had three more children. But if he and his clan struck many other conservative Carolinian leaders as overbearing and self-centered, Rhett often did work with allies and appeal to voters, at least in the early stages of his career. Evangelical religion provided one way to identify with ordinary people, as he converted during the Nullification controversy and was a devout proponent of temperance.

Although Rhett's radicalism often put him out of step with the commercial community in Charleston, the city was a center of his operations through his longtime involvement with the Charleston *Mercury*. His brother-in-law John Stuart bought the newspaper from its founder Henry L. Pinckney when the latter was elected to Congress in 1833, and he generally continued to support Rhett politically even after Rhett's sister left the editor, taking their children with her, in despair over Stuart's alcoholism. Rhett's political ally John Heart bought part of the newspaper in 1849, after which Rhett largely directed the editorial policy of the paper before he went to the Senate. Around the time he retired from that body, his nephew William Taber became Heart's partner. Rhett, who had bought a grand home at the corner of Thomas and Vanderhorst Streets, practiced law in Charleston and enjoyed the outlet for his opinions that the *Mercury* afforded. His son Edmund became an editor in 1856. When Edmund's criticisms of A. G. Magrath soon led to Taber's death in a duel with Magrath's brother, Robert Barnwell Rhett provided his oldest son, Robert Barnwell Rhett Jr., with the funds to buy Taber's share. Two years later this namesake bought full control of the paper with proceeds from his father's sale of thirty-one slaves to Langdon Cheves. As the Rhett organ, the *Mercury* was the most strident and quotable voice of Southern radicalism.

The rising tide of secession briefly restored Rhett's political fortunes. After his admirer William Lowndes Yancey of Alabama broke up the 1860 Democratic national convention in Charleston in protest against the failure of the party platform to call for Congressional protection of slavery in the federal territories, Rhett served as a delegate to the follow-up convention that completed the rupture of the Democratic party. Charleston elected him to the secession convention, though he was only the seventh-highest votegetter, and he helped to draft the Ordinance of Secession. The convention named him one of the state's delegates to the Provisional Confederate Congress. Rhett evidently had some hopes that this meeting in Montgomery would elect him president or that he would be named secretary of state, neither of which was realistic. He was active in the framing of the Confederate constitution and successfully promoted a single six-year term for the president, though he was bitterly disappointed by the defeats of his proposals to permit reopening of the Atlantic slave trade and to declare explicitly that only slaveholding states could belong to the Confederacy.

Frustrated that more conservative, or pragmatic, politicians had commandeered the movement that he felt he had started, Rhett became a vitriolic critic of the Davis administration. The war soon degenerated into one defeat after another for him. The fall of Beaufort in November 1861 turned his boyhood home into a federal office. Despite the wartime eagerness for news, subscriptions to the *Mercury* fell sharply amid the sentiment for Confederate unity. Rhett started renting out his grand Charleston home and in 1863 sold it to George A. Trenholm. He ran for election to the Confederate Congress in the same year, expecting incumbent Lewis Ayers to step aside in his favor, but Ayers had the temerity not only to run but to win. When the Union Army arrived on one of his plantations in February 1865, Rhett fled to Alabama. He returned to South Carolina the next winter to help Robert Barnwell Rhett, Jr., restart the *Mercury* and help his son Alfred resume planting. But the *Mercury* folded in November 1868 after assailing Reconstruction for two years, and Rhett lost his plantations to foreclosure sales a few years later. He spent his last years living in New Orleans with one of his daughters and her husband, a former staff officer for Gen. P. G. T. Beauregard. The cause of death was evidently the skin cancer that had forced Rhett to undergo a series of operations that eventually removed almost all of his nose.

The decision to bury Rhett at Magnolia illustrates one of the reasons for the establishment of the cemetery. His biographer reports that Rhett had expressed a desire to be buried alongside his father in the family vault at St. Philip's Church but that the location of James Smith's remains had been lost in the shifting of caskets and bones over the years. Rhett was laid to rest near his first wife and other family members in a plot that long remained unmarked until the installation of a single stone inscribed only with the name Rhett.

Robert Goodwyn Rhett (1862–1939)

Mayor and Historian of Charleston   MAP LOCATION: SOUTHEAST 50

Robert Goodwyn Rhett was the leading citizen of Charleston in his day. He was mayor of Charleston, president of the U.S. Chamber of Commerce, president of the People's Bank, and author of an important book about the city. Charleston's signature dish, she-crab soup, was invented in his kitchen.

Rhett was born in Columbia, the son of Albert Moore and Martha (Goodwyn) Rhett. He was the great-nephew of Robert Barnwell Rhett. R. G. Rhett was raised in and around Charleston and received his secondary education at Porter Military Academy and Episcopal High School in Alexandria, Virginia. He received a master's degree from the University of Virginia in 1883 and a law degree from the same institution the following year.

Rhett quickly became a member of the Charleston bar and was one of the founding members of the firm that became Trenholm, Rhett, Miller and Whaley. He was also prominently involved in commerce and banking in Charleston. He played a leading part in the fertilizer industry in Charleston until his firm was acquired by the Virginia-Carolina Chemical Company. In 1896 he was made president of the South Carolina Loan and Trust Company. Three years later he became controlling stockholder and president of the People's National Bank of Charleston. As its president, Rhett oversaw the acquisition of the Dime Savings Bank and the First National Bank. While he was president, the People's Bank built as its headquarters Charleston's first "skyscraper," the People's Building at Broad and State Streets. Rhett founded the Commercial Club of Charleston and also served at various times as the president of seven other business groups.

Rhett's political career began with his election to the city council in 1895. He served as an alderman until his election as mayor of Charleston in 1903. He remained in that office until 1911. While in city government, Rhett was instrumental in the building of Murray Boulevard and in the establishment of the Charleston Navy Yard. He was one of the early developers of what is now called North Charleston.

Mayor Rhett hosted William Howard Taft at his home on three separate occasions. During one of Taft's visits, Rhett's butler and cook accidentally added crab roe to the crab soup and she-crab soup was born. History does not record how many bowls America's largest president consumed.

When Rhett completed his second term as mayor, he declined to seek reelection, but he remained an active force in commercial circles locally and nationally. He was a participant in the construction of the Francis Marion Hotel. He was elected president of the U.S. Chamber of Commerce from 1916–1918. He was chairman of War Savings for South Carolina in World War I. From 1920 to 1926 he was chairman of the South Carolina Highway Commission. In that position, he led the way for the bridging of the Savannah River at Savannah, the bridging of the Ashley River, and the bridging of the Santee River near Kingstree.

Despite his many accomplishments, Rhett's life was not an unbroken string of successes. He lost a close race for the U.S. Senate to Ellison D. Smith in 1908. His greatest disaster came with the failure of the People's National Bank in 1932. The failure of the bank not only crippled Rhett's finances but also the finances of the city. Charleston, which deposited its funds with People's, was left for all practical purposes bankrupt.

Undeterred, Rhett proceeded with the great project of his late years, a history of Charleston. He finished *Charleston: An Epic of Carolina* (1940) shortly before his death of uremic poisoning. The book was published posthumously to great acclaim.

JAMES HENRY RICE, JR. (1868–1935)

Conservationist   MAP LOCATION: NORTHEAST 14

James Henry Rice was a winner of the field shooting championship of the world who realized that game was being killed too rapidly. He knew that there would soon be no hunting at all if conservation measures were not taken. He devoted his life and pen to the cause of conservation thereafter.

James Henry Rice was born at Riverlands Plantation near Ninety-Six, South Carolina, shortly after the Civil War. He graduated from the Ninety-Six High School and was briefly enrolled at South Carolina College. Of his college experience, Rice later wrote, "I consider my college course the most lasting injury I ever received." He quickly recovered, however, and worked in a variety of jobs as teacher, editor, publishing agent, and land manager. In 1895 he became editor of the *Colonial Record of South Carolina* and the Columbia *Evening News*. He wrote editorials for *The State* in the late 1890s and was successively editor of *The Field* and *The South Carolina Field*.

He served as secretary of the Audubon Society from 1907 to 1910 and as field agent of the National Association of Audubon Societies from 1910 to 1913. Simultaneously he was the chief game warden of South Carolina and an inspector for the U.S. Biological Survey from 1913 to 1917.

Most of all, James Henry Rice will be remembered as a writer. He wrote several books, of which the most notable were *Glories of the Carolina Coast* (1925) and *The Aftermath of Glory* (1934).

CLEMENTS RIPLEY (1892–1954)
KATHARINE BALL RIPLEY (1898–1955)

Authors   MAP LOCATION: NORTHEAST 2

Clements Ripley was a transplanted Charlestonian who became famous as a writer of novels, short stories, and movies. He was born in Tacoma, Washington, but came from old New England roots. A graduate of Taft School and Yale, where he was an editor of the *Yale Review,* he joined the Army almost immediately upon his graduation in 1916 and was eventually stationed at Camp Jackson. There he met and fell in love with the daughter of William Watts Ball, Katharine. They married in 1919. Ripley left the service with the rank of captain in 1920.

For a number of years Mr. and Mrs. Ripley tried to make a living by farming peaches in the hills of North Carolina. They failed miserably. Ripley supported his family by writing pulp fiction. A serial he wrote for *Adventure* magazine, *Dust and Sun,* was brought out in hardcover in 1929 and Ripley was on his way. He became a regular contributor to the *Saturday Evening Post* and in short order published *Devil Drums* (1931), *Black Moon* (1933), *Murder Walks Alone* (1935), *Gold Is Where You Find It* (1936), *Clear for Action* (1940), and *Mississippi Belle* (1942).

While he was achieving success as a novelist, Ripley was also in demand in Hollywood. In 1934 he received $30,000 for the rights to his short story, "A Lady Comes to Town," at that time the highest price ever paid for film rights to a short story. Several of his other works were adapted for film, including *Gold Is Where You Find It* as a vehicle for Olivia de Havilland. Ripley wrote the screenplays for *Love, Honor, and Behave* (1936), *Buffalo Bill*

(1944), and *Old Los Angeles* (1948). His most lasting achievement was the adaptation, in a collaboration that included John Huston, of *Jezebel* (1938), which won Bette Davis an Oscar and is widely acknowledged as her greatest role.

Mr. and Mrs. Ripley always maintained a home in Charleston and finally retired here in 1947. Ripley never stopped writing. His last short story "A Christmas Tale" was published by the *Saturday Evening Post* shortly before his death.

Clements Ripley gave the lie to the idea that an outsider could not be accepted in Charleston. His humor and spirit made him beloved to the wide range of friends he made here. His reputation is only burnished by the writings of his son, Warren Ripley, an important Charleston historian and long-time president of the Charleston Library Society.

Katharine Ball Ripley was born in Charleston, the daughter of William Watts Ball and Faye Witte Ball. The daughter, wife, granddaughter, niece, and first cousin of Charleston writers, she was an important author herself. She wrote uncounted short stories and three books: *Sand in My Shoes* (1931), the story of her failed experiment growing peaches; *Sand Dollars* (1933), a memoir of the stock market crash; and *Crowded House* (1936), a novel of manners about Charleston.

ROSWELL SABINE RIPLEY (1823–1887)

Confederate General   MAP LOCATION: SOUTHWEST 59

R. S. Ripley was a key figure in the Civil War military operations around his adopted home of Charleston. Born in Worthington, Ohio, he attended West Point and ranked seventh in the graduating class of 1843. (Ulysses S. Grant ranked twenty-first.) He served with distinction as an artillery officer in the Mexican War and soon afterward published a history of that conflict. After seeing further action against the Seminoles in Florida, he was assigned to garrison duty at Fort Moultrie. While there he married the widow Alica Middleton Sparks. He resigned his commission a few months later in March 1853 and settled in Charleston, working at least part of the time as an agent for a rifle company. He led the state troops that seized Fort Moultrie when Maj. Robert Anderson shifted base to Fort Sumter in December 1860. Four months later, Ripley was the Confederate officer in immediate command of the artillery at Fort Moultrie that poured hot shot into Fort Sumter and started the fire that prompted Anderson's surrender.

Promoted to brigadier general, Ripley commanded the Department of South Carolina until the Confederacy merged it into a larger army led first by Robert E. Lee and later by John C. Pemberton. Ripley had some differences of opinion with Lee and a serious clash with Pemberton, in which his fiery temper drew fuel from his superior knowledge of the area. Over local protests he asked to be relieved of duty in Charleston and was sent to D. H. Hill's division in Virginia. He fought with the Army of Northern Virginia from the Peninsula Campaign through Antietam, where he was wounded in the throat but staunchly managed to rejoin his brigade on the field. Meanwhile civic leaders pressed for his reassignment to Charleston, now under the command of P. G. T. Beauregard. He returned in late 1862 and assumed responsibilities well beyond those of most brigadiers, as Beauregard repeatedly observed in recommending him for promotion. But once again he came into conflict with his commanding officer, particularly during the finger-pointing that followed the loss of Morris Island in September 1863. Friction intensified after Maj. Gen. Samuel Jones replaced Beauregard in April 1864. These strains often turned a spotlight on Ripley's drinking or as British observer Arthur J. L. Fremantle put it, his "occasional rollicking habits." Called in to resolve a dispute between Ripley and Jones, Beauregard recommended in late 1864 that Ripley be removed from Charleston, "which offers such great temptations and facilities for indulging in his irregular habits." Local leaders again rallied to Ripley's defense. He quietly went on furlough and played little part in the rest of the war.

After the war Ripley worked for a while in England, again in the rifle business, before settling in New York. He died of a stroke in that city. Upon learning that Ripley had asked to be buried in Charleston, Mayor William Ashmead Courtenay arranged for the return of the body and with the permission of Ripley's family selected a prominent site in Magnolia for the grave. The monument placed there by the Confederate Survivors Association bears an inscription saluting the "GAY CHIEFTAIN" that is excerpted from a poem Henry Timrod wrote in Ripley's honor when the general was the toast of Charleston.

George Calvin Rogers, Sr. (1889–1964)

Educator and Football Coach   MAP LOCATION: NORTHEAST 15

Dr. George C. Rogers dedicated his life to education. He fought for increased funding for the education of black students at a time when that was a courageous thing to do. He was born in Charleston, the son of Anna Simmons and John Ellsworth Rogers. He graduated from the High School of Charleston in 1906 and was a city scholarship student at the Citadel, from which he graduated in 1910. He held a master's degree from Columbia University and received an honorary doctorate from the Citadel in 1955. He and his wife, the former Helen Bean, had two children.

Rogers's life was learning. He taught at Georgia Military Academy briefly after his college graduation and then returned to Charleston. He was the principal of Courtenay School from 1912 to 1936. He coached football at the Citadel for much of this period, first as head coach and later as line coach. He won the South Carolina football championship against much larger powers (Clemson, South Carolina) in 1915 and 1916 and was fired in both years. He served as acting superintendent of Charleston schools in 1934 before becoming principal of Memminger School in 1936. He became superintendent of Charleston city schools in 1946 and served in that capacity until his retirement in 1955. After he retired, he served as administrative director of the College of Charleston's branch at Conway, which is today Coastal Carolina University. For many years he was a board member of the Avery Institute, Charleston's premier seat of learning for young African Americans.

GEORGE CALVIN ROGERS, JR. (1922–1997)

Historian   MAP LOCATION: NORTHEAST 16

The dean of South Carolina historians in his generation, George C. Rogers, Jr., illustrates the principle that there is really no history, only autobiography. He was a child of the Charleston Renaissance, growing up on Tradd Street as the artistic and literary efflorescence consolidated into a civic identity. He graduated from the College of Charleston in 1943 and served in the Air Force meteorology service during World War II. Determined to become a historian after his discharge, he enrolled in the University of Chicago to work with Avery Craven, the mentor of Rogers's mentor at the College of Charleston, Harold Easterby. But like many Charleston Renaissance luminaries, Rogers had little interest in the Civil War era, which was Craven's area of specialization. Enchanted by England while stationed outside London in 1945, he spent a year in Edinburgh on a Rotary Fellowship and wrote his doctoral dissertation on the Puritan revolutionary Sir Henry Vane. His first academic position was at the University of Pennsylvania, where he finally gained his bearings when a Philadelphia archivist directed him to the newly acquired papers of William Loughton Smith, a prominent South Carolina politician of the post-Revolutionary era. By 1958 Dr. Rogers was on the faculty at the University of South Carolina, working on a book about Smith and embarked on the life he had imagined as a boy on Tradd Street.

Dr. Rogers soon established himself as the preeminent historian of the Charleston elite from the late colonial period through the Federalist era. His *Evolution of a Federalist: William Loughton Smith of Charleston* (1962) provided a thoroughly detailed portrait of not only its title figure but of all the major contending personalities and factions in South Carolina politics after independence. The stylish *Charleston in the Age of the Pinckneys* (1969) offered an elegiac overview of the transformation of a vital, sensuous, cosmopolitan eighteenth-century seaport into an economically declining, intellectually and socially closed city that would serve as a home to nullification and secession. In 1965 he became an editor of *The Papers of Henry Laurens* (16 vols., 1968–2003), a project he headed for many years. He declared that the moderate, steadfast, and resolute Laurens was his hero and long hoped to write his biography.

These interests estranged Dr. Rogers from some influential trends in historical scholarship. At the same time that researchers were focusing closely on small communities to reconstruct the lives of ordinary men and women who had not left collections of papers and could be studied only through census, probate, tax, and other local records, Dr. Rogers published *The History of Georgetown County, South Carolina* (1970), an immensely informative but conceptually traditional survey concentrating on the planter gentry. He later collaborated with his former students Lawrence S. Rowland and Alexander Moore on the first volume of *The History of Beaufort County, South Carolina* (1996). Detached from the newer forms of social and political history, Dr. Rogers was particularly critical of the increased scholarly attention to the black majority of early South Carolina. He felt that emphasis on slaves' resistance to their oppression, celebrated as the center to their forging of a distinct African-American culture, lost sight of a mutuality between blacks and whites in the history of the state. As he drifted from the national currents of the profession he took on more commissioned projects and became more active in state historical institutions. Most noteworthy among his sponsored work was *Generations of Lawyers: A History of the South Carolina Bar* (1992). He served as editor of the *South Carolina Historical Magazine* from 1964 to 1969 and later as a member of the board of managers and president of the South Carolina Historical Society. He was also chair of the South Carolina Commission on Archives and History from 1984 to 1990 and chair of scholarly activities for the state Tricentennial Commission. At his retirement in 1986 he was Caroline McKissick Dial Professor of History and chair of the History Department at the University of South Carolina.

Dr. Rogers once wrote that the central theme of South Carolina history was "a recurring search for stability, for a balance in human affairs." If a debatable claim for a state that has produced such unstable extremists as Robert Barnwell Rhett and Ben Tillman, that thesis aptly describes Dr. Rogers himself. He was a true gentleman of the sort that he envisioned personifying the state. Every year he memorized the names of all of his students on the first day of class, not merely to demonstrate his photographic memory but because it was the courteous thing to do. He was a charming host, a congenial wit, and a master gardener. An excellent dancer, his own sense of balance famously included an ability to do the Charleston with a glass of champagne balanced on his head. His burial in Magnolia appropriately brought this academic exile home permanently.

JANE BACHMAN HASKELL ROSE (1856–1935)

Author   MAP LOCATION: SOUTHWEST 60

Jane "Jennie" Bachman Haskell Rose was one of the first Charleston women, if not the first, to make a living from writing and one of the first married women of her set to work for wages. She was born in Charleston, the youngest daughter of William and Eve (Bachman) Haskell and a granddaughter of Audubon's friend and collaborator Dr. John Bachman. She was graduated from Miss Kelly's School and taught for many years at the Confederate Home College. In 1886 she married Arthur Gordon Rose, who died in 1891.

The then Miss Haskell published her first story, "Unfinished," at the age of sixteen in *Frank Leslie's Magazine.* She was to publish prolifically throughout her life in such magazines as *Godey's Lady's Book, Belford's Monthly Magazine, Cosmopolitan, Youth's Companion, Vogue,* the *Christian Herald, All-Story Weekly,* and *Antiques.* Mrs. Rose wrote a novel originally titled *The City of Disaster* which was published as *Adam Kent's Choice* under the pseudonym "Humphrey Elliott" in 1889.

Rose was the first female stenographer hired by the *News and Courier.* She served as secretary to both Francis Warrington Dawson and, after his death, to James C. Hemphill. In this capacity, her duties were not only secretarial. She also wrote editorials, articles on historical themes, and book reviews. Through this position, she became editor of the *Exposition Magazine,* the journal of the South Carolina Interstate and West Indian

The Confederate Home College in the early twentieth century.
Courtesy of the South Caroliniana Library, University of South Carolina

Exposition. At the close of the exposition she wrote the *History of the Exposition.* She also edited *Alexander's Weekly* from 1902 to 1906.

The work for which Rose is most remembered today is Charleston's most beloved (and scariest) children's story, *Little Mistress Chicken.* It is the true story of Catherine Chicken, a Berkeley County colonial child, and of her ordeal being tied by a cruel schoolmaster to a tombstone in Strawberry Chapel Churchyard overnight. The story was first published serially in *Youth's Companion* in 1894 and brought out as a book several years later. The work has been republished many times and remains a popular local legend.

At the end of her life Mrs. Rose published frequently in *Antiques* magazine. Her expertise in the fields of Charleston-made antique furniture, silver, and clocks did much to bring national attention to these then-forgotten works of art.

JOHN RUSSELL (1812–1871)

Bookstore Owner and Publisher   MAP LOCATION: SOUTHWEST 61

A town without a good bookstore is like a body without a brain. Charleston has always been fortunate in having outstanding bookstores. The symbiotic relationship between

Charleston's writers and bookstores reached its apogee in the years before the Civil War in Russell's Bookstore.

John Russell was the proprietor. He was born in Charleston in 1812. His father died soon after Russell's birth, and his mother remarried a Mr. Jones by whom she bore two sons and a daughter. One son, Edward C. Jones, was the principal architect of Magnolia Cemetery. Early on, Russell was employed in the bookstore of John B. Beile. He worked as an accountant for a time and joined Jacob Sass in the firm of Russell and Sass in 1840 as an auctioneer and commercial merchant. He opened his "literary emporium" sometime in the 1840s. Though he moved several times, Russell's Bookstore would always be the sun in Charleston's literary solar system.

Russell made sure to stock his store with both classics and the books of the day. He made his store comfortable for the literati of the town and allowed books to be borrowed for a night. He quickly achieved a large following. He placed comfortable chairs and tables in the back of the store and soon had the literary lights of Charleston coming by on a daily basis. William Gilmore Simms, W. J. Grayson, Henry Timrod, Paul Hamilton Hayne, Basil Gildersleeve, Bishop Patrick Lynch, John Dickson Bruns, F. Peyre Porcher, Mitchell King, and James Louis Petigru all patronized Russell's regularly. Eventually, Russell started a magazine that drew upon his distinguished patronage. The magazine, *Russell's Magazine,* was a success until shortly before the Civil War.

Besides the magazine, Russell encouraged literature by publishing books of his patrons. Russell brought out a number of books by William Gilmore Simms, including *Areytos: or, Songs of the South* (1846), *Cassique of Accabee* (1848), and *Poems Descriptive, Dramatic, Legendary and Contemplative* (1853). He published Catherine Gendron Poyas's *The Huguenot Daughters, and Other Poems* (1849), as well as the most famous poem to come out of his store, W. J. Grayson's *The Hireling and the Slave* (1854). During the war he published D. F. Jamison's *Life and Times of Bertrand Du Guesclin: A History of the Fourteenth Century* (1864), considered one of the finest books issued in the South during the Confederacy.

Russell's bookstore was pillaged and virtually destroyed by Yankee forces. As late as 1870, he published William Henry Trescot's *Memorial of the Life of J. Johnston Pettigrew, Brigadier General of the Confederate States Army.* Russell tried to reopen his bookstore at the end of his life, but with no success. He died in November 1871, mourned by all of Charleston's intellectual elite.

BENJAMIN HUGER RUTLEDGE (1829–1893)

Confederate Soldier   MAP LOCATION: SOUTHEAST 52

Benjamin Huger Rutledge was one of the youngest signers of the Ordinance of Secession and a gallant fighter for the Confederacy in the Civil War. He was born in Stateburg, South Carolina, and educated by private tutors until he was sent to Dr. Muhlenberg's Academy in Long Island, New York. He entered Yale as a sophomore and graduated with honors in 1848. He did post-graduate studies for a year at Yale in philosophy and metaphysics before returning to Charleston to read law under James Louis Petigru. He was admitted to the bar and eventually became a partner of William Whaley. In 1858 he became captain of the Charleston Light Dragoons.

Rutledge served throughout South Carolina in the early phases of the Civil War and was cited for bravery at the Battle of Pocotaligo. In May 1864, Rutledge, by this time a colonel in command of a regiment, was ordered to Virginia, where he fought until the end of the year. In December, he and his troops were sent back to South Carolina in a desperate and ultimately futile attempt to slow Sherman's advance.

After the war he again took up the practice of law, this time in partnership with Henry Young, formerly judge advocate general on the staff of Robert E. Lee. During Reconstruction, Col. Rutledge reorganized the Charleston Light Dragoons as one of the paramilitary organizations that proved so helpful to Wade Hampton in effecting "Redemption." Rutledge was elected to the legislature in 1876 and served until 1880 while at the same time becoming a major general of the South Carolina volunteer troops.

For his remaining years, Gen. Rutledge was much in demand as a speaker on political and historical topics. Late in life he oversaw a course of reading and study for his young, orphaned office boy. The boy grew up to be the U.S. senator and secretary of state James F. Byrnes.

GEORGE HERBERT SASS (1845–1908)

Lawyer and Poet MAP LOCATION: SOUTHEAST 48

George Herbert Sass was a lawyer with a taste for literature. Fortunately he excelled in both pursuits. G. H. Sass was born in Charleston, the son of Jacob Keith and Octavia (Murden) Sass. His father, as the president of the Bank of Charleston (which later merged into South Carolina National Bank and much later still became part of Wachovia Bank), had his son educated in the best private schools in the city. George Herbert Sass furthered his education at the College of Charleston, from which he received a B.A. in 1867.

After graduation Sass read law in the office of Charles Richardson Miles and began the practice of law in 1869. He became master-in-equity of Charleston in 1883 but always continued his literary leanings. He was a fine poet and was often called upon to compose poems for commemorative occasions. He served as literary editor of the Charleston *News and Courier* even as his law practice grew by leaps and bounds. After Sass published a collection of his poetry, *The Heart's Quest* (1904), under the pseudonym Barton Grey, the Columbia *State* opined that he ranked "as a poet, first since Timrod." His poem *Ode to the Confederate Dead* is quoted in the memorial tablet to the Confederate dead in St. Michael's Church.

In 1883 Sass married Anna E. Ravenel, the daughter of Dr. St. Julien Ravenel and Harriott Horry Rutledge Ravenel. Mr. and Mrs. Sass are buried next to her parents. Their son, Herbert Ravenel Sass, was one of the great nature and history writers of the South.

Jacob Frederic Schirmer (1803–1880)

Diarist   MAP LOCATION: SOUTHEAST 54

Jacob F. Schirmer was a cooper in a town and a time when barrels were in short supply. He was prominent in many German-American organizations. For many years he was the president of the Corporation of St. John's Lutheran Church. He was treasurer of the German Friendly Society for forty-three years. Were it not for a curious writing habit, Schirmer would be a squib in a genealogist's journal.

Fortunately for history, Schirmer kept a meticulous journal of the happenings in Charleston from 1826 until his death. His journal was so precise and accurate that it was admitted as evidence in courts. More importantly, Schirmer's diary has become an indispensable resource for historians and is virtually ubiquitous in any account of nineteenth-century Charleston. It has been largely reprinted in the pages of the *South Carolina Historical Magazine*.

John Schnierle (1808–1869)

Mayor of Charleston   MAP LOCATION: SOUTHEAST 55

John Schnierle was a fine lawyer who spent most of his time in public service. He was born in Charleston and graduated from the South Carolina College with distinction. He entered the bar soon thereafter and quickly had a large practice.

Schnierle became mayor in 1842 upon the death of Mayor Jacob F. Mintzing. He was then elected to a series of full terms during 1842–1846 and 1850–1852. While mayor, he was also head of the fire department and colonel of the Sixteenth Regiment of the South Carolina Militia. He eventually rose to the rank of major general in the S.C. Militia. He also served as a South Carolina state representative for a number of years.

An incident described in the collection of letters *No Chariot Let Down: Charleston's Free People of Color on the Eve of the Civil War* (1984), edited by Michael P. Johnson and James L. Roarke, offers a glimpse of Schnierle's character. After the Denmark Vesey uprising, owners were prohibited from emancipating their slaves in South Carolina. To get around this law, slaves who would otherwise have been emancipated often had a trust relationship with a white owner who would hold title and provide some protection to the "slave" but allow him to live in all respects as a free man. Schnierle had such a relationship with a man. When the city police guard began to try in 1860 to enforce the slave tag laws and force these otherwise emancipated "slaves" back into slavery, many whites in the trust arrangement simply gave in. Not Schnierle. When the guard threatened the man with whom Schnierle had the trust agreement, Schnierle defied the guard to touch the man and threatened to beat to death any member of the guard who tried.

WILLIAM HAYNE SIMMONS (1784–1870)

Author   MAP LOCATION: SOUTHEAST 56

William Hayne Simmons tried his hand at many different vocations, including physician, soldier, planter, legislator, poet, and essayist. He was born in Charleston, the son of Susannah (Bulline) and John Simmons. He received a medical degree in 1806 from the University of Pennsylvania, the leading medical school in the United States for much of the nineteenth century. During the War of 1812 he served as a private in the South Carolina Militia, after which he was elected to the South Carolina House of Representatives from St. Philip and St. Michael (Charleston) and served one term.

A planter with lands in the Colleton District, Simmons left South Carolina for the Florida Territory, where he established a citrus plantation. He also wrote. He published the poetry collection *Onea: An Indian Tale* in 1820 and *Notices of East Florida, with an Account of the Seminole Nation of Indians* in 1822. Together with his brother, the author James Wright Simmons, he wrote *American Sketches: By a Native of the United States* (1827), a set of essays published in London and aimed at the English market.

Simmons left a lasting legacy in his involvement with the political and diplomatic aspects of the expansion of the United States into Florida. When whites turned their attention to north central Florida, Simmons served on a two-person committee charged with identifying a site for the territorial capital that would be convenient both to West Florida interests centered in Pensacola and East Florida interests headquartered in St. Augustine. The committee selected the village of Tallahassee, then inhabited by several hundred Seminoles who greeted Simmons and his partner warmly but who firmly opposed giving up their land. The dispossession was an important incident in the events that led to the second Seminole War (1835–1842), in the course of which Simmons's citrus plantation was destroyed.

Moving back to South Carolina, Simmons returned to the practice of medicine. He also revised and expanded *Onea,* publishing the resulting collection of poems in 1857 as *Alasco.* His old friend William Gilmore Simms praised Simmons's work as a beautiful blending of the descriptive and contemplative but criticized him for wasting his gift through indolence. The two men died only three days apart in June 1870.

WILLIAM GILMORE SIMMS (1806–1870)

Author   MAP LOCATION: SOUTHWEST 62

The preeminent man of letters in the South during the mid–nineteenth century, William Gilmore Simms is a towering figure in the intellectual history of Charleston. He can nevertheless be an elusive figure. He was so phenomenally productive that it can be difficult to get a fix on the broad shape of his career. He published more than eighty books, including two dozen novels, and left enough uncollected writing to fill another twenty volumes,

William Gilmore Simms.
Courtesy of the South
Caroliniana Library,
University of South Carolina

much of it in the ten or so periodicals he edited at one time or another. Moreover, he did not fit the antebellum Charleston stereotype of a well-bred, fastidious cultural conservative. He was a modestly born, rather bumptious enthusiast of contemporary trends. Although he did take a keen interest in the past, he ignored the classics and wrote sensational tales of adventure and the frontier. He visited New York City regularly and participated actively in its literary life. But he was in his way a thorough Charlestonian.

Simms's attachment to Charleston was more complex than that of most people who were born and died here. The son of a tavernkeeper, he was entrusted to his maternal grandmother shortly before the age of two when the death of his baby sister and their mother so shocked his father that his hair turned white within a week. When the father sent for his only child eight years later upon establishing himself in Mississippi, the grandmother refused. Young Simms successfully resisted an uncle who tried to seize him on the streets to carry him to the Southwest. Eventually a judge let the boy decide whether he would live with his father or remain in Charleston. Simms chose the center of Lowcountry civilization. The intertwining of his feelings about his home, his mother, his father, and his vocation invites endless psychological speculation.

Simms plunged into the center of local intellectual life by the time he was in his early twenties, and a simple narrative account of his subsequent literary activities would take up many pages. In his early years concentrated on poetry, with an interesting sidelight as the editor of a Unionist newspaper during the Nullification controversy. He started writing novels in the 1830s and established himself as a leading author by 1835, when he published both *The Yemassee,* an Indian adventure romance, and *The Partisan,* the first in his interconnected series of novels about the Revolutionary War in South Carolina. The latter tale introduced Simms's most famous character, Lieutenant (later Captain) Porgy, a corpulent, philosophical, and humorous planter reminiscent of Falstaff and also of Simms himself. Porgy is the central character of *The Sword and Distaff* (1852), which under the revised title *Woodcraft* (1854) is now Simms's most frequently read and admired book. Another important historical novel, set in late seventeenth-century Charleston, is *The Cassique of Kiawah* (1859). Simms also wrote in many other genres of fiction, including the tall tale, the comedy of manners, and the crime novel, not to mention full shelves of poetry, history, and literary criticism.

At the age of twenty Simms married Anna Malcolm Giles, with whom he had one daughter before his wife's death in 1832. Four years later he married Chevillette Eliza Roach, the nineteen-year-old daughter of wealthy planter Nash Roach. Installed by his father-in-law on a four-thousand-acre plantation near Orangeburg named Woodlands, Simms took up the life of a planter-writer while maintaining a Charleston base in a Smith Street house that Roach supplied. Simms's second wife gave birth to fourteen children during their marriage, the last one only a year before she died in 1863. By that time she and Simms had buried nine of their children, two of them on the same day. The house on Smith Street burned in an accidental fire in 1860, as did Woodlands two years later. Looking back on these sorrows and on his unsatisfied craving for recognition gave a haunting quality to his father's warning that if Simms stayed in his home city his talents "would be poured out like water on the sands. Charleston—*I know it only as a place of tombs.*" Simms reflected years later that "I can mournfully say the old man was right. All that I have has been turned to waste in Charleston which has never smiled on any of my labors . . . . *And I too know it as a place of tombs.*"

Simms did not always feel so alienated from his home. He found time to participate in a variety of civic discussions and initiatives. It was entirely in character that he would agree to deliver his long poem "The City of the Silent" at the dedication of Magnolia Cemetery. Barnwell County sent him to the state legislature for a term in 1844–1846, and he later came within a vote of election as lieutenant governor. His political success and its limits partly reflected his association with his closest friend, James Henry Hammond, one of many warm confidantes. The intellectually minded Charlestonians who made up the Conversation Club excluded Simms from membership, mostly because he talked too much and listened too little, but he was the presiding spirit of the salon that gathered at Russell's Bookstore, and he served as a mentor to Henry Timrod, Paul Hamilton Hayne, and William Porcher Miles. He joined wholeheartedly in support for secession and offered extensive detailed suggestions in anticipation of the artillery war that would take place in Charleston harbor.

The Civil War came home extremely painfully to Simms when his rebuilt house at Woodland [Woodlands]—and even more distressingly, his magnificent separate library with 12,000 carefully selected volumes and numerous historical manuscripts—burned to the ground in February 1865 in a fire set either by some of Sherman's bummers or by some of Simms's slaves. Ironically, Simms and his family had fled from Sherman's advance shortly earlier to seek safety in Columbia, the burning of which Simms witnessed and soon described in an anguished volume, *Sack and Destruction of the City of Columbia, S.C.* (1865).

Simms's death in 1870 prompted numerous tributes. He would have been pleased that the proprietors of Magnolia Cemetery buried him in a lot originally set aside for a monument to Calhoun. Local admirers commissioned a memorial for White Point Garden, featuring a bust of Simms by John Quincy Adams Ward, dedicated in 1879. Simms has long since slipped, however, into the dustbin of authors read only by literature professors. A coterie of academics regularly promotes his rediscovery, often with the unappealing argument that he was as good a novelist as James Fenimore Cooper, but publishers interested in broader audiences have not been persuaded. After more than a quarter-century the Library of America has not acknowledged Simms, and none of his major books available in paperback. Simms himself recognized that he had fallen short of his ambitions. He asked to have his grave marked by a broken column with the epitaph, "Here lies one, who after a reasonably long life, distinguished chiefly by unceasing labor, has left all his better works undone."

ALBERT SIMONS (1890–1980)

Preservationist   MAP LOCATION: SOUTHEAST 57

Albert Simons exercised a greater influence on the present appearance of Charleston than any other person in the twentieth century. The values he imprinted on the city landscape were the hallmarks of his own personality. Respect for continuity with the past—or at least, a particular vision of the past—was typical of his congenial temperament. A warm, thoughtful person with a self-effacing sense of humor, he did his most important work in collaboration with close personal friends. The city he strove to realize was similarly a harmonious ensemble. It would be artistically creative and economically thriving while preserving the idealized community ethos of the colonial and Federal periods. If somewhat limited in openness to different heritages and viewpoints, Simons's preservation efforts helped to establish the basic framework for modern Charleston.

Born on Montague Street, Simons was the son of a physician and the nephew of William Martin Aiken, supervising architect of the Treasury Department under President Grover Cleveland. He attended the College of Charleston before earning B.S. and M.S. degrees in architecture at the University of Pennsylvania, where he studied with the distinguished French architect Paul Cret. Simons then studied architecture in Europe during 1912–1913. His first professional employment was as a draftsman for the prominent Baltimore architect Lawrence Hall Fowler. When the business contraction following the outbreak of World War I obliged Fowler to let him go, Simons taught architecture at Clemson until he returned to Charleston in 1916 to join the firm of Todd, Simons & Todd. There he worked on his first renovation project, the installation of bathrooms at the William Washington House on South Battery. Shortly before enlisting in the Army for World War I, he prepared the architectural drawings for Daniel Elliott Huger Smith and Alice Ravenel Huger Smith's *The Dwelling Houses of Charleston* (1917).

Simons's participation in that landmark volume foreshadowed his postwar immersion in the cultural life of the Charleston Renaissance, which influenced his architecture at least as much as his professional training. He was a member of the Etchers' Club, the Society for the Preservation of Negro Spirituals, the Poetry Society of South Carolina, the Carolina Art Association, and the Charleston Library Society, serving as president or chairman of the last three groups at various times. He also lectured on art appreciation at the College of Charleston. He became a trustee of that school and also of the Charleston Museum. In these organizations he enjoyed excellent working relations with the other leading figures of the revitalization movement, to many of whom he was kin. He expanded his network in 1917 with his marriage to Harriet Porcher Stoney, who was also active in many local initiatives.

The architectural firm that Simons formed with Samuel Lapham in 1920 contributed significantly to the development of historic preservation in Charleston. Simons took the lead in cultivating donor support for the restoration of the Heyward-Washington House, a key stage in the maturation of the Society for the Preservation of Old Dwellings, and Simons & Lapham did the design work for the project. The firm restored several plantation houses during the 1920s and demonstrated a historically informed sensibility in the new buildings they designed for individuals and institutional clients. The partners also collaborated on *The Early Architecture of Charleston* (1927), commissioned by the American Institute of Architects, and joined with Simons's brother-in-law Samuel Gaillard Stoney, Jr., to produce *Carolina Plantations of the Low Country* (1938).

Simons's greatest influence, however, came with the legal consolidation of historic preservation in the planning and zoning ordinance of 1931. Simons was from the outset the dominant force on the Board of Architectural Review established to regulate modifications in the exterior appearance of buildings in the designated historic district. He remained in that position for more than forty years, tactfully but fastidiously imposing his aesthetic tastes down to the level of the designs of balustrades and the selection of paint colors. Often drafting officially sanctioned suggestions for homeowners proposing renovations, he defined the history to be preserved as the period closing by the mid–nineteenth century. He had little sympathy for Victorian architecture, which perhaps did not seem old enough or vulnerable enough to need protection but which was also often self-absorbed, idiosyncratic, and chaotic. He focused his efforts on the built heritage of white elites, a standpoint typical of his background and era that assumed enormous importance because Simons's influence extended to planning for development in the city and later in the county as well. His advice helped to shape the initial mapping of the properties that deserved protection, and along with Sam Stoney, Alice Ravenel Huger Smith, and a few other friends, he served on the Regional Planning Committee that conducted a more

The Heyward-Washington House before restoration. Courtesy of the Library of Congress

extensive survey of significant structures in 1939–1940 and produced *This Is Charleston* (1944). Moreover, Simons took a central role in city and federal planning for the clearance of slums in the historic district, funded primarily by the New Deal. This process relocated African Americans and working-class whites from the showcase area to housing projects in other parts of the city. As a result, the preservation district became more segregated on racial and class lines than it had ever been in the history of the city.

In addition to his involvement with local organizations and his service as a public official on the city and county planning and zoning commissions, Simons was prominent in professional circles. He became a fellow of the American Institute of Architects in 1934 and held many of its most prestigious positions of responsibility. He was also made a fellow of the National Academy of Design and the Royal Academy of the Arts. The College of Charleston named its fine arts center for him. His influence was well captured by preservation scholar Charles Hosmer's observation that "It might not be an exaggeration to say that the whole historic district of Charleston emerged as a grand design from the drawing board of Albert Simons."

The Heyward-Washington House after restoration. Courtesy of the Library of Congress

James Simons II (1813–1879)
James Simons III (1839–1919)

Speakers of the South Carolina House of Representatives   MAP LOCATION: SOUTHWEST 63

James Simons pére and fils led eerily similar lives. James Simons II was born in Charleston, the son of Capt. James Simons, a Revolutionary soldier under Col. William Washington and later collector of the port of Charleston by appointment of President Washington.

James II studied at the College of Charleston for a brief time before he transferred to South Carolina College, where he graduated with first honors in the class of 1833. He then read law in the firm of Eggleston and Frost and was admitted to the bar in 1835. He was elected to the South Carolina House of Representatives in 1842 and continuously re-elected for twenty years. In 1850 he was elected speaker of the South Carolina House, a position he held for twelve years during some of South Carolina's most troublous times. He originally opposed secession but embraced the movement in 1860.

Simultaneous with his political rise, Simons advanced in rank in the South Carolina Militia. At the time of secession, he was brigadier general in charge of its Fourth Brigade. Among his responsibilities was the defense of Charleston and its harbor. Though he was outranked by Beauregard, he was in immediate charge of the South Carolina troops who fired the first shots on Fort Sumter. A dispute with Gov. Pickens led Gen. Simons to re-sign his commission in the state militia and reenlist as a private in the Marion Artillery. He served with that unit for a short while until his health forced him to retire.

After the war Gen. Simons again took up the practice of law with his son, James Simons III. Gen. Simons was widely regarded at his death as the foremost equity lawyer of his day. He was president of the South Carolina Society of the Cincinnati and vice-president general of the national society.

James Simons III also studied at South Carolina College, from 1856 to 1858, before he went abroad to complete his education at the University of Leipzig. He returned to Charleston in 1860 and had just been admitted to the bar when war broke out. Simons joined Bachman's Brigade, a company of German volunteers attached to Hampton's Legion and the Army of Northern Virginia. He saw action in all the major battles of Virginia, Maryland, and Pennsylvania and became captain in command of the company by war's end.

After the war James III joined his father in the practice of law in the firm of Simons and Simons. After "Redemption," he was elected to the South Carolina House of Repre-sentatives where, like his father, he served as speaker from 1882 to 1890. He was ousted from the speakership by Ben Tillman's populist revolution of 1890 and declined to offer for reelection to the House thereafter. He continued to practice law and to make himself available for public service, particularly in the interests of education. He was president of the trustees of the High School of Charleston and was for many years the chairman of the local school board. After his death, James Simons Elementary School was named in his memory.

Like his father, Simons was president of the South Carolina Society of the Cincinnati and vice-president general of the national organization. He also served as president of the *News and Courier.*

KATHERINE DRAYTON MAYRANT SIMONS (1890–1969)

Author   MAP LOCATION: SOUTHWEST 64

Katherine Drayton Mayrant Simons was under her own name and two pseudonyms an extremely successful poet, novelist, and historical writer. Born in Charleston, the daughter of Kate Drayton (Mayrant) and Sedgwick Lewis Simons, Miss Simons was educated at Brownfield Academy in Summerville and Converse College in Spartanburg.

Sometimes using the pseudonym Kadra Maysi, Simons published three books of poetry: *Shadow Songs* (1912), *The Patteran* (1925), and *White Horse Leaping* (1951). She also wrote *Stories of Charleston Harbor* (1930). She achieved her greatest success and fame as a romantic novelist under the name of Drayton Mayrant, the author of *A Sword from Galway* (1948), *The Running Thread* (1949), *First the Blade* (1950), *Courage Is Not Given* (1952), *The Red Doe* (1953), *Always a River* (1956), *Lamp in Jerusalem* (1957), and *The Land Beyond the Tempest* (1960). She was one of Charleston's most commercially successful and prolific writers.

ROBERT BENTHAM SIMONS, SR. (1888–1971)

Naval Officer   MAP LOCATION: SOUTHEAST 57

Robert Bentham Simons was one of the few commanders at Pearl Harbor who wasn't asleep at the switch when the Japanese launched their surprise attack. He was born in Charleston, the son of Confederate soldier Thomas Grange Simons III and Serena Daniel Aiken Simons. He graduated from Annapolis in 1911 and saw action in the numerous Caribbean disturbances in Cuba, Haiti, Santo Domingo, and Nicaragua that preceded World War I. In World War I, he was a first lieutenant on board the *U.S.S. Florida* in the North Sea.

On December 7, 1941, then-Captain Simons was in command of the *U.S.S. Raleigh* in Pearl Harbor. Capt. Simons was on the bridge during the attack when the *Raleigh*'s anti-aircraft guns shot down five Japanese planes despite the fact that the *Raleigh* was bombed and torpedoed during the action. Due to Capt. Simons's quick response, one sailor from the *U.S.S. Arizona* was saved when men from the *Raleigh* cut a hole in the bottom of the *Arizona*'s sunken hull. Simons saw action throughout the war and retired in 1947 with the rank of rear admiral.

After his return to Charleston, Simons taught history in local schools and completed the family genealogy, *Thomas Grange Simons III, His Forebears and Relations* (1954). The Simons genealogy is fascinating and comes as close as any book probably ever will to cutting the Gordian knot of Charleston bloodlines.

THOMAS YOUNG SIMONS, JR. (1828–1878)

Lawyer and Newspaper Editor   MAP LOCATION: SOUTHWEST 65

Thomas Young Simons, Jr., was one of Charleston's finest antebellum trial lawyers, a signer of the Ordinance of Secession, a Confederate officer, and an editor of the Charleston *Courier*. Simons was born in Charleston, the son of prominent physician Thomas Y. Simons and Margaret Anderson (Ballentine) Simons. He attended the College of Charleston for two years in his mid-teens and enrolled in Yale in 1844. He graduated in 1847. He was a tutor at the High School of Charleston for two years while he read law. He was admitted to the bar in 1850. He quickly became one of the leaders of the Charleston trial bar. He was well known for his extraordinary preparation and consequent success in trials. He delivered the Washington's Birthday Address before the Washington Light Infantry in 1850 and was thereafter much in demand as a public speaker.

Simons was elected to the South Carolina House of Representatives from 1854 to 1860 and became a voice against the plan of "separate secession," by which South Carolina would secede without other states. He was an ardent opponent of the Know Nothing Party and its ideas. Simons was a delegate to the 1860 Democratic National Convention, which split and eventually saw half the delegates go to a separate convention in Baltimore. Soon afterward he was a delegate to the secession convention and signed the Ordinance of Secession on December 20, 1860.

During the Civil War, Simons served first as a captain of the Charleston Light Infantry (Gaillard's) 27th South Carolina Volunteers and later as a judge advocate general. After the war, he became editor of the Charleston *Courier* in September 1865. He held that position until the paper was acquired by Riordan, Dawson, and Co. and merged with the Charleston *News* in April 1873. He was an organizer of the Union Reform Party of South Carolina, which sought to combine elements of the Republican and Democratic parties.

Simons was a leading member of the Taxpayers' Conventions of 1871 and 1874 and served on the executive committees of those bodies. He discovered that $22,000,000 of state bonds had been issued for a debt that was supposedly less than $10,000,000 under Governor Scott and publicized this fact in the Charleston *Courier*. He testified before the United States Congress on this issue and thus did much to establish the idea in the national mind that South Carolina's Reconstruction government was hopelessly corrupt.

Simons took a trip to Europe in 1876 in an attempt to relieve his failing health. He returned to Charleston in 1878 and was elected corporation counsel of the city, but he died before he could assume the office.

CHARLES HENRY SIMONTON (1829–1904)

Jurist   MAP LOCATION: SOUTHEAST 58

Charles Henry Simonton was a distinguished soldier, lawyer, legislator, author, and judge. He was born in Charleston and received his secondary education at Doctor Bruns's high school. He attended the College of Charleston for a year before transferring to South Carolina College, where he was first honor graduate in 1849.

After a brief time spent teaching, Simonton read law and soon afterwards became a member of the bar. He was a member of the South Carolina House of Representatives immediately before the Civil War and was also captain of the Washington Light Infantry. After serving for a while as acting adjutant and inspector general for South Carolina, he entered the Confederate Army as a captain in the part of the Washington Light Infantry that formed the Eutaw Battalion of the 25th South Carolina Volunteers. He quickly rose to the rank of colonel in command of the regiment. He saw action in the Lowcountry and in Virginia before he was captured at Town Creek, North Carolina, in February 1865. He remained a prisoner of war for the final months of the war.

Capt. Charles H. Simonton (center) and fellow members of the Washington Light Infantry encamped on Sullivan's Island early in the Civil War. Courtesy of the U.S. Army Military History Institute

Simonton served in the constitutional convention of 1865 and in the legislature of 1865–1866, in which he was elected speaker of the House. He left the legislature during Reconstruction and played an active role in the Democratic resistance. Upon "Redemption," he returned to the legislature from 1877 to 1886, serving as chairman of the Judiciary Committee. Throughout this time he was also one of the leading lawyers in Charleston, practicing with Theodore G. Barker until President Grover Cleveland appointed Simonton to the U.S. District Court bench in 1886. After Simonton had served seven years on the bench, President Cleveland elevated him to the U.S. Court of Appeals for the Fourth Circuit. Judge Simonton retained this position until his death.

Simonton published numerous addresses and legal treatises, the most notable of which was *The Federal Courts, Their Organization, Jurisdiction and Procedure* (1898).

SLAVE TRADERS

The economy of the Old South and more particularly of South Carolina and more particularly still of Charleston in all its glory was based upon slave labor. Almost all the white inhabitants of the city and surrounding regions owed whatever comfort and degree of "civilization" they achieved to the exploitation of imported and native African Americans

The Old Slave Mart Museum, located in the remaining building of the Chalmers Street slave auction complex built by Thomas Ryan and later owned by Ziba Oakes. Courtesy of the Old Slave Mart Museum

who were held in lifetime bondage to serve at the whim of white masters. Yes, there were black freedmen, and even some black freedmen who owned slaves, but they were much more the exception than the rule.

This is the humiliating, embarrassing fact that blights our history. It is the reason that no man can brag of Charleston's antebellum history without blocking out the fact that all the achievements and wealth of Charleston's white citizenry were borne upon the backs of its black chattel. White South Carolinians are often so embarrassed by their ancestors' part in the system that they will not admit to this immortal blot upon their honor, though the very concept of Southern honor was rooted in slavery and its maintenance as an institution—a "peculiar" institution indeed.

An anecdote from the great Charleston lawyer Gedney M. Howe, Jr., is a vehicle to understanding the complex difficulties in acknowledging our painful past. Someone once asked him why the South had to sunder the Union and fight the Civil War, to which he replied: "If you called my sister a whore, then sir, I'd have to fight you. If you called my sister a whore, and she was a whore, why then, sir, I'd have to kill you."

Charleston was for many years the capital of slavery. From Charleston came not only slavery's great defenders and advocates, but also its beneficiaries, the planters and the traders. The slave traders made most of their livelihood from the sale of human flesh. Ironically, after the Civil War most of the slave traders (who were, after all, salesmen) went into the real estate and insurance business without even changing the typeface in their newspaper advertisements.

If Charleston was the capital of slavery, Magnolia is logically the burial place of the most successful of the slave traders. Prominent examples are:

THOMAS NORMAN GADSDEN (1808–1866) was a grandson of the radical incendiary Christopher Gadsden, whose "Don't Tread on Me" rattlesnake flag was a potent symbol of the American Revolution. His cousins included Christopher Gadsden, Episcopal bishop of South Carolina, and James Gadsden, who negotiated the Gadsden Purchase, which gave the United States what would become southernmost Arizona and New Mexico. Bancroft identifies Gadsden as far and away the high-volume slave trader of his time. His success was extraordinary. By the time of the war, Gadsden was one of the wealthiest of the wealthy Charlestonians. He lived in the Broad Street home that had been built by John Rutledge and inhabited by Gen. John McPherson. Gadsden died shortly after the death of slavery. MAP LOCATION: SOUTHEAST 13

ZIBA B. OAKES (1806–1871) saw his opportunities and took them. Originally from Maine, he became one of Charleston's most prosperous slave traders. After the war, he was one of those who continued to amass wealth as a real estate and insurance salesman. He served two terms as a member of city council. A collection of letters to Oakes, edited by Edmund Lee Drago under the title *Broke by the War: Letters of a Slave Trader,* was published in 1991. MAP LOCATION: SOUTHEAST 42

JOHN S. RIGGS (1829–1899) was another high-volume slave trader who achieved postbellum acclaim as a benefactor of mankind. He was a multi-term city councilman and had great success after the Civil War as a real estate and insurance salesman. He gave much of his fortune to charity. MAP LOCATION: SOUTHEAST 51

THOMAS RYAN (1800–1866). Until 1856 sales of slaves in Charleston were held in the open, usually in the area just north of the Exchange building. The growing abolitionist spirit and Northern reports of families being torn apart and slave owners selling their own mixed-race children caused more than a little negative press from the pens of Northern journalists who made their way south. After a series of particularly truthful articles, the city fathers decided that it would be best if slave-trading was conducted in a more controlled setting. Ryan's Auction Mart, built by city alderman Thomas Ryan, was the most extensive of these facilities. At Ryan's, slaves coming to market could be conveniently kept at "Ryan's Nigger Jail" on Queen Street, which abutted the Chalmers Street property. Slaves were sold behind the building, out of public view. Ryan is buried in an unmarked plot almost directly behind the pyramid of W. B. Smith. MAP LOCATION: SOUTHEAST 53

Frederic Bancroft's *Slave-Trading in the Old South* (1931) and Michael Tadman's *Speculators and Slaves: Masters, Traders, and Slaves in the Old South* (1989) identify many other slave-traders who are buried at Magnolia, including Thomas Alexander, Robert Austin, J. Russell Baker, J. E. Bowers, Jacob Cohen, Louis DeSaussure, G. DeWitt, Joseph W. Faber, William Allston Gourdin, J. P. LaBorde, Hutson Lee, Francis Nipson, T. L. Rodgers, J. S. Ryan, Anthony J. Salinas, Seth Spencer, T. A. Whitney, Henry Willis, Sr., and Henry Willis, Jr.

ALICE RAVENEL HUGER SMITH (1876–1958)

Artist, Author, and Preservationist   MAP LOCATION: SOUTHWEST 66

Alice Ravenel Huger Smith was the single most important person in the cultural life of Charleston in the twentieth century. Her art and writings brought attention of the exact right sort to Charleston and did much to ensure the physical preservation of the city she loved. Her civic activities led to her part in the first comprehensive survey of Charleston architecture. In addition she was one of the founders of the Historic Charleston Foundation which, with the Preservation Society, saved scores of buildings and whole neighborhoods when their destruction seemed inevitable.

It is for her art, however, that "Miss Alice" has obtained immortality. She was *the* great artist of the Charleston Renaissance. Her work inspires more than local pride. She and Mississippi's Walter Inglis Anderson are recognized as the finest artists the South produced in the first half of the twentieth century. For most of her life she stayed where she was and painted what she knew. The reason her art is so enduring is that she came to know her place so well that she could paint entire landscapes accurately from memory. She was regional in the sense that Faulkner was regional or Winslow Homer was regional. She was a realist with a romantic's heart.

"Miss Alice" was born at the very end of Reconstruction and spent a great deal of her life celebrating what had gone before her. She had impeccable Charleston ancestry, as her mouthful of a name indicates. On her father's side she was descended from Sen. Daniel Elliott Huger and from Robert Smith, first Episcopal bishop of South Carolina and founder of the College of Charleston. On her mother's side she was descended not only from the Ravenels, but also an aberrant branch of the Winthrops of Massachusetts who

Alice Ravenel Huger Smith, *Charleston Doorway, 92 Church Street.* Courtesy of LaVonne N. Phillips

wandered south for health and business reasons. She grew up in what is now called "genteel poverty" at 69 Church Street, her only home throughout her long life. The great influence in her life was her father, Daniel Elliott Huger Smith. She ascribed to him god-like knowledge and followed his every suggestion without question. Together, they collaborated on some of her best works.

Smith received what has repeatedly been described as "the formal schooling of a woman of her time and place," which is to say, very little. She received rudimentary training in painting and drawing at the Carolina Art Association but was almost entirely self-taught in art. She had little if any exposure to Impressionism, yet she would eventually display an extraordinary talent for light and immediacy that she gained from the same source as the Impressionists, the Japanese.

She began her career as an artist by doing decorative work on dance programs, fans, and cards. She painted watercolor sketches of local vendors. She became popular for the watercolor portraits she did of local families in the first decade of the century. All the while, she was honing her skills as a draftsman.

Her pencil drawings of life at Chicora Wood were used as the illustrations in Elizabeth Waties Allston Pringle's book *A Woman Rice Planter* (1913). With her father she produced a portfolio, *Twenty Drawings of the Pringle House in King Street, Charleston,* in 1914. She continued her architectural pencil studies of Charleston in *The Dwelling Houses of Charleston* (1917), which she illustrated and co-wrote with her father. *Dwelling Houses* was the first attempt at a comprehensive architectural and historical study of Charleston. Like Harriott Horry Rutledge Ravenel's *Charleston: The Place and the People* (1906), the Smiths' book achieved a wide audience outside of Charleston and was instrumental in attracting favorable attention to Charleston in the colonial revival that followed World War I.

At about this same time, Alice Smith was beginning to study the print collection of her cousin (and some say, beau) Motte Alston Read. He had been a professor at both Harvard and the College of Charleston but had been forced to resign due to ill health. Read's extensive collection of Ukiyo-e woodblocks influenced the direction of Smith's art for the remainder of her life. The only other acknowledged influence on her work was that of the New York artist Birge Harrison, who visited Charleston frequently around 1910.

Energized by her encounter with Read's print collection, Smith began to do woodblocks herself. She produced several dramatic prints before she abandoned woodblocks. She would use the lessons she learned from woodblocks in the watercolors that occupied her for most of her artistic life.

In 1923 Smith was instrumental in establishing the Charleston Etchers' Club, which numbered in its nine original members Alfred Hutty, Elizabeth O'Neill Verner, Antoinette Rhett, Minnie Mikell, John Bennett, and Leila Waring, and two Boston artists who wintered in Charleston, Ellen Day Hale and Gabrielle deVeaux Clements. Smith abandoned etching after she had created only six images, but the association was of note in the history of American printmaking.

Charleston in the twenties was in the midst of what is now acknowledged as "the Charleston Renaissance." Smith was the leader of the visual artists of this time in much the same way that John Bennett was the leader of the writers. Smith had inherited Motte Alston Read's house on Atlantic Street at his death in 1920, and she set up her studio there.

Leila Waring, Anna Heyward Taylor, and Elizabeth O'Neill Verner all established their studios in the same block. Smith encouraged these artists by sending them clients and by helping to bring their work to public notice through shows and correspondence with out-of-town galleries and museums. Together with many of the other artists and writers of the Charleston Renaissance, Smith collaborated on *The Carolina Low-Country*, which was published in 1931.

In 1924 Smith and her father collaborated on a biography of the nineteenth-century Charleston miniaturist Charles Fraser. Smith also owned Fraser's sketchbook, which she eventually gave to the Gibbes Gallery of Art. In 1940 this sketchbook was published with notes and an introduction by Smith as *A Charleston Sketchbook, 1796–1806.*

In 1935 Smith contributed seventeen watercolors as illustrations for naturalist Herbert Ravenel Sass's *Adventures in Green Places.* In 1936, Smith and Sass collaborated again, this time on Smith's most ambitious project, *A Carolina Rice Plantation of the Fifties.* In this book, Smith evoked the bygone rice culture that had been the source of Charleston's great antebellum wealth. She produced thirty watercolor scenes of life on a rice plantation for the book. Smith donated the original watercolors to the Gibbes Gallery of Art. In the introduction to the book, Smith set down her great subject:

> Throughout my life I have been trying to paint the rice-planting section of South Carolina: that long strip of flat lowlands lying within the influence of tides which extended to about forty or fifty miles from the sea. The marshes, the fields and forests, the canals, "the settlements," and the many other marks of a great industry, have been noted down by me for many years. I have seen much of it disappear and the remnants are vanishing year by year.

The watercolors for *Carolina Rice Plantation* constitute Smith's finest body of work. The book was the culmination of her period of greatest creativity, the 1920s and 1930s. During this time Smith exhibited widely throughout the United States and Europe.

During World War II Smith opened her home to sailors and soldiers and cut down on her painting. In the early 1940s she participated in the architectural survey of Charleston that was eventually published as *This Is Charleston.* The survey photographed and ranked the importance of many of the antebellum buildings of the city. It remains a valuable resource for architectural historians today.

Smith was one of the founders of the Historic Charleston Foundation in 1947. The Foundation has saved literally hundreds of historic structures that were in danger of demolition or disfiguring alteration.

In 1950 Smith edited two books dealing with her family. *The Mason Smith Family Letters, 1860–1868,* which she co-edited with historian Arney Childs, describes the privations, deaths, and diseases her family endured as it dealt with war and sunk from wealth to poverty. She also edited and introduced her father's memoirs, *A Charlestonian's Recollections, 1846–1913,* which he had written at her behest years before.

A group of Smith's friends and admirers put together a small volume of tributes to her on her eightieth birthday, *Alice Ravenel Huger Smith of Charleston, South Carolina, An Appreciation* (1956). Among the tributes, that of Albert Simons perhaps best caught her spirit:

Alice Ravenel Huger Smith, or 'Miss Alice,' as she is familiarly known to us, is the distinguished exponent of higher provincialism. Basically she has preserved to the present day the refinements of an eighteenth-century culture inherited from many generations of Charleston forbears but to this she has added a Maude Adams-like quality of sprightliness and charm that is entirely her own. Beneath the gay smile and graceful good humor that is always so disarming there is an undercurrent of intensity of purpose flowing from a compelling affection for her native land. Those who have seen her water-colors and remember a winter's dawn in the Low Country with the opalescent mists brooding over the marshes know that she has cast a spell over these lonely reaches and claimed them for her domain.

Smith continued to work until shortly before her death in 1958. In 1993 the Carolina Art Association published Martha Severens's *Alice Ravenel Huger Smith: An Artist, a Place and a Time* together with Alice Smith's own unpublished *Reminiscences.* Severens has long been Smith's most valuable and perceptive critic and champion. Her volume did much to excite a new national interest in Smith's work.

Daniel Elliott Huger Smith (1846–1932)

Author   MAP LOCATION: SOUTHWEST 66

D. E. Huger Smith attained importance in his own right as a memoirist, but he is best remembered as the father and collaborator of Charleston's finest artist, Alice Ravenel Huger Smith. He was born in Charleston and educated privately until he entered the University of Virginia. He left the University of Virginia in 1863 at the age of seventeen to join the Confederate Army in the coastal defenses of South Carolina. After the war, he became a cotton exporter.

With his daughter Alice, he wrote *The Dwelling Houses of Charleston* (1917), a seminal work that is still an authoritative source. They also joined forces on a life of their kinsman, Charles Fraser. Smith's most important work was *A Charlestonian's Recollections, 1846–1913* (1950), which was written at the insistence of his daughter Alice and published posthumously due to her perseverance. The *Recollections* provide some of the most important views of a high-born, yet poverty-stricken, Charlestonian in the years following the Civil War. Many of his letters from the Civil War are included in *Mason Smith Family Letters, 1860–1868* (1950), edited by his daughter Alice together with Arney Childs.

William B. Smith (1815–1892)

Banker   MAP LOCATION: SOUTHEAST 59

William B. Smith was a self-made man who achieved extraordinary success in business. After his death his family erected and entombed his remains in the pyramid mausoleum, Magnolia Cemetery's most imposing monument.

The pyramid mausoleum of William B. Smith. Courtesy of the Magnolia Cemetery Trust

Smith left school at the age of fifteen to seek his fortune in the cotton factorage business that was successively Hutchins and Company; Wisward, Jones and Company; Jones and Smith; and finally, William B. Smith and Company.

Mr. Smith had the Midas touch. Among his other business ventures, he was president of the Union Bank from 1857 to 1872, through panics, war, and depression. He was an alderman in the administration of Mayor John Wagener. He was part of the Charleston delegation that sought from President Hayes the removal of Federal troops. When Smith died, his net worth was over two million dollars.

Among his descendants were Richard Smith Whaley, chief justice of the U.S. Court of Claims, and William B. S. Whaley, who built Olympia Mills and Whaley Mill in Columbia.

Mary Amarinthia Snowden (1819–1898)

Paragon of Confederate Womanhood   MAP LOCATION: SOUTHEAST 60

As the founder and longtime president of the Ladies Memorial Association of Charleston, Amarinthia Snowden is an important figure in the history of Magnolia Cemetery. Those contributions were part of her broader exploration and expansion of the opportunities that the secession movement and its aftermath afforded for women's participation in public life.

Born in Charleston, Amarinthia Yates attended school in Philadelphia during the five years that her mother brought her children to that city for their education. On her return to Charleston she received instruction at Madame Talvande's well-known school. Miss Yates completed her education at Dr. Elias Marks's seminary in Barhamville. One of her classmates was Ann Pamela Cunningham, organizer of the movement to preserve Mount Vernon.

Shortly after Miss Cunningham launched that campaign, Miss Yates invited a group of Charleston women to the drawing room of her Church Street home in January 1854 to begin an effort to build a monument to John C. Calhoun. She took the role of treasurer in the Ladies Calhoun Memorial Association (LCMA), which raised about $40,000 before the Civil War, much of it in two benefit bazaars that were unusual initiatives for women in the Old South. As treasurer, she was responsible for protecting the LCMA's fund during the war. In a famous incident, she saved the ladies' assets amid the burning of Columbia by sewing the securities into her petticoat before she fled the city. The story is recorded in the inscription on the Calhoun Monument that the LCMA put up in Marion Square after the war.

Miss Yates married Dr. William Snowden in 1857 and soon had two children, but she did not restrict herself to domestic duties during the war. The LCMA provided the nucleus for the Soldiers' Relief Association of Charleston, and Mrs. Snowden was again the most active member. She led the collection and distribution of clothing, bandages, brandy, and other provisions sent to military hospitals and soldiers in the field. She volunteered her services as a nurse at hospitals in South Carolina, and after the Second Battle of Manassas she traveled to Virginia to care for wounded men near the front lines. She also drew on her fund-raising experience. She and the other LCMA members sponsored a Ladies' Gunboat Fair in 1862 to raise money for a ship that would position the Confederacy for a more aggressive attack on the blockade. In early 1865 she organized an elaborate fair held in the South Carolina State House. Known as the Great Bazaar, the event raised about $350,000 for the Confederacy, in part because Mrs. Snowden had received authority to import liquor through the blockade as space permitted. Though prominent in the wartime North, such fairs were uncommon in the Confederacy, and perhaps for that reason Mrs. Snowden's ventures are sometimes said to have been the models for the fund-raising bazaar in *Gone With the Wind* at which Rhett buys a dance with Scarlett.

Mrs. Snowden assumed the presidency of the Ladies Memorial Association when it formed in 1866, and she remained in that position until her death. In that role she was instrumental in the development of the Confederate section of Magnolia, including arrangements for the making of soldiers' headstones, the repatriation of the fallen dead from Gettysburg, and the commissioning of the Defenders of Charleston monument and several other monuments in the cemetery. As president she also helped to direct the annual Memorial Day exercises at Magnolia.

At the same time, she launched another important postwar initiative in 1867 by establishing the Home for the Mothers, Widows, and Daughters of Confederate Soldiers. She and her sister Isabella Snowden, both widowed, mortgaged their home to pay the first year of rent for the capacious building on Broad Street. The Confederate Home provided a residence for several dozen female survivors of soldiers for no charge or an affordable fee, but it quickly came to center on the education of Confederate daughters. After sending these girls to Charleston schools for several years, the Confederate Home set up its own school in 1870. Mrs. Snowden even sought to have the fund for the Calhoun Monument transferred to the Confederate Home as an endowment, a proposal supported by most women but blocked by men (particularly Calhoun's son-in-law, Thomas G. Clemson, who wanted the endowment for a state college he hoped to establish on Calhoun's old estate). The school recognized that young women would increasingly support themselves. It prepared them to be schoolteachers and later provided training in secretarial skills. This emphasis on resourceful independence was appropriate for Mrs. Snowden's institutional legacy.

At Mrs. Snowden's death, one South Carolinian observed that "as Wade Hampton must ever be our typical South Carolina Confederate soldier, so must Mary Amarinthia Snowden remain the type of the South Carolina Confederate woman." Both are honored in plaques on the Defenders of Charleston monument in Magnolia. In 1917 the General Assembly and the United Daughters of the Confederacy placed a marble memorial tablet to Mrs. Snowden in the rotunda of the State House.

Yates Snowden (1858–1933)

Historian   MAP LOCATION: SOUTHEAST 60

Yates Snowden was one of the most beloved historians of South Carolina for the last thirty years of his life. Though he published little in his lifetime, his influence is still felt. He was born in Charleston, the son of physician William Snowden and Mary Amarinthia (Yates) Snowden. His father died of typhoid during the war, and his mother removed to Columbia, then thought to be safer than Charleston. As a boy Snowden witnessed the burning of Columbia after the surrender of the city to Sherman. Forever after, Snowden retained an enmity for all things Northern. Ironically, his best friend in later life was an Ohio Yankee, John Bennett.

Snowden was an 1879 graduate of the College of Charleston and admitted to the bar in 1882. He soon found he was ill-fitted for life as a lawyer and took up journalism. He published and edited the *Berkeley Gazette* for several years and joined the staff of the *News and Courier* in 1886. He was at the *News and Courier* for seventeen years, rising to the position of associate editor. He also served as the Charleston correspondent for the New York *Tribune.*

During all this time, Yates Snowden accumulated knowledge and books on South Carolina history. He was widely acknowledged as the great authority on the subject. He agreed to help put together a history of South Carolina in the early years of this century. The publishing company that put the history together was interested primarily in Snowden's reputation. Though Snowden contributed virtually nothing to it, a five-volume *History of South Carolina* was published under Snowden's name in 1920, to his horror. The history is rife with errors and so pained Snowden that he rarely commented on it.

Snowden was appointed head of the history department of the University of South Carolina in 1904, and after a year of post-graduate study at Columbia University he assumed the professorship which he would hold for the remainder of his life. Snowden was a ubiquitous figure on campus, flying about in his academic gown. He was an avid collector of arcane Caroliniana, and was always willing to share his collection with visiting scholars or perplexed freshmen. He possessed an encyclopedic knowledge of the details of South Carolina history. He knew more about who did what to whom and why in eighteenth-century South Carolina family scandals than most South Carolina historians knew about John C. Calhoun. For all this, and for his extraordinary wit, he was beloved.

Most of what little he published was sentimental verse and worse. Best remembered are his poem "A Carolina Bourbon," first published in the *Southern Bivouac* in 1886 and his *Memories of the Early Seventies* (1924). Nothing he published ever caught his spirit or the depth of his knowledge.

After his death the University of South Carolina a published booklet of obituaries, tributes, and remembrances, *In Memoriam, Yates Snowden (1858–1933),* that gives some idea of the veneration in which Professor Snowden was held. But it was not until the publication of *Two Scholarly Friends: Yates Snowden—John Bennett Correspondence, 1902–1932,* edited by Mary Crow Anderson (1993) that contemporary readers and scholars could begin to appreciate the adulation that Professor Snowden inspired. John Bennett was a transplanted South Carolinian who shared most of Snowden's enthusiasms. Their correspondence is witty, scandalous, and full of the excitement and ephemera of South Carolina history. In this book, Yates Snowden finally has an appropriate monument. Snowden was buried in the Yates family plot facing away from his family and towards the city of Charleston, always his greatest love.

Magnolia Cemetery is home to a rich variety of birds. Courtesy of the Magnolia Cemetery Trust

ALEXANDER SPRUNT III (1898–1973)

Ornithologist   MAP LOCATION: NORTHWEST 16

Alexander Sprunt was an environmentalist before the term was popular. He was one of the great ornithologists of his time. He was born in Rock Hill, South Carolina, where his father was the Presbyterian minister. He moved to Charleston early in his life when his father accepted the pulpit of First (Scots) Presbyterian Church.

Mr. Sprunt was educated in the public and private schools of Charleston and received his undergraduate education at Davidson College. His principal education came as the protégé of Arthur T. Wayne, the great ornithologist of his time. Mr. Sprunt joined the staff of the Charleston Museum in 1924 and served until 1930. He also studied at the U.S. National Museum and the Museum of Natural History in New York. In 1934 he became Southern supervisor for the Audubon Society and a spokesman for conservation and the preservation of vital habitats.

In 1947 Sprunt received a Guggenheim Foundation fellowship that allowed him to finish his masterpiece, *South Carolina Bird Life* (1949), which he co-authored with E. Burnham Chamberlain. His other books include *Dwellers of the Silences* (1931), *An Album of Southern Birds* (1953), *Florida Bird Life* (1954), *Life in the Everglades* (1955), *North American Birds of Prey* (1955), and *Carolina Lowcountry Impressions* (1964). He also co-edited

Warblers of America (1957) with Ludlow Griscom. Mr. Sprunt was an intimate friend and collaborator of Roger Tory Peterson. Mr. Sprunt was one of the last people to see Bachman's warbler and the ivory-billed woodpecker, although state legislator—and later judge and College of Charleston president—Alexander Sanders saved the Congaree Swamp from logging and set the old-growth hardwood forest on the path to protection as a National Park Service site when he conveniently heard the ivory-billed woodpecker there in the 1970s.

Clement H. Stevens (1821–1864)

Confederate General   MAP LOCATION: SOUTHWEST 67

Clement H. Stevens was descended from a family distinguished by military service. Before the Civil War he was a successful businessman, the cashier of the Planters and Mechanics Bank of Charleston, and a member of the firm of Hacker and Pickens, railroad contractors. He invented and constructed a land battery on Morris Island that was fortified with railroad T-iron. It is perhaps the first armored fortification ever built.

Stevens was wounded at the Battle of Manassas. After recovery, he helped to raise the 24th South Carolina Infantry and served as its first colonel. In this capacity he was one of the Confederate heroes of the Battle of Secessionville, near Charleston, and later fought with Gen. States Rights Gist's brigade in the Vicksburg campaign. He fought with extraordinary courage at Chickamauga and was again severely wounded. Early in 1864, he was promoted to brigadier general and commanded a Georgia brigade throughout the Atlanta campaign. He was mortally wounded in the attack at Peach Tree Creek and died of his wounds five days later. Originally buried at St. Paul's Episcopal Church in Pendleton, his body was moved to the family plot at Magnolia after the war.

Peter Fayssoux Stevens (1830–1910)

Superintendent of the Citadel and Bishop   MAP LOCATION: SOUTHWEST 67
of the Reformed Episcopal Church

Peter Fayssoux Stevens was in one part of his life a defender of slavery. Later, he became a champion of black freedpeople. He was born in Florida, the younger brother of Clement H. Stevens. He and his family moved to Pendleton, South Carolina, upon the outbreak of the Seminole War. After his father's death, Stevens enrolled in the South Carolina Military Academy (the Citadel) and graduated as valedictorian in 1849.

Stevens served for two years as a civil engineer with the Laurens and Yorkville Railroad before his appointment as a professor of the Arsenal Academy in Columbia, South Carolina, in 1852. He became a professor of mathematics at the Citadel in Charleston in January 1853. In 1859 he became superintendent (president) of the school.

After South Carolina seceded from the Union, Major Stevens was ordered by Gov. Pickens to occupy Morris Island and "fire on any vessel entering the harbor bearing the

United States flag." Soon enough, Col. Stevens and his Citadel cadets had opportunity for action when the *Star of the West* sailed into Charleston harbor on January 9, 1861, in an attempt to reprovision Fort Sumter. The cannons under Col. Stevens went into action and turned back the *Star of the West* in what some historians regard as the first military engagement of the Civil War.

Col. Stevens eventually became commander of the Iron Battery designed by his brother, Clement H. Stevens, on Morris Island. He was commander of this fort during the firing on Fort Sumter on April 12, 1861. He resigned from the Citadel and the Confederate forces in August 1861 to prepare to enter the Episcopal ministry, for which he had been studying for some time before the war. But soon after his resignation the Union forces took Port Royal and Hilton Head, and Col. Stevens felt it incumbent upon himself to offer his services once again. He organized the Holcombe Legion, named for South Carolina first lady Lucy Holcombe Pickens. He saw action at Second Manassas, Rappahannock, Boarsboro Gap, and Sharpsburg. He finally retired from the army to pursue his calling as an Episcopal minister.

As a minister, he served a number of South Carolina parishes, including Upper St. John's, St. Stephen's, Epiphany (Eutawville), St. Paul's (Eutawville), Trinity (Pinopolis), Grace Church (Anderson), and St. Luke's (Newberry). The Reverend Stevens was tireless in his vocation and particularly devoted to his ministry to former slaves.

After the 1874 schism in which Bishop George David Cummins of the Diocese of Kentucky broke with the Episcopal Church because he felt it was becoming too "Roman" in its emphasis on ritual, Rev. Stevens joined the new Reformed Episcopal Church and became the first bishop in South Carolina. The Reformed Episcopal Church became essentially a church of high-born African Americans and remains so to this day. Bishop Stevens remained tireless in his evangelical duties until the end of his life. By the time of his death, he was the oldest surviving alumnus of the Citadel.

JOHN STOLLE (1835–1909)

Artist   MAP LOCATION: SOUTHEAST 61

John Stolle was a German immigrant who made a name for himself as a fine portrait painter in late-nineteenth-century Charleston. He was born in Germany, probably in Dresden. He made the acquaintance of Gabriel Wesley Dingle of Charleston when Dingle was studying at the University of Göttingen shortly before the Civil War. After the war Dingle, who was then a member of Charleston City Council, noted the poor condition of the portraits in City Hall chambers and suggested that the city hire Stolle to restore them.

Stolle came to Charleston around 1882. As there were no other portrait painters living in Charleston, he stayed and soon attracted a large clientele. Stolle painted not only from life but also from photographs and was much in demand to copy ancestral portraits. His portraits of Mayor William Ashmead Courtenay, William Enston, Henry Horlbeck, Francis Marion, and Gen. Andrew Pickens are in City Hall. He painted numerous portraits for the Charleston Library Society. His portrait of John Wagener hangs in the church that Wagener founded, St. Matthew's Lutheran Church.

Stolle was hurt in a trolley car accident and died of the effects of his injuries a year later.

ARTHUR JERVEY STONEY (1889–1962)

Businessman and Poet   MAP LOCATION: SOUTHEAST 62

Arthur J. Stoney was an insurance and real estate salesman who wrote doggerel about the Charleston area and its denizens in his spare time. Stoney was born in Charleston and attended local schools and the College of Charleston. He served on the Mexican border with the Charleston Light Dragoons and was commissioned a lieutenant with the Thirtieth Infantry Division in Europe during World War I. After his discharge from the Army he went into the real estate and insurance business, eventually becoming owner of the insurance firm of William S. Hastie & Sons.

Stoney's penchant for writing humorous and often wicked doggerel about Charleston and its inhabitants brought him some measure of local fame. After his death, Emmett Robinson compiled a volume of these verses as *A Miscellany of Doggerel Rhymes* (1964). One of Stoney's regular targets was Judge J. Waties Waring. When Charleston's most venerable brothel, The Big Brick, was threatened with destruction, he wrote the following poem with clear allusions to Judge Waring's youthful recreation:

> Is it true, what everyone's saying?
> Tell me it isn't so!
> Shall the best known building in the town,
> At the hands of the wreckers go?
>   Anchored in hallowed tradition,
>   Honored in song and story;
>   The Big Brick represents the days,
>   When one lawyer was in his glory.
> Wire this noted lawyer,
> One of our legal lights.
> He must save the glorious old Big Brick,
> Where he spent his happiest nights.
>   He was King of the Tenderloin;
>   Big Brick was his Palace Hall;
>   And the girls were wild with excitement,
>   When the lawyer was coming to call.
> The Madam's smile was wide for him,
> He could charge up any amount.
> For he was one patron of the Brick,
> Who enjoyed a charge account.

The lawyer is old, his youth long past;
He can only dream and repine.
But he was a master swordsman once,
And the Big Brick should be his shrine.
Stay the hand of the wrecker,
And send up a mighty cry!
The Big Brick must stand forever,
To remember that lawyer by.
If it is gone, save some bricks from the wreckage;
Build a vault, where he'll rest when he's dead.
In death, as in life, let that lawyer sleep,
Though alone, in a Big Brick bed.

The building that housed the Big Brick has recently been the headquarters of the Historic Charleston Foundation.

Stoney's wife, **Anne Montague Stoney** (1898–1989), was a native of Middleburg, Virginia, and a graduate of Ashley Hall School and Hollins College. She was the first president of the Charleston Junior League and co-edited the enormously popular *Charleston Receipts* (1950) with Mary Vereen Huguenin. Many of Arthur J. Stoney's verses are published in *Charleston Receipts.*

Mrs. Stoney's father, **Robert Latane Montague** (1870–1930), was secretary-treasurer of the company that developed North Charleston. Montague Avenue, in North Charleston, is named in his memory. He is buried with his daughter and son-in-law.

SAMUEL GAILLARD STONEY, SR. (1853–1926)

Agriculturalist   MAP LOCATION: SOUTHEAST 63

Samuel Gaillard Stoney, Sr., was neither the first nor the last of Charlestonians who attempted to raise a dike against the tides of change that washed away much of old Charleston and her environs, but his life and influence were archetypal. When Capt. Stoney died, those in a position to know knew that what was left of the Charleston he had attempted to revive was dead. Though others, most notably his oldest son and namesake, attempted to carry on his work, the cause was lost and thus incurably romantic (or vice versa).

S. G. Stoney, Sr., was born in 1853, the son of Samuel D. Stoney and his wife Harriet Porcher (Gaillard) Stoney. He was born too late to participate in the war that destroyed the way of life he hearkened to, yet too soon to avoid its disastrous effects. He claimed the feudal heritage of the "Old South" early in life to the point that he was a leader in attempting to revive the medieval blood sport of tilting. Stoney was a master tilter. He earned his military title as captain of the Charleston Light Dragoons, a troop more ancient than the nation it served.

He earned his living in a dying culture, as president of the West Point Rice Mill, where much of the rice of that industry was processed in its last days. He spent his final years and the large endowment of the South Carolina Agricultural Society in an attempt to revive the rice industry, to no avail. Rice was, by the twentieth century, cheaper to grow in Arkansas, Louisiana, and Texas. Rice was soon a by-gone memory in South Carolina.

Capt. Stoney was recognized as a preserved relic of a time gone by, even in his lifetime. John Bennett, who married Mrs. Stoney's sister, wrote *The Treasure of Peyre Gaillard* about him and dedicated the work "to S. G. S." Stoney's ownership of Medway Plantation and personal supervision of its deer drives are the source of several literary productions. His status in Charleston society is suggested by some of the positions he held: president of the Agricultural Society, president of the St. Cecilia Society, chairman of the board of vestryman of Old Goose Creek Church, vestryman of St. Michael's Church, vice-president of the French Huguenot Society, vice-chairman of the board of commissioners of the Charleston Orphan House, and president of the board of trustees of the Charleston Museum. Nice work if you can get it.

Capt. Stoney's wife **Louisa Cheves Smythe Stoney** (1868–1939) was no distaff ornament. She was named for her grandmother, Louisa Cheves McCord, and was the daughter of Augustine Thomas Smythe and Louisa Rebecca McCord Smythe. Mrs. Stoney was for her time a civil rights leader, though she would have shunned such a title. She was an organizer with Clelia McGowan of the Interracial Committee and a founder of the "colored" Y.W.C.A. on Coming Street.

She was an accomplished artist and writer. She edited and wrote the introduction to her grandfather's papers, *Autobiographical Notes, Letters, and Reflections, by Thomas Smythe, D. D.* (1914). She enlarged, edited, and wrote a new introduction for the nineteenth-century work by John Beaufain Irving, *A Day on the Cooper River* (1932). She wrote and compiled the recipes in *Carolina Rice Cook Book* (1901), a classic that has recently been expanded and explicated in Karen Hess's *The Carolina Rice Kitchen: The African Connection* (1992).

An amusing anecdote is told by a member of the Smythe family of the naming of Mrs. Stoney's second son. It is said that shortly after the boy's birth, Mrs. Stoney presented him to her brother, the famous lawyer Augustine Thomas Smythe, with the statement, "I intend, with your permission, to name this boy Augustine Smythe Stoney for you, next to my husband, my ideal."

Smythe: "I would not inflict such a perpetual torment on so defenseless a being."

Mrs. Stoney: "What can you mean? Though you are a lawyer, you are still honorable, and a gentleman."

Smythe: "Consider his monogram."

Thus **Augustine Thomas Smythe Stoney** (1895–1949) was named. A. T. S. Stoney was a surveyor and soldier. As a soldier he fought in both world wars and attained the rank of lieutenant colonel. As a surveyor he saw much of the Lowcountry and produced beautiful maps of its plantations and habitations in books spearheaded by his brother Samuel Gaillard Stoney, Jr., such as *The Carolina Low-Country* (1931) and *Plantations of the Carolina Low Country* (1938). He was an accomplished etcher. The Gibbes Museum owns a particularly fine Stoney etching of Medway, his boyhood home.

Samuel Gaillard Stoney, Jr. (1891–1968), is not buried at Magnolia but at St. James, Goose Creek. Yet he cannot lie beyond the purview of this book. He was Charleston's most tireless promoter. Though he valued a story above fact, he was sought out for historical accounts. Like his father, he sought to preserve the past, and he was largely successful in a collaborative effort to preserve Charleston's physical fabric. He lived to see a second invasion of Yankee troops anxious to discover Charleston's treasures. Capt. Stoney died in his own bed of the lingering effects of pneumonia, surrounded by family and friends. Sam Stoney, Jr., died alone of a self-inflicted gunshot wound. Both deaths were seen as the end of the "Old South." Both were.

WILLIAM NELSON TAFT (1847–1889)

Carpetbagger   MAP LOCATION: NORTHWEST 17

Plainly stated, William Nelson Taft was what was called, in a simpler day, a carpetbagger. Born in Providence, Rhode Island, he served as a private in Company B of the Third Rhode Island Heavy Artillery. Settling in Charleston after the war, he became active in local politics. As county coroner from 1870 to 1872 he was assailed by Democrats as the only person ever to have made a fortune from the fees generated by that office. He served as a state senator for Charleston County from 1876 to 1880. He received the plum patronage position of Charleston postmaster from President Chester A. Arthur in 1881 and remained in that position until 1885. He would also hold the positions of brigadier general in the South Carolina National Guard, Republican National Executive Committeeman from 1880 to 1884, and delegate to the 1888 Republican National Convention.

Sen. Taft was known for his fondness for the ladies, and in November 1878 was shot, non-fatally, by J. C. Millar, whose wife had allegedly been receiving Taft's attentions. In 1881 he was married to Mary Richardson Moses Bowen, daughter of Reconstruction governor Franklin Moses and widow of Reconstruction congressman Christopher Columbus Bowen.

Taft's wife, Mary, sold to black freedpeople parts of Hillsboro Plantation, which she inherited from her first husband, Congressman C. C. Bowen. The community which resulted is today known as Maryville.

GEORGIANNA RAOUL HORRY PALMER TOWNSEND (1882–1979)

The Duchess of Wadmalaw   MAP LOCATION: NORTHWEST 18

Georgianna Townsend was a pickle queen, or rather, "Duchess." She was born in Pinopolis in Berkeley County of an old Berkeley County family. She began putting up her pickles in the 1920s and gained a tremendous local reputation for their good flavor. In 1930, she introduced the Duchess brand of Palmetto Pickles and achieved national success. She became well known as the Duchess of Wadmalaw, and that title adorns her tomb.

Ashley Hall in the early 1890s, after George Alfred Trenholm sold the residence to Charles Otto Witte, who installed the aviary for exotic birds. Courtesy of the Historic Charleston Foundation

George Alfred Trenholm (1807–1876)

Merchant and Confederate Financier   MAP LOCATION: SOUTHWEST 68

One of the wealthiest businessmen in the mid-nineteenth-century South, George Alfred Trenholm played a key role in the economic operations of the Confederacy long before he succeeded his friend and fellow Charlestonian Christopher Memminger as the secretary of the treasury.

Trenholm was the grandson and son of merchants who had seen revolutions. The original American settler left Charleston for New York City because of his Loyalist sentiments, and his son brought the family back to Charleston to escape from the 1793 uprising in Saint-Domingue, where he had married the daughter of a French landowner. Sixteen years old when his father died, George Alfred Trenholm went to work for John Fraser & Company, an import-export firm that maintained an extensive cotton trade. He became a partner in the firm in 1835 and the senior partner and principal owner in 1853. The affiliated Fraser, Trenholm & Company provided a base of operations in Liverpool, and Trenholm Brothers served as the New York branch office. At its peak under Trenholm's management, Fraser & Company is said to have been able to ship 20,000 bales of cotton in a morning.

Trenholm's wealth and crucial position in the local economy made him a vital member of many enterprises. He was a longtime director of the Bank of Charleston and the South Carolina Railroad and was one of the chief promoters of the Blue Ridge Railroad. He served in the state legislature from 1852 to 1856. His family long maintained its principal residence at Ashley Hall, later the original building of the Ashley Hall School.

Trenholm was a strong advocate of secession, and his political principles and business interests converged in his support for the Confederacy. His shipping enterprises made him a central figure in blockade running, which has led to the implausible suggestion that he was Margaret Mitchell's model for Rhett Butler in *Gone With the Wind*. Trenholm's firms owned or operated approximately sixty vessels during the war, and he leased substantial space to the Confederate government for the importation of munitions and other war matériel. He devoted additional cargo capacity and outbound freight to valuable commodities in private trade. It was estimated in November 1862 that John Fraser & Co. had shipped seven-eighths of the cotton to leave the Confederacy. Trenholm's international connections also positioned him to aid Confederate finances. Fraser, Trenholm & Co. in Liverpool served as a depository for Confederate funds in Europe and as a financial agent for the government. In exchange for Confederate securities received in Charleston, Fraser, Trenholm & Co. issued letters of credit that allowed Confederate agents to draw funds from European banks. This arrangement made Fraser, Trenholm & Co. the financial base for Confederate agents seeking to influence public opinion, buy arms, arrange loans, or otherwise transact business in England and elsewhere abroad.

Trenholm was a logical choice to succeed Memminger as secretary of the treasury in July 1864, although the nomination drew some allegations that Trenholm had profited excessively from the war. He had made a lot of money, though he had invested heavily in Confederate bonds and had foregone some speculative opportunities by focusing much of his blockade-running activities on government contracts. As secretary he was an able man in an impossible situation. He fled Richmond with the rest of the cabinet and was arrested in Columbia in June 1865. The federal government held him in prison until October 1865.

Trenholm returned after the war to the firms he had left upon his appointment as secretary, but his companies fell into bankruptcy in 1867. He reorganized his cotton brokerage as George A. Trenholm & Son and remained a prominent figure in business circles. In 1874 he went back to the state legislature as one of five Democrats elected to the General Assembly through a bipartisan arrangement to divide the eighteen-member Charleston delegation. His admirers regarded his willingness to serve in the biracial Republican-dominated legislature as another of his public sacrifices and maintained that the stress of the position contributed to Trenholm's death at the end of the session.

WILLIAM LEE TRENHOLM (1836–1901)

Business Leader   MAP LOCATION: SOUTHWEST 68

William L. Trenholm, like his father, George Alfred Trenholm, made more than one fortune and served his country as a high-ranking Treasury Department official. Although born to privilege, Trenholm never displayed the indolence so characteristic of wealthy young men of his generation. He was educated at the school of Christopher Cotes in Charleston. He graduated with second honors in the class of 1855 of South Carolina College.

After graduation he went to work for his father's firm, John Fraser & Co., and became the firm's agent in Liverpool. He returned to Charleston in the winter of 1861 to help organize a military company that would become known as the Rutledge Mounted Riflemen. He served with distinction throughout the war and was severely wounded at Cold Harbor. He advanced to the rank of lieutenant colonel during his service.

Trenholm had served as an alderman of the city of Charleston during the war and served again from 1875 through 1877. With his father, he started a new, very successful business after federal government seizures had forced Fraser & Co. into bankruptcy. Trenholm became a perceptive critic of the city's commercial development. His controversial speech before the Charleston Board of Trade in 1869 included the startling line, "We must forget to defer to senility, we must learn to respect and to make use of youth." His speech at the centennial celebration of the Chamber of Commerce in 1884 electrified the city. In it he criticized the old attitudes and businessmen who had stifled Charleston's growth before and after the war. He warned that the brightest and most enterprising of Charleston's young men were leaving rather than staying in the stagnant pool that was Charleston's business environment.

Trenholm again courted controversy at a bankers' convention in Atlanta in 1885 by going against the Southern sentiment and calling for continuance of the gold standard. President Cleveland was so impressed that he appointed Trenholm to the important and newly created position of civil service commissioner. Soon afterwards, President Cleveland further expressed his confidence in Trenholm by appointing him comptroller of the currency. Few Southerners received such high federal appointments in the late nineteenth century. Trenholm's appointments were all the more striking in that his father had been secretary of the treasury for the Confederacy and had been imprisoned for treason by the Union forces after the Civil War.

In 1889 Trenholm became president of the American Surety Co. in New York, joining the drain of Charleston business talent he had described. He later served as president of the North American Trust Co. He died in 1901. He is buried beside his father beneath a modest marble slab that bears only his dates and initials.

Don H. Doyle's *New Men, New Cities, New South: Atlanta, Nashville, Charleston, and Mobile, 1860–1910* (1990) offers a fine analysis of Trenholm's importance to the postbellum Charleston economy.

Frederich August Richard, Count von Strensch
L'Estrange de Blackmere (1867–1941)

Gentleman Friend   MAP LOCATION: SOUTHEAST 38

What is a German count who only visited Charleston a few times doing buried in Charleston? The answer is Mary Wilkerson Middleton Pinckney Lee. As recited on his stone, the count was a noted neurologist, an artillery officer of Saxony, and a special envoy of the Court of Saxony to the United States.

He became the "great, good friend" of one of the grande dames of Washington society, the aforementioned Mrs. Lee, when she was widowed for the second time. Upon his death Mrs. Lee had his remains buried alongside those of her two husbands, Gustavus M. Pinckney and Robert E. Lee III. At the end of the count's epitaph, Mrs. Lee had engraved the enigmatic initials "S.W.H.G.B." The meaning of the initials is probably lost to the ages.

CORNELIUS IRVINE WALKER (1842–1927)

Confederate Soldier   MAP LOCATION: SOUTHWEST 69

C. Irvine Walker served as an officer in the Confederate Army and in higher-ranking positions in its postwar incarnations. He was born in Charleston, the son of printer and publisher Joseph Walker. He attended the King's Mountain Military School and graduated at the head of his class from the South Carolina Military Academy (later the Citadel) in 1861. He enlisted almost immediately in the 10th Regiment of South Carolina Volunteers. Initially appointed adjutant of the unit, he eventually rose to the rank of lieutenant colonel. He suffered a near-fatal wound at the Battle of Atlanta.

After the war Walker joined his father's company when it was reorganized as Walker, Evans and Cogswell. He eventually became manager of the company and remained at its helm until 1900.

Walker founded the Carolina Rifle Club in 1869 with a group of other veterans. This sort of paramilitary organization played a crucial part in the "Redemption" of the South Carolina government by white Democrats in 1876. The Carolina Rifle Club was such a large and well-organized group that it was received into the South Carolina Volunteers as a battalion. Walker was later promoted to the position of brigadier general of the Sixth Brigade.

Walker lobbied persistently in the press and with the legislature for the reestablishment of the Citadel after its closing at the conclusion of the war. His work finally saw fruition when the Citadel was reopened in 1882.

Walker was also involved in the organization of the United Confederate Veterans. He was the first commander of the South Carolina Division, succeeded Wade Hampton as commander of the Army of Northern Virginia, and became commander-in-chief of the United Confederate Veterans on the death of Gen. George W. Gordon in 1911. He resigned in 1912 and was made honorary commander-in-chief for life.

Walker wrote prolifically on the history of South Carolina and the Civil War. Among his books and pamphlets were *Rolls and Historical Sketch of the Tenth Regiment, South Carolina Volunteers* (1881), *The Carolina Rifle Club* (1904), *The Romance of Lower Carolina* (1915), *The Life of Lt. Gen. Richard Herron Anderson of the Confederate States Army* (1917), *History of the Agricultural Society of South Carolina* (1919), and a posthumous volume, *What the World Owes the South for Secession* (1927).

William Aiken Walker, *Cabin Scene.* Courtesy of LaVonne N. Phillips

WILLIAM AIKEN WALKER (1839–1921)

Artist   MAP LOCATION: NORTHWEST 19

In his day William Aiken Walker was known as a "character," an itinerant artist who sold pictures to tourists for a few dollars. He could carry a tune and tell a good story. Today he is recognized as the most important artist of the postbellum South, and his paintings command prices in the hundreds of thousands of dollars.

Walker was born in Charleston in 1839 (not 1838 as his tombstone states), the son of an Irish immigrant father and a Charleston mother. He served in Hampton's Legion during the Civil War and was wounded at Seven Pines. He later did civilian service for the Confederate Engineer Corps, where his skills in graphic arts were put to use in drafting and cartography.

Walker stayed in Charleston for a few years after the war, but by 1869 he was painting in Baltimore. For the rest of his life he would consider Charleston home but would only occasionally visit here. His real home was the resorts of the South, where he would sell his works to tourists and sometimes barter art for food and lodging.

Walker painted all sorts and varieties of Southern scenes: landscapes, children's portraits, still lifes of fish. He is most widely recognized today for his depictions of the lives of African Americans after slavery. Walker's style was painterly, yet relatively unadorned. He depicted a way of life somewhat sentimentally but basically factually. He typically sold his paintings for between two and twenty dollars. He was popular and made a good living for an artist of his time.

At the close of his life, he returned to Charleston and died at the home of his nephew George William Walker at 134 Cannon Street.

It was not until several decades after Walker's death that his work began to be nationally recognized. *William Aiken Walker: Southern Genre Painter* (1972) by August P. Trovaioli and Roulhac B. Toledano intensified the interest in Walker's work, which had been pioneered by Charleston dealer Herman Schindler. Today his work is voraciously sought out by museums and collectors alike. The largest private holders of Walker paintings include Jay Altmayer, Oprah Winfrey, Jack Warner, the Gulf States Paper Collection, and Logan Sewell. In 1995 Robert M. Hicklin, Jr., the most important dealer in Walker's works and other Southern historical art, published Cynthia Siebels's much expanded, definitive biography of Walker, *The Sunny South: The Life and Art of William Aiken Walker.*

Dorothy Thomson Waring (1900–1988)

Artist   MAP LOCATION: SOUTHEAST 64

Dorothy Waring led a quiet life as a legal secretary. In her spare time, she was Charleston's finest botanical artist. Miss Waring was born in Charleston, the daughter of Joseph Ioor Waring and Emma Thomson Taber Waring. Her only sibling was Dr. Joseph I. Waring, Jr., beloved physician and historian, for whom the Waring Historical Library at the Medical University of South Carolina is named.

Miss Waring was a graduate of Ashley Hall and studied at Hollins College. She was legal secretary to Robert McC. Figg, one of Charleston's finest attorneys. She was also a student of Alfred Hutty and taught for a time in the early 1930s at the Gibbes Gallery School. She illustrated a number of books, notably Loutrel Briggs's *Charleston Gardens* (1951). Her delicate watercolors are both scientifically and aesthetically pleasing. They are her most important legacy.

Elizabeth Avery Hoffman Waring (1895–1968)

Civil Rights Leader   MAP LOCATION: SOUTHEAST 65

Without question, Elizabeth Avery Hoffman Waring was the most vilified woman in Charleston in the 1940s and 1950s. Time has proven, however, that she was on the right side of history, for she was Charleston's most outspoken advocate of racial equality long before such a stance was popular, or even safe.

Mrs. Waring was born in Detroit, Michigan, in 1895, the daughter of Mr. and Mrs. John Avery. Her second husband, Henry Hoffman, and the then Mrs. Hoffman were good friends and bridge partners of Judge and Mrs. J. Waties Waring in the 1940s. When Judge Waring fell in love with the beautiful, younger Mrs. Hoffman, Charleston society was aghast. Judge Waring obtained a Florida divorce from his first wife, Annie Gammell Waring, and promptly married the by-then divorced Mrs. Hoffman in June 1945. Judge Waring's rulings after their marriage were blamed as much on Mrs. Waring as on the Judge, "blame" which Mrs. Waring would have proudly accepted.

Mrs. Waring's status as a spokeswoman for civil rights was such that in 1950 she was invited to appear on the NBC program *Meet the Press*. Though she and Judge Waring were already ostracized from Charleston society, she made no friends with her declaration that the people of Charleston were "sick, confused, and decadent . . . full of pride and complacency, introverted, morally weak, and low." In the same year she and Judge Waring held an integrated luncheon for the benefit of the cameras of *Collier's* magazine. Their reward was a cross burnt on the sidewalk in front of their house at 61 Meeting Street.

After Judge Waring's retirement from the bench in 1952, he and Mrs. Waring moved to "exile" in New York, where they continued to fight for civil rights until their deaths in 1968.

JULIUS WATIES WARING (1880–1968)

Jurist   MAP LOCATION: SOUTHEAST 65

The life of J. Waties Waring presents much of Charleston's history in its enfolding arrogance, racism, and enmities. Waring is the supreme enigma of Charleston history. He is still widely *hated* today, decades after his death and more than a half-century after his judicial decisions set in motion the drama and triumph of *Brown v. Topeka Board of Education* (1954).

Waring was the privileged son of a privileged family. Like his siblings, he was brilliant. He was born in 1880 in Charleston, the son of Edward Perry Waring and Anna Thomasine Waties. He traced his ancestry in Charleston to Benjamin Waring, who arrived here in 1683. Waties Waring attended the University School in Charleston and the College of Charleston, from which he graduated with second honors in the class of 1900. Due to his family's reduced circumstances after the Civil War he was unable to afford law school but instead followed the customary career path of a Charlestonian of his day by reading law in the office of a prominent Charleston attorney, in Waring's case the stellar John Pendleton Kennedy Bryan. He married Annie Gammell (1879–1954) in 1913. Annie was a devotee and intimate of Sarah Bernhardt. (Bernhardt's inscribed photograph to Annie is framed and on display on the second floor of the Charleston Library Society.) In 1914 Waring was made an assistant U.S. attorney for South Carolina's eastern district. His life and career trajectory from that point should have been as easy as it was easily predictable.

For a time it was so. He gained valuable experience and much credit in established Charleston through his successful prosecution of the *Liebenfels* case, in which he was pitted against the Irish-Catholic former and future mayor John P. Grace. In 1920 he joined forces with another young Charleston blue-blood, David A. Brockinton, with whom he remained partners until his elevation to the federal bench. Brockinton was married to the daughter of future South Carolina governor Wilson Harvey, whose second wife was

A luncheon at the Waring home at 61 Meeting Street in 1950. Clockwise from top are Judge Waring, Lillian Wilson, John Fleming, Mildred Guenveur Cherry, journalist Samuel Grafton (obscured), Elizabeth Waring, Susan Butler, Septima Clark, Ruby Cornwell, Roscoe Wilson, and Corinne Guenveur. Courtesy of the Moorland-Spingarn Research Center, Howard University

Waring's sister Margaret. The entangling bonds of society, kinship, and professional life exemplified by this relationship are the very stuff and substance of Charleston to this day.

Waring prospered in private practice, but he always stayed knee-deep in city and state politics, for he was a man of great ambition. He was particularly close with a young cotton factor, Burnet Maybank, who became mayor in 1931. He became Maybank's right-hand man and city attorney. He was also campaign manager for that most notorious of racist Southern politicians, U.S. senator Ellison "Cotton Ed" Smith. Waring proved himself an aggressively successful political lawyer and an arch-segregationist in his early legal career. Given his arrogance, racism, intellect, and political and familial connections, Waring was the obvious candidate for U.S. District Court judge when Ernest Cochran committed suicide in 1934. Blood, or blood-in-law, is thicker than water, however, and Maybank successfully pushed for the nomination of Frank K. Myers (Maybank's father-in-law) over the candidacy of Waring. Though the relationship of Maybank and Waring was not destroyed, the incident soured and colored the dealings between the men for the rest of their lives.

Myers's term ended with his life in 1940, and after some frantic New Deal political machinations, Waring soon assumed what he had long regarded as his rightful seat as U.S.

District Court judge for the eastern district of South Carolina. His early judicial career was unremarkable but energetic. He cleared clotted dockets and displayed a remarkably workman-like attitude toward friend and foe alike. His opinions were generally short and unappealable. He was a great believer in the finality of a decision—except in matters of the heart.

The central fact of J. Waties Waring's life was his divorce from his first wife, Annie Gammell Waring and his marriage to Elizabeth Avery Hoffman Waring (his second marriage, her third). This was at a time when divorce was not yet legal in South Carolina. Whatever one may think of Waring's later rulings, however one might admire Waring's courage in flying against tradition, one can only conclude that Waring acted as the cad in the divorce.

After a marriage of thirty-one years and one daughter, during which Anne Gammell Waring endured infidelities, career disappointments, and worse, the judge took up with the distaff half of one of their favorite couples, Mr. and Mrs. Henry Hoffman, heirs to a New England textile fortune. In February 1945 Judge Waring told his wife that he wanted a divorce on his terms, and he wanted as part of the settlement the house that she had brought to the marriage. "Miss Annie" dutifully obeyed her husband and obtained a Florida divorce. For the rest of her life, she lived in a rented kitchen house around the corner where she pined for her former husband and died nine years later of what Charlestonians universally agreed was a broken heart.

The new Mrs. Waring soon replaced Eleanor Roosevelt as "that woman" in Charleston conversation. The Warings were ostracized in the society in which Judge Waring had formerly been lionized. Coupled with a new perspective on racial matters, Waring's ostracism resulted in a series of rulings on civil rights cases that were to contribute to the end of *de jure* segregation. Waring's evolution from arch-segregationist to integrationist certainly suggests that vengeance against his former life and education by his Northern wife played no small part in his decisions.

Waring's partner in justice was a young black lawyer with the NAACP, Thurgood Marshall. Beginning in 1943–1944 with the case of *Duvall v. Seignous,* Waring ruled repeatedly against the time-honored segregation orthodoxy that Marshall challenged. *Duvall* involved the question of whether black public school teachers deserved the same pay as their white counterparts; Judge Waring concluded that they did.

The case of *United States v. Shull* solidified and "radicalized" Waring's view of racial justice in South Carolina. Isaac Woodard was a black U.S. Army veteran from Winnsboro, South Carolina, honorably discharged from service at Camp Gordon near Augusta, Georgia, in February 1946. During his bus trip home, Woodard was removed from the bus as a result of his "uppity" behavior and back-talk to the bus driver when the bus stopped in Batesburg, South Carolina. He was then beaten with a blackjack by the town's chief of police Lynwood Shull and permanently blinded. When local authorities refused to prosecute Chief Shull, he was indicted under federal law. Judge Waring conducted the trial in November 1946 and consistently ruled racist arguments and testimony out of order. Despite Judge Waring's rulings, the jury debated only twenty-five minutes before returning a verdict of not guilty. As a direct result of this outrage, President Truman ordered the racial integration of the U.S. armed services.

The next important case for Waring involved similar high stakes. *Elmore v. Rice* was a challenge to South Carolina's "white primary." After the U.S. Supreme Court ruled in *Smith v. Allwright* (1944) that "white primaries" were unconstitutional, Gov. Olin Johnston attempted to circumvent the court's ruling by making the Democratic Party a "club," whose nominee alone would be on the state's ballot in November. Of course, the Democratic "club" would be all white. Judge Waring rejected this charade and ruled in July 1947 that "it is time for South Carolina to rejoin the Union. It is time to fall in step with other states and to adopt the American way of conducting elections."

Waring's divorce, remarriage, and pro–civil rights rulings only hardened the Warings' almost complete ostracism from Charleston society. They also hardened Waring's resolve to undermine segregation and to cut off those (including family) who had not yet expelled Waring and his new wife from Charleston society. The case of *Briggs v. Elliott* would decide forever Waring's place in Charleston and in history.

Briggs v. Elliott grew out of a Clarendon County case in which a Summerton minister Joseph DeLaine convinced a number of local African Americans to put their livelihoods and lives on the line by challenging the patently unequal treatment dished out by the local school board. Thurgood Marshall, the lawyer for the plaintiffs, initially filed the case as a simple question of the equality of services offered under *Plessy v. Ferguson.* Judge Waring (in a possible affront to judicial ethics) invited him to challenge the entire system of segregation. A three-judge federal court ruled over Judge Waring's spirited dissent that Clarendon's system was unequal but that segregation was still the law. That 1951 dissent was the first judicial opinion in a string which would eventually culminate in *Brown v. Board,* as Judge Waring was the first federal judge to find that "segregation is per se inequality."

After his retirement in 1952, Judge and Mrs. Waring went into self-imposed "exile" in New York City. There they became outspoken civil rights activists and found honor for their efforts. Judge Waring did not return home to Charleston permanently until his death. At his funeral, hundreds of blacks came to pay posthumous respects. Fewer than a dozen whites joined them.

In one of the many ironies of the Warings' lives, Elizabeth Waring's second husband, Henry Hoffman (1874–1952), is buried in Magnolia, beside his second wife, Julia Grimke Young Hoffman. Thus, all the participants in South Carolina's divorce of the century lie in the same ground, strange bedfellows indeed.

The most thorough work on Judge Waring is Tinsley E. Yarbrough's *A Passion for Justice: J. Waties Waring and Civil Rights* (1987).

LAURA WITTE WARING (1877–1975)

Author   MAP LOCATION: NORTHWEST 20

One of the six daughters of Charles Otto and Charlotte Sophia (Reeves) Witte, Laura W. Waring was educated at Miss Kelly's School in Charleston and Miss Hersey's School in Boston. She was married to Thomas R. Waring, Sr., for many years the editor of the Charleston *Evening Post.* She authored a charming and informative memoir of her privileged late-nineteenth-century childhood, privately published as *You Asked for It* (1941). The book has been republished under the title, *The Way It Was in Charleston* (1980).

Thomas Richard Waring, Sr. (1871–1935)

Newspaper Editor   MAP LOCATION: NORTHWEST 20

A native Charlestonian, T. R. Waring was from 1897 to 1935 the editor of the Charleston *Evening Post*. During much of this period, his brother-in-law, William Watts Ball was editor of the morning paper, the *News and Courier*. Together they exercised a powerful influence on Charleston and its early-twentieth-century history.

Mr. Waring was born in Charleston and was a graduate of Porter Military Academy and Hobart College. He married Laura Witte, one of the famous Witte sisters, and was the father of Rosamond W. Salmons, prominent lawyer Charles Witte Waring, and the great editor Thomas R. Waring, Jr.

In addition to his editorial duties, Waring was an early and important preservationist and one of the first chairmen of the Board of Architectural Review. He contributed the chapter "Charleston, Capital of the Plantations" to *The Carolina Low-Country* (1931), published by the Society for the Preservation of Spirituals.

Thomas Richard Waring, Jr. (1907–1993)

Newspaper Editor   MAP LOCATION: NORTHWEST 20

Tom Waring inherited a famous journalistic name and enlarged upon it. He was an inheritor of segregation and fought for it. History gave him integration, and after a desperate struggle, he ultimately joined in smoothing its way.

Waring was born in Charleston and educated at Porter Military Academy. He graduated in 1927 as valedictorian at the University of the South at Sewanee, Tennessee, where he was a member of Phi Beta Kappa. His father, the editor of the Charleston *Evening Post,* refused to hire him, but his uncle by marriage, William Watts Ball, editor of the morning *News and Courier,* recognized his talents and hired him on the spot. Waring soon went north as a reporter for the New York *Herald Tribune*. He remained there for a number of years until his return to Charleston as a reporter, again for the *News and Courier*. By 1942 he was elevated to managing editor and, on the death of W. W. Ball, to editor.

As editor of the *News and Courier,* Waring became a national figure in opposition to integration. His situation was all the more poignant in that one of the leaders of desegregation was his uncle and neighbor, U.S. District Court judge J. Waties Waring. As staunchly opposed to Communism as he was to integration, Waring was one of Fidel Castro's earliest and most vociferous editorial opponents.

When it became patently clear that racial integration was to become fact, Waring recognized his mistake and was the sponsor of Arthur J. Clement, the first African-American member of the Charleston Rotary Club.

Mr. Waring wrote a chapter of his first cousin Beatrice St. J. Ravenel's *Charleston Murders* (1947) and edited and wrote an introduction for the new edition of his mother Laura Witte Waring's memoir, *The Way It Was in Charleston* (1980).

Mr. Waring was unfailingly kind and generous with his time, recollections, library, and friendship. He was the very model of a Charleston gentleman.

WILLIAM WAY (1876–1974)

Episcopal Cleric   MAP LOCATION: SOUTHWEST 70

William Way was one of the longest serving rectors in the history of the South Carolina Episcopal Diocese. He was born in Weaverville, North Carolina, and attended the public schools of Asheville. He was graduated from the General Theological Seminary in New York. He was rector of Grace Episcopal Church in Charleston from 1902 until his retirement in 1948 and rector emeritus until his death. He received a doctor of divinity degree from the University of South Carolina in 1922 and a doctor of sacred divinity degree from the General Theological Seminary in 1948.

In his long life Dr. Way served as president of the New England Society and the South Carolina Historical Society, and as chairman of the South Carolina Historical Commission. He wrote two fine histories, *The History of the New England Society of Charleston* (1920) and *The History of Grace Church* (1948).

His son, **William Way, Jr.** (1907–1956), was a native of Charleston who founded the first university school dealing with transportation at the University of Tennessee in 1948. He was a graduate of the University of North Carolina and attended graduate school at the University of Pennsylvania. His book, *The Clinchfield Railroad: The Story of a Trade Route Across the Blue Ridge Mountains* (1931), explained an important, if neglected, area of South Carolina history. At the time of his untimely death from a heart attack, Professor Way was head of the transportation department at the University of Tennessee.

FREDERICK THEODORE WEBER (1883–1956)

Artist   MAP LOCATION: SOUTHWEST 71

Frederick Weber lived a peripatetic life. He lived abroad for much of his youth and used the training he received in Paris to become one of the most acclaimed portrait painters and etchers of his time.

Weber was born in Columbia, South Carolina, and spent his formative years there and in Summerville. His father's business took the family to Germany when Weber was a young boy. He was educated at the Königlich Joachimsthalsches Gymnasium in Berlin, from which he graduated in 1903. His native talent and growing interest in art caused him to turn his eyes to Paris, where he studied at the Académie Humbert in 1905–1906, the Académie Julian in 1910–1911, and the École des Beaux-Arts in 1910–1913. At these schools he studied under the French academicians Ferdinand Humbert, Jean Paul Laurens, and Raoul Verlet. While at the Beaux-Arts, he won the prestigious Prix Talrich and exhibited his works in the salon of the school. Shortly after the completion of his studies he moved to New York City, where he scored easy success as a society portrait painter. He was also active as an etcher and served a term as president of the Brooklyn Society of Etchers.

For most of his working life, Weber maintained homes in New York and Florida and kept in close touch with relatives and friends in his native South Carolina, particularly his beloved mother, Julia Nixon Weber, a native Charlestonian. During the Civil War, the teenaged Julia Nixon had become the head of her family when her father was away. When her young sister died of diphtheria, Julia bought a family plot in Magnolia Cemetery and registered it in her father's name. When her son the internationally acclaimed artist died on Long Island, New York, the wanderer returned to South Carolina forever and now rests between his mother and his wife.

His work is represented in all major South Carolina museums as well as at the governor's mansion in Columbia. His portrait of Mayor Thomas P. Stoney hangs in City Hall chambers in Charleston. His work is part of the permanent collections of the Metropolitan Museum, the Brooklyn Museum, the Museum of American Art, the Library of Congress, and the Bibliothèque Nationale.

EDWARD LAIGHT WELLS (1839–1917)

Confederate Soldier   MAP LOCATION: SOUTHWEST 66

Edward Wells was a native New Yorker who came south to fight for the Confederacy and returned to Charleston after the war to write histories and found a distinguished family. His grandfather's second wife was Sabina Elliott Huger Wells, sister of Daniel Elliott Huger, and the prominent New York family sympathized strongly with the South. When it became apparent that Wells might be drafted into the Union army, he took a steamer from New York to Nassau and ran the blockade into Charleston, where he joined the Charleston Light Dragoons. He fought valiantly throughout the war with that unit, participating in campaigns throughout Virginia and the Carolinas. Over the course of the war he had three horses shot from under him.

After the war Wells became a successful cotton factor and an historian. In 1869 he married Anna Mason Smith, sister of D. E. Huger Smith. He published three books: *A Sketch of the Charleston Light Dragoons, from the Earliest Formation of the Corps* (1888); *Hampton and His Cavalry in '64* (1899); and *Hampton and Reconstruction* (1907). As he had full access to his friend Gen. Hampton and his papers, Wells's books are still valuable primary resources today.

Wells's son and namesake, Edward L. Wells, Jr., was an American hero in France in World War I. He is buried with his troops near Argonne. Wells the dragoon's granddaughter, Anna Wells Rutledge, virtually invented the study of South Carolina art history.

RICHARD SMITH WHALEY (1874–1951)

Politician and Jurist   MAP LOCATION: SOUTHEAST 59

Richard Smith Whaley was a prominent politician in Charleston and an important judicial officer for the country in the first half of the twentieth century. He was born in Charleston and educated at Episcopal High School in Alexandria, Virginia, the University of South Carolina, and the University of Virginia, from which he received his law degree in 1897.

Soon after Whaley's entrance to the bar he joined the firm co-founded by his kinsman by marriage Robert G. Rhett, which became Trenholm, Rhett, Miller, and Whaley. He also quickly launched his political career. He was an early associate of James F. Byrnes, a friendship that stood him in good stead throughout his political and judicial career. Whaley was a South Carolina representative from 1900 to 1913, serving as speaker from 1907 to 1910. He was elected to succeed U.S. representative George S. Legaré upon the congressman's death in 1913 and served in Washington until 1921, when he declined to seek reelection. He was appointed judge of the U.S. Court of Claims by President Herbert Hoover in 1930 and was elevated to chief justice of that court by President Franklin D. Roosevelt in 1939.

Chief Justice Whaley retired in 1947 and died in 1951. He was entombed in the pyramid built by his grandfather William B. Smith.

WILLIAM MAY WIGHTMAN (1808–1882)

Methodist Bishop   MAP LOCATION: SOUTHEAST 66

William M. Wightman was an educator, preacher, writer, editor, and Methodist bishop. He was born in Charleston and graduated from the College of Charleston in 1827. He was licensed to preach during his senior year at the College and quickly became a favorite of Dr. (later Bishop) William Capers. Wightman was employed as an agent to raise funds for Randolph-Macon College in Virginia in 1834 and soon became a professor of English literature at that school.

Wightman resigned as professor when he was made presiding elder of the Cokesbury District of South Carolina. In 1840 he became editor of the *Southern Christian Advocate,* the Methodist magazine for South Carolina, Georgia, Florida, and Alabama. During this period, he also frequently published the travel writings of his brother-in-law, George Walton Williams, whose first wife was Wightman's sister Louisa. Williams remained close to Wightman, even after the death of Louisa. Williams was one of the most devout and generous lay members of the Southern Methodist Church; his friendship was important to Wightman's career.

Wightman played a prominent proslavery role in the sectional schism of the Methodist church and the subsequent expansion of southern colleges. Benjamin Wofford's will made him a member of the founding board of Wofford College in Spartanburg, South Carolina, and he was named the first president of the institution in 1854. He held this position for several years until he was named chancellor of Southern University in Greensboro, Alabama. For the second time he oversaw the early growth of a strong young liberal arts college. He presided at Southern University until 1866, when he was made a bishop of the Methodist Church.

Bishop Wightman was recognized as a scholar and moving orator. His biography of Bishop Capers, first published in 1858, was highly praised in the popular press of the day and reprinted several times.

George Walton Williams (1820–1903)

Businessman   MAP LOCATION: SOUTHWEST 72

George Walton Williams was Charleston's great entrepreneur both before and after the Civil War. He was a key figure in mercantile and banking circles and was to a considerable degree responsible for the continuation and success of Magnolia Cemetery.

Williams was born near North Cove, North Carolina, but moved with his family at an early age to the Nacoochee Valley in northeast Georgia. There his father made his fortune and young George was first exposed to business. Williams also embraced the strict Methodism of his parents. For the remainder of his life, he was a teetotaler and would allow no alcohol sold in any of his businesses (though alcohol sales were sometimes as much as fifty percent of a wholesale grocer's business). He early showed a penchant for trading, and though he had little if any formal education he set out at the age of seventeen for Augusta, Georgia, without the blessing or help of his then prosperous family. He immediately began work for David Hand, a prominent wholesale grocer. Within three years, Williams had bought out Hand's partner and was a member of the firm of Hand and Williams. Williams was at that time and always an extremely hard worker, and through his efforts the business grew almost geometrically.

By 1852 Williams expanded to Charleston and established the wholesale firm of George W. Williams and Company. Shortly after, he established his growing family here. His first wife was born Louisa Wightman, of an old Charleston Methodist family. Her brother was William May Wightman. She and Williams had seven children. Three of the children died before the age of three in Augusta. The surviving children and Mrs. Williams all died of the prevailing fevers shortly after the move to Charleston. They are buried in a separate plot in Magnolia Cemetery from where G. W. Williams and his second family are buried.

Despite these personal tragedies, Williams continued to experience phenomenal business success. Charlestonians elected Williams an alderman of city council in 1857. He was quickly made chairman of the Ways and Means Committee. In addition he was a supervisor of the High School of Charleston and one of the great patrons of the Charleston Orphan House.

At the commencement of the Civil War, Williams was one of the most successful young men of the South. He was a principal in two of the major mercantile businesses in the

George Walton Williams, from the frontispiece to his *Sketches of Travel in the Old and New World* (1871). Courtesy of the South Caroliniana Library, University of South Carolina

country; he was a leader in the civic and social life of Charleston; and he was newly married to a Georgia girl. Eventually, they would have six children.

When the war came, Williams went all out for the South, but he also invested heavily in land, gold, and English banks. He and his firm became a (if not the) main supplier of Charleston's material goods during the war. In 1862 he became chairman of the Subsistence Committee. The committee's purpose was to see that supplies reached the city at a cost which its residents could pay. Williams was also at the fore of those who sought to feed the poor of the city and the virtually ubiquitous widows and orphans of the war who would otherwise have faced starvation. Despite his help to the Confederacy and Charleston, Williams was criticized as a war profiteer. He defended himself and his company by challenging his accusers to "try their hand at merchandizing, and if they can succeed in furnishing goods at prices satisfactory to the buyers, they will be entitled to the gratitude of the entire country."

When it became obvious in February 1865 that the defense of Charleston was no longer possible, Confederate forces retreated. Mayor MacBeth entrusted to G. W. Williams and W. H. Gilliland the duty of rowing across the harbor and surrendering the city to Col. Bennett of the Union forces. After the surrender Williams continued his relief activities and was credited with the saving of many lives and the relief of much suffering. Williams was one of the first to apply for a pardon on August 23, 1865, and was one of the earliest to receive one as "he had in no way participated in the late rebellion" and throughout the war had "devoted himself to the relief of the poor of Charleston and suspended all business pursuits."

After the war Williams had sufficient capital in land, bonds, and British sterling to pay back his partners in the North and start business anew. He grew only more wealthy. He was instrumental in the founding of literally scores of Charleston businesses, notably the First National Bank and the Carolina Savings Bank. Through the latter business, he became the principal stockholder and chairman of the board of trustees of Magnolia Cemetery until his death.

The imposing monument over his grave is not the only reminder of Williams's life. He built the largest residence in Charleston (now called the Calhoun Mansion) at 16 Meeting Street in 1876. He also wrote a number of books on his travels, businesses, and origins. Among them are *Sketches of Travel in the Old and New World* (1871); *Nacoochee and its Surroundings* (1874); *Advice to Young Men* (1896); and *History of Banking in South Carolina from 1712 to 1900* (1900).

The eminent Southern historian E. Merton Coulter's *George Walton Williams: The Life of a Southern Merchant and Banker, 1820–1903* (1976) is an excellent biography of Williams.

EOLA WILLIS (1856–1952)

Artist and Historian   MAP LOCATION: SOUTHWEST 73

Eola Willis was a prolific writer and one of Charleston's finest artists before the Charleston Renaissance. She was the daughter of a blockade runner, Maj. Edward Willis. She was educated in the schools of Charleston and New York. She studied at the Art Students League under William Merritt Chase and Rhoda Holmes Nicoll and studied history, literature, and drama at Columbia University.

Willis wrote on historic topics for the Charleston *Evening Post* and published widely in such magazines as *Harper's, Century, Atlantic Monthly, Antiquarian, Antiques,* and *Youth's Companion.* Her greatest work was her book, *The Charleston Stage in the XVIII*

Century (1924). Miss Willis was an incorporator of the Society for the Preservation of Old Dwellings (now the Preservation Society of Charleston) and a charter member of the Footlight Players. Her papers are in the Charleston County Library.

ROBERT WILSON (1838–1924)

Physician and Episcopal Cleric   MAP LOCATION: SOUTHWEST 74

Robert Wilson was a noted physician and Episcopal minister who found time to write for the major periodicals of his day. After his death his writings were collected by his children as *Half Forgotten By-Ways of the Old South* (1928). Dr. Wilson was born and educated in Charleston. He practiced medicine in Berkeley County in the early part of his life but found himself increasingly pulled by a religious vocation. To that end, he moved to Columbia shortly before the Civil War to study with the noted Episcopal divine Peter J. Shand. In addition to receiving training from Dr. Shand, he fell in love with and married his daughter Nanna Shand. During the Civil War, Dr. Wilson served as a surgeon at the Wayside Hospital in Columbia. Afterwards he was rector for a time at the Church of the Holy Cross in Stateburg, South Carolina. He then removed to the Episcopal Church at Easton, Maryland, on the Eastern Shore. He served there for many years and was much beloved by the people.

In the closing years of his life Dr. Wilson returned home to Charleston, where he continued to write. His son, **Robert Wilson, Jr.** (1867–1946), was himself a noted physician, professor of medicine at the Medical College of South Carolina, and eventually dean of the Medical College. He and his father are buried in the family plot at Magnolia.

CHARLES OTTO WITTE (1823–1908)

Banker   MAP LOCATION: SOUTHWEST 56

Charles Otto Witte was a German immigrant who achieved immense and almost immediate success before the Civil War. After the war he became one of the leading bankers of the Southeast and fathered six girls who were famous for their beauty, ability, and intelligence. Karl Otto Witte was born in Blomberg, Lippe-Detmold, Hanover, and was educated in the Hanover Lyceum as a farmer. He was the third child in a family of ten and came to New York at the age of twenty-three with the intention of buying an estate and becoming a farmer. He anglicized his name upon his arrival in America.

When he saw that agriculture was not the most promising field in America, he became engaged in the import-export business. In 1847 he moved to Charleston, where he worked as a clerk for Herman Thierman. Within two years he opened his own grocery and commission business in Charleston. He was so successful that he considered himself retired at the beginning of the Civil War.

Shortly after Lee's surrender, Witte fell in love with and married Charlotte Sophia Reeves of Charleston. They had a two-year honeymoon in Europe. When they returned Witte became involved with the People's National Bank as an investor and director. By

1870 he was its president. He would remain in that position until he sold his interest in the bank to Robert Goodwyn Rhett in 1899. By that time he and a few other prominent Charleston businessmen had organized the Security Savings Bank, of which he was president until his death.

Mr. Witte was known to be extraordinarily indulgent of his wife and six daughters. Each of his daughters was herself a strong personality and made a good marriage, and each made a name for herself outside the constraints of wife and mother in the early twentieth century. His daughter Laura Witte Waring's memoir *The Way It Was in Charleston* provides a loving portrait of the Witte family.

According to Witte's granddaughter Beatrice St. Julien Ravenel, his tombstone was designed and made by Louis Comfort Tiffany.

WILLIAM BLACK YATES (1809–1882)

Sailors' Friend   MAP LOCATION: SOUTHEAST 60

"Parson Yates," as he was known to all, was the beloved chaplain of the Charleston Port Society for forty-six years. The older brother of Amarinthia Yates Snowden, he spent part of his youth in Aberdeen, Scotland, where his parents moved to educate their children. After he returned to the United States, he was the patient in a widely reported operation by the famous surgeon Valentine Mott, who took out much of Yates's left clavicle, without anesthesia, to remove a malignant tumor. During his convalescence Yates started to prepare for the ministry. He studied at Virginia and Princeton and was one of the first graduates of the Theological Seminary of Columbia.

After serving at various churches, Parson Yates began his life's mission in 1836 when he became chaplain of the Port Society. The organization had been founded thirteen years earlier, the second of its kind in the country, in an attempt to reform the raucous sailors that the busy harbor brought to the city. Parson Yates became a leader of the local Washingtonian temperance movement and also took an interest in discouraging prostitution. He preached at the Seamen's Bethel from a pulpit shaped like the prow of a ship. Lettered in gold on the front of the pulpit were the words "He Taught Them Out of a Boat." Known for his melodramatic sermons and animated gestures, Parson Yates paralleled in style and setting his famous contemporary Rev. Edward Thompson Taylor, memorably described as Father Mapple in *Moby-Dick*.

In 1859 the Port Society realized one of Parson Yates's most innovative proposals by establishing the Charleston Marine School on the two-hundred-ton brig *Lodebar*. The floating school aimed to provide practical nautical training as well as instruction in English and mathematics to city boys who had been living on the streets. The state soon began to provide additional funding in hopes that an increase in Southern sailors would diminish the number of Northern seamen on ships docking in Charleston. With the outbreak of the war, the state began to think of the Marine School as a naval complement to the Citadel. But the school was forced to relocate to Orangeburg in 1863 and collapsed by the end of the war. Parson Yates also helped to establish a Sailors' Home in Charleston. He continued his ministry at the Seamen's Bethel until his final illness.

Henry Edward Young (1831–1918)

Lawyer   MAP LOCATION: SOUTHEAST 67

Henry Edward Young was a well-educated lawyer who became judge advocate general on the staff of Gen. Robert E. Lee. He was educated in what was then Prussia at the University of Berlin, from which he received a law degree. At the commencement of the Civil War, he held the rank of first lieutenant in the South Carolina Militia. He was promoted to captain in September 1861 and served with Generals Drayton, Jones, Longstreet, and Anderson before he became an assistant advocate general and later judge advocate general of the Army of Northern Virginia. He was promoted to major in 1864.

At one point, Young was offered the position of judge advocate general of the entire Confederate Army, but he declined on Lee's request that he remain on the general's staff. He was with Lee until Appomattox and saw action during all of the campaigns of Virginia and at Antietam and Gettysburg. He was twice wounded.

After the war Young became a partner with Benjamin Huger Rutledge in the firm of Rutledge and Young. After the death of Col. Rutledge he practiced with his son Arthur in the firm of Young and Young. The firm survives today in Charleston as Young, Clement Rivers LLP.

Major Young was the last surviving member of Lee's staff when he died at his home at 22 Legaré Street on April 9, 1918.

MAPS AND THEMATIC TOURS

These lists illustrate one approach to exploring Magnolia Cemetery. More names could be added to several of categories below, particularly the select sample of Confederate soldiers and sailors. Many other themes would also make for fascinating groupings, such as socialites, members of Congress, lawyers, doctors, journalists, entrepreneurs, ministers and missionaries, naturalists, or important figures in the histories of the local schools and colleges. The maps and index to this volume are valuable tools for constructing tours.

Artists and Writers before the Charleston Renaissance

William Elliott, Emma Susan Gilchrist, William J. Grayson, Caroline Howard Gilman Glover Jervey, Hugh Swinton Legaré, Louisa S. McCord, Elizabeth Waties Alston Pringle, Harriott Horry Rutledge Ravenel, Jane Bachman Haskell Rose, George Herbert Sass, William Hayne Simmons, William Gilmore Simms, Yates Snowden, John Stolle, William Aiken Walker, Frederick Theodore Weber, Eola Willis

Artists, Writers, and Preservationists of the Charleston Renaissance

Mary Wilson Ball, John Bennett, Susan Pringle Frost, Isabella Bowen Heyward, Helen von Kolnitz Hyer, Ned Jennings, Samuel Lapham, Harriet DuBose Kershaw Leiding, Minnie Robertson Mikell, Marguerite Cuttino Miller, Josephine Pinckney, Beatrice Witte Ravenel, Antoinette Rose Guerard Rhett, Albert Simons, Alice Ravenel Huger Smith

Confederate Soldiers and Sailors

Capt. Langdon Cheves, Jr., Gen. James Conner, Gen. Wilmot Gibbes DeSaussure, Capt. Edward Downes Frost, Maj. Robert C. Gilchrist, Lt. John Grimball, Capt. Edwin Lindsley Halsey, Pvt. Robert Little Holmes, Horace Lawson Hunley and crew members of the *Hunley,* Adm. Duncan N. Ingraham, Gen. Micah Jenkins, Gen. Arthur Middleton Manigault, Capt. John C. Mitchel, Jr., Col. Benjamin Huger Rutledge, Gen. Roswell Sabine Ripley, Gen. James Simons II, Col. Charles H. Simonton, Gen. Clement H. Stevens, Col. Peter Fayssoux Stevens, Col. C. Irvine Walker, Pvt. Edward L. Wells, Maj. Henry E. Young

Crime and Vice

William C. Corrie, Frank Hogan, J. Elmore Martin, Dr. Thomas Ballard McDow, Judge Robert Withers Memminger, Belle Percival, Beatrice St. Julien Ravenel, Mary Mack Martin Ravenel

Intendants and Mayors of Charleston

Thomas Bennett, Jr. (Intendant, 1812–1813), George Dwight Bryan (1887–1891), William Ashmead Courtenay (1879–1887), George Irving Cunningham (1873–1877), John F. Ficken (1891–1895), Christopher S. Gadsden (1887), P. C. Gaillard (1865–1868), Tristram T. Hyde (1915–1919), Henry W. Lockwood (1938–1944), Burnet Rhett Maybank (1931–1938), Robert Goodwyn Rhett (1903–1911), John Schnierle (1842–1846, 1850–1852), E. Edward Wehman, Jr. (1944–1947).

Signers of the Ordinance of Secession

Alexander Henry Brown, Charles Pinckney Brown, Andrew William Burnet, Langdon Cheves, Jr., Benjamin Faneuil Dunkin, Robert Newman Gourdin, William Gregg, Isaac Hayne, John H. Honour, Andrew Gordon Magrath, John S. O'Hear, Robert Barnwell Rhett, Benjamin Huger Rutledge, Thomas Young Simons. (Other notable secessionists include James Conner, Alfred Huger, William D. Porter, William Gilmore Simms, and George Alfred Trenholm.)

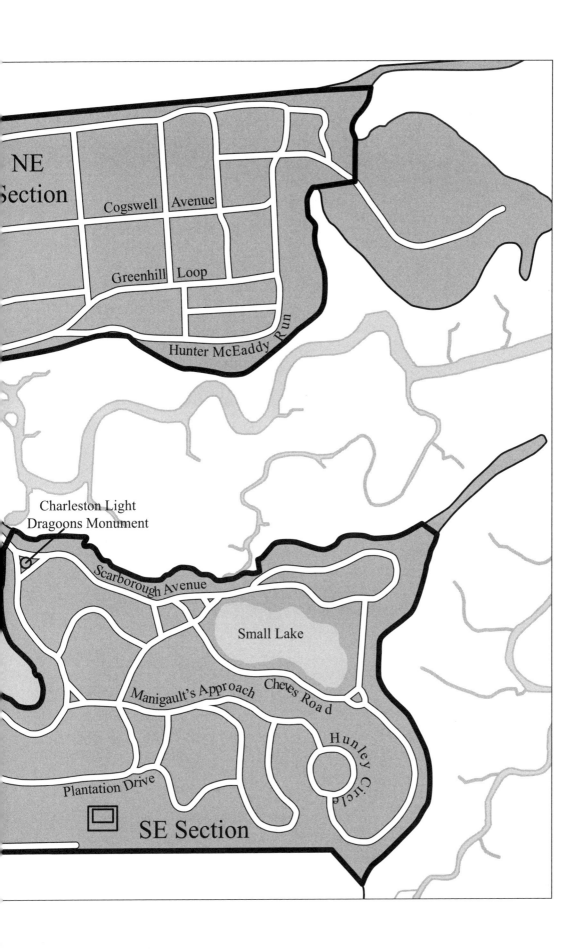

NE
Section

Cogswell   Avenue

Greenhill   Loop

Hunter McEaddy Run

Charleston Light
Dragoons Monument

Scarborough Avenue

Small Lake

Manigault's Approach   Cheves Road

Hunley Circle

Plantation Drive

SE Section

Northwest

1. Henry Brown
2. William Coombs Dana
3. Robert Cogdell Gilchrist and Emma Susan Gilchrist
4. J. Ross Hanahan
5. James Calvin Hemphill
6. Alfred Huger (1876–1938)
7. Tristram Tupper Hyde
8. Fanny Mahon King
9. Andrew Kroeg
10. George Swinton Legaré and William Storen Legaré
11. Margaret Simons Middleton
12. Frank Withers Munnerlyn, Jr.
13. Frank Kerchner Myers
14. Belle Percival
15. Louise Bouknight Poppenheim and Mary Barnett Poppenheim
16. Alexander Sprunt III
17. William Nelson Taft
18. Georgianna Raoul Horry Palmer Townsend
19. William Aiken Walker
20. Laura Witte Waring, Thomas Richard Waring, Sr., and Thomas Richard Waring, Jr.

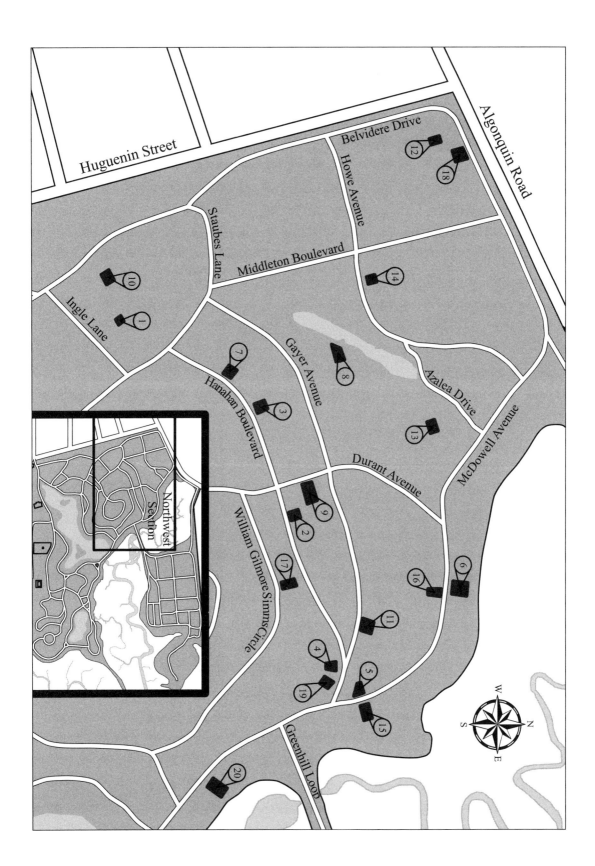

Northeast

1. Mary Wilson Ball
2. William Watts Ball, Clements Ripley, and Katharine Ball Ripley
3. John Bennett
4. Leon Dunlap
5. Simon Fogarty
6. Elizabeth Berkeley Grimball
7. Frank Hogan
8. Helen von Kolnitz Hyer
9. Louie Boyd Jenkins and Margaret Quante Jenkins
10. Clarence William Legerton
11. Mary Vardrine McBee
12. Robert Withers Memminger
13. Ted Ashton Phillips, Jr.
14 James Henry Rice, Jr.
15. George Calvin Rogers, Sr.
16. George Calvin Rogers, Jr.

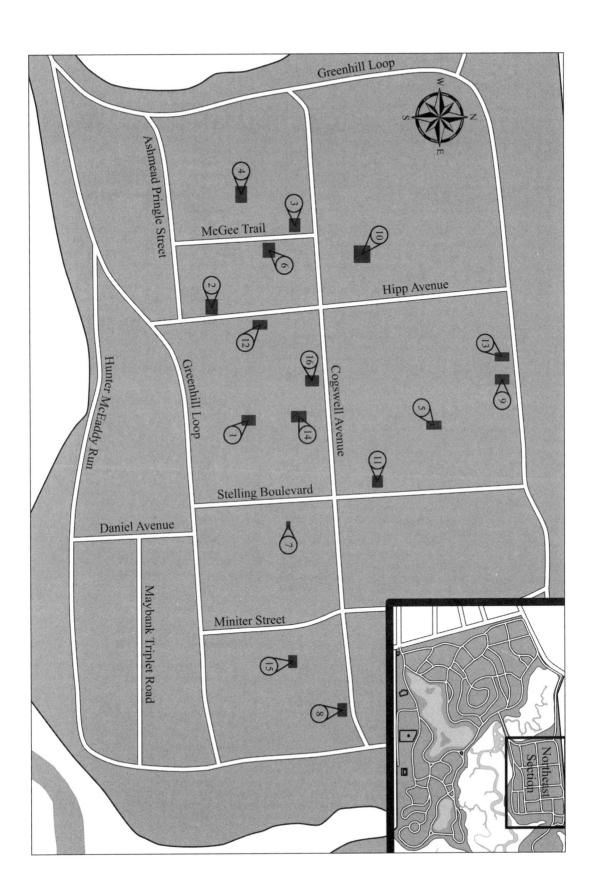

1. William Aiken, Jr.
2. Rufus Calvin Barkley
3. Samuel Murray Bennett, Jr.
4. Oliver James Bond
5. William Hiram Brawley
6. William Izard Bull and William Bull
7. Andrew William Burnet
8. Daisy Breaux Calhoun
9. William Carrington
10. Edward Burnham Chamberlain
11. Cogswell Family
12. James Conner
13. William C. Corrie
14. William Ashmead Courtenay
15. George Irving Cunningham
16. James W. Duckett
17. Anne Carson Strohecker Grimball Watt Elliott
18. William Elliott
19. John Frederick Ficken
20. Robert McCormick Figg
21. Edward Frost and Edward Downes Frost
22. Susan Pringle Frost
23. Christopher Schultz Gadsden
24. James Schoolbred Gibbes
25. Frank Gilbreth, Jr.
26. William J. Grayson
27. William Gregg
28. Robert Emmet Gribbin
29. George Daniel Grice
30. John Grimball
31. Edwin Lindsley Halsey
32. Isaac William Hayne
33. Isabel Bowen Heyward
34. Henrietta Emogene Martin Hoagg
35. Mary Vereen Huguenin
36. Edward Iredell Renwick Jennings
37. Samuel Lapham
38. Mary Wilkerson Middleton Pinckney Lee, Robert E. Lee III, Gustavus M. Pinckney, and Frederich August Richard, Count von Strensch L'Estrange de Blackmere
39. Harriette DuBose Kershaw Leiding
40. Henry Whilden Lockwood
41. Andrew Gordon Magrath
42. Louis Manigault
43. J. Elmore Martin
44. Burnet Rhett Maybank
45. Helen Gardner McCormack
46. Clelia Peronneau Mathewes McGowan
47. Clara Gooding McMillan and Thomas Sanders McMillan
48. Minnie Robertson Mikell
49. Marguerite Cuttino Miller
50. John S. Mitchell
51. Nelson Mitchell
52. L. Harry Mixon
53. Josephine Pinckney
54. Elizabeth Waties Allston Pringle
55. Harrison Randolph
56. Beatrice Witte Ravenel, Beatrice St. Julien Ravenel, and Charles Otto Witte
57. Motte Alston Read
58. Antoinette Rose Guerard Rhett
59. Roswell Sabine Ripley
60. Jane Bachman Haskell Rose
61. John Russell
62. William Gilmore Simms
63. James Simons II and James Simons III
64. Katherine Drayton Mayrant Simons
65. Thomas Young Simons, Jr.
66. Alice Ravenel Huger Smith, Daniel Elliott Huger Smith, and Edward Laight Wells
67. Clement H. Stevens and Peter Fayssoux Stevens
68. George Alfred Trenholm and William Lee Trenholm
69. C. Irvine Walker
70. William Way and William Way, Jr.
71. Frederick Theodore Weber
72. George Walton Williams
73. Eola Willis
74. Robert Wilson and Robert Wilson, Jr.

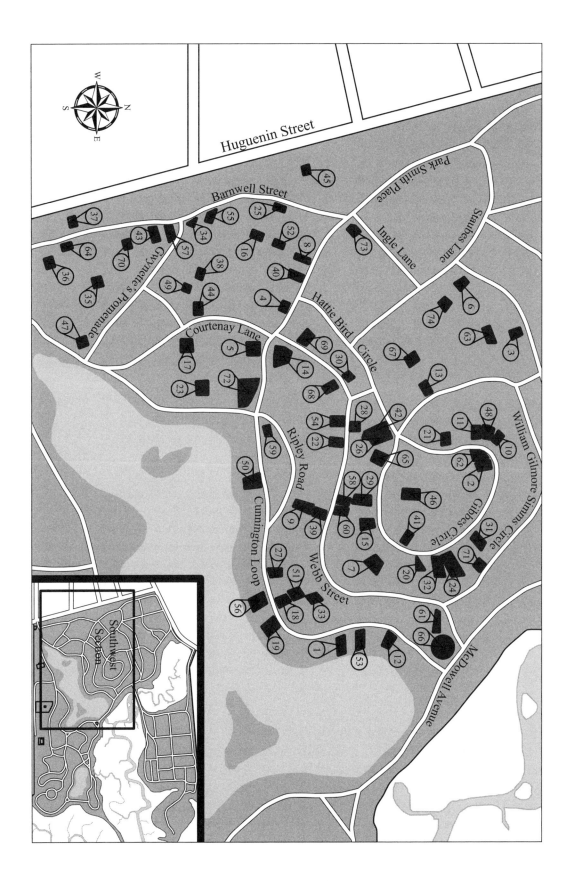

SOUTHEAST

1. Thomas Bennett, Jr.
2. Washington Jefferson Bennett and Andrew Buist Murray
3. Arthur LeRoy Bristol
4. Alexander Henry Brown
5. Charles Pinckney Brown
6. George Dwight Bryan
7. James Butler Campbell and Celia Campbell
8. Langdon Cheves, Louisa S. McCord, and Langdon Cheves, Jr.
9. Wilmot Gibbes DeSaussure
10. Benjamin Faneuil Dunkin
11. John Ewan and William Ewan
12. John H.L. Fuller
13. Thomas Norman Gadsden
14. Peter Charles Gaillard
15. Henry Gourdin and Robert Newman Gourdin
16. Johnson Hagood
17. Wilson Godfrey Harvey
18. John Edwards Holbrook
19. Robert Little Holmes
20. John H. Honour
21. Henry B. Horlbeck
22. Alfred Huger (1788–1872)
23. Daniel Elliott Huger
24. Francis Kinloch Huger
25. William Harleston Huger
26. *H. L. Hunley* crew members
27. Duncan Nathaniel Ingraham
28. Micah Jenkins
29. Caroline Howard Gilman Jervey
30. Theodore Dehon Jervey
31. King of the Clouds
32. Hugh Swinton Legaré
33. Timothy Willard Lewis
34. Robert Whilden Lockwood and Thomas J. Lockwood
35. William Turner Logan
36. Sarah Buchanan Preston Lowndes
37. Arthur Middleton Manigault
38. Thomas Ballard McDow
39. Nathaniel Russell Middleton
40. John C. Mitchel, Jr.
41. Mohammedans
42. Ziba B. Oakes
43. John Sanders O'Hear
44. Leonard Talbert Owens
45. Princess Henrietta Pignatelli
46. William Dennison Porter
47. Harriott Horry Rutledge Ravenel and St. Julien Ravenel
48. Mary Mack Martin Ravenel and George Herbert Sass
49. Robert Barnwell Rhett
50. Robert Goodwyn Rhett
51. John S. Riggs
52. Benjamin Huger Rutledge
53. Thomas Ryan
54. Jacob Schirmer
55. John Schnierle
56. William Hayne Simmons
57. Albert Simons and Robert Bentham Simons, Sr.
58. Charles Henry Simonton
59. William B. Smith and Richard Smith Whaley
60. Mary Amarinthia Snowden, Yates Snowden, and William Black Yates
61. John Stolle
62. Arthur Jervey Stoney, Anne Montague Stoney, and Robert Latane Montague
63. Samuel Gaillard Stoney, Sr., Louisa Cheves Smythe Stoney, and Augustine Thomas Smythe Stoney
64. Dorothy Thomson Waring
65. Elizabeth Waring and J. Waties Waring
66. William May Wightman
67. Henry Edward Young

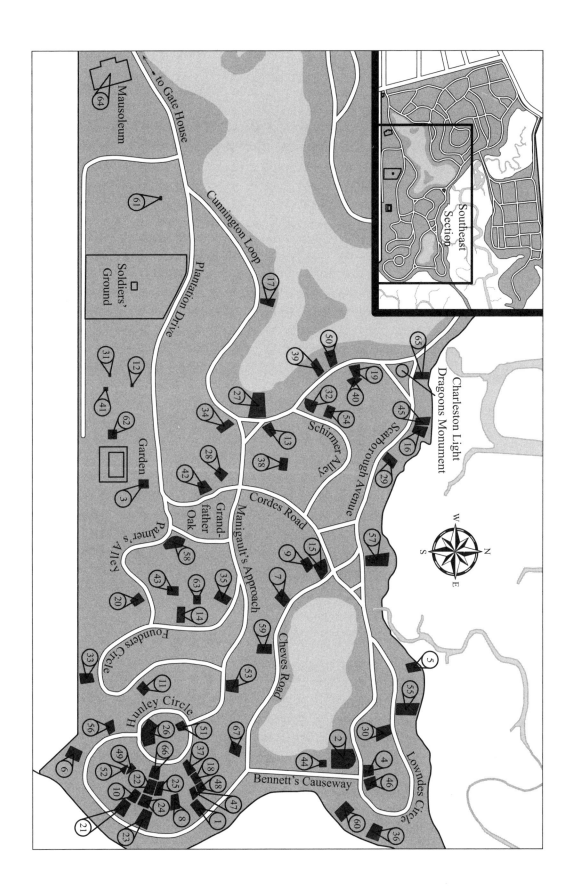

AFTERWORD

Alice McPherson Phillips

At the age of four, my father knew the names of all the U.S. presidents and, I've been told, readily recited them to any eager listener. The same youthful excitement flared in his eyes every time he had the chance to share his knowledge of history. If ever I needed an answer, he was sure to have it, and when he did not, he would humor me with a stream of entertaining speculation. I fail to recall the slightest hint of a suppressed spirit even in his days of fading.

Excepting a few trips to Walt Disney World, our family vacations revolved around visiting points of historical interest. Twice we drove to Niagara Falls and back, stopping at every major historic city, and some not so major ones, along the way and out of the way: Richmond; D.C.; Dover; New York; Philadelphia; Charleston, West Virginia; Boston; Stowe; and Trenton, New Jersey to name a few. Dressed in pinafores and Velcro-tabbed shoes, my sister, Sarah, and I followed our parents around museum after museum as Dad explained the significance of various exhibits, hoping to spark our enthusiasm. The last vacation we took with him in 2004 was the start of a self-designed "Civil Rights Tour of the South," although by that time he was not well enough to continue past Atlanta, the first stop.

At home in Charleston, he was the same, always instinctually seeking to learn something new and wanting to impart that nature to his children. Every Saturday morning, I could expect to hear his uneven gait growing less faint outside my bedroom door, a gentle knock, and an animated invitation to accompany him to the weekly flea market at the Gaillard Municipal Auditorium. Every first and third Sunday of the month, I could expect the same kind of invitation for a trip to Roumillat's Auction House down Highway 17. And perhaps only because we were Ted's children, Sarah and I went with him nearly every time.

We followed him from the Gibbes Museum of Art to the line of antique stores on King Street, from the Battery in White Point Gardens to—of course—Magnolia Cemetery. Sometimes in Charleston's scorching heat and sweltering humidity, we would be out there with him, cooling ourselves with homemade fans while he wandered among the gravestones, examining inscriptions and taking notes. When, at age thirteen, the appeal of visiting the same hot, buggy, boring place full of dead people began to dwindle for me, he refueled my interest by letting me drive his 1996 blue Ford Escort wagon around and around the circle bounding the *Hunley* crew graves and sometimes even across the causeway to the newer plots at Greenhill, while he wandered the tombstones with his legal pad and fountain pen. Today, I often drive the same Escort, fondly known as the

"Limousine," around the graveyard alone, stopping by the water to admire the dozens of wading white wood ibises before arriving at my destination on the far side of Greenhill: the resting place of Ted Phillips.

I never thought Magnolia Cemetery would be a happy place again. But some curious presence comforts me, and I have probably visited Magnolia more frequently in the few years since Dad's death than I ever did with him. There are many places I worried would never again bring happiness to my family. Visiting Harvard was probably the hardest, when I competed in their annual debate tournament the winter of my senior year of high school. I could vaguely remember perusing the Coop, Harvard's bookstore and souvenir shop, and gazing for the first time upon the bronze ibis on the dome of the Lampoon Castle, where Harvard's whimsical undergraduate publication, the *Lampoon,* is composed. Dad's dear college friend and Leverett House roommate, Mike Reiss, showed my mother and me through the Castle's circular library and into the Sanctum, where the random-thought notebooks from each year have been stored in tall, dark wooden cabinets. We flipped through a volume from 1980 only to encounter a familiar scrawl: "Craziness at the Kong . . ." presumably referring to a wild night at the infamous Hong Kong bar on Massachusetts Avenue. Picturing a nineteen-year-old Ted, dancing on the tables and bodysurfing down the stairs of the *Lampoon* offices, I could not suppress a smile.

Being at Harvard, even twenty-seven years after his graduation, gave me a fuller picture, I believe, of who my father really was, beyond the basic biographical information. For a man as rich in life as Dad, it is not enough to know merely that he was born in Easley, S.C., in 1959, and that he was raised in Lynchburg, S.C., until his family moved to Charleston before he was a teenager. Raised in a generation starkly different from his, I never felt like my twelve years at his alma mater, Porter-Gaud, could give me an adequate representation of his childhood the way Harvard and his college friends reconstructed his college experience. But regardless of the places I see or the stories I am told, there are many things about my dad that I will never be able to imagine with assured accuracy. One thing, however, that I have learned for certain is that my father was a fighter in every sense of the word. He fought to preserve justice in the courtrooms. He fought for historic preservation in Charleston. And he fought hardest of all to preserve his own life.

After getting a law degree from the University of South Carolina in 1986, he acted as a clerk for the late Honorable James M. Morris. Before joining the Public Defender's Office, he worked as a prosecutor for the Ninth Judicial Circuit. As a public defender, he specialized in cases concerning drugs and related crimes. While my mother was expecting my sister in 1992, he played a critical role in jump-starting a case involving the constitutional rights of pregnant women who had abused drugs and had been mistreated by hospital officials and the police. The case, *Crystal M. Ferguson et al. v. City of Charleston,* was won much later at the judgment of the United States Supreme Court. I believe my father considered his role in this case among his greatest achievements.

My dad served on the Brown Fellowship Cemetery Committee, the Board of Trustees of Magnolia Cemetery, and, finally, the Preservation Society of Charleston, first as a board member and then as vice president and secretary for several years. He annually volunteered our 1690s Bermuda Stone home for public tours to raise money for historical preservation.

The beautiful Charleston art collection with which Dad filled the house made 141 Church Street a unique stop on the walking tours. He frequented rallies and even stood between crumbling single houses and wrecking balls, in the company of other Preservation Society members. He stood his ground against greedy developers, and where his strong will could not triumph, his charm always did.

Ted Phillips's greatest battle was fought in secret, beyond the public eye. Not even some of his closest friends were aware of his protracted struggle with AIDS. Nor were my sister and I told until we were old enough to start understanding the infinite implications. The circumstances of his contracting the virus are uncertain. He was diagnosed in late 1993, not long after the birth of my sister. Over the years, the effectiveness of his treatment depended precariously on how long it took the virus to mutate and become resistant to his current drug combination. Apparently there were many close calls. By some miracle, HIV bypassed the rest of our family, so my mother was able to stand by and care for my father through his hardship.

AIDS did not define my father, but it was a major part of his life. I grew up believing it was normal for fathers in their mid-thirties to sleep all the time; to not work; to take twenty-five pills per day. I guess like the flea market, auction, cemetery, and other historic outings, I took it for granted that beyond his immeasurable brilliance, he was, after all, just a typical father.

As his illness progressed, my father left the law profession and instead stayed home, amusingly characterizing himself as a "recovering lawyer." He did not fall apart like many people would have. Instead, he channeled his energy into his family, his research, and his writing. For the 2001 book *Charleston in My Time,* he contributed a biography of local artist and friend, West Fraser, to introduce the beautiful volume of Fraser's Charleston paintings. The bulk of his time, however, he poured into *The City of the Silent,* a biographical history of Magnolia Cemetery. As an elementary school student and also an aspiring writer, I would tease him about how long he took to write the book. His retort was always the same: for every sentence of the manuscript he produced, he must first invest at least an hour's research. His writing echoed his eloquent, witty voice, as well as his hard work. As his friend and fellow writer, Josephine Humphreys, once said, Ted's book was more than his lifework; it was his baby. He always made a fuss when even his mother and typist, LaVonne, tried to alter his words.

With the tragic realization that he was unlikely to ever leave room 543 of Roper Hospital, he asked that his first college roommate, Tom Brown, and I finish his masterpiece in his stead. Here it is. I can only hope that he would be satisfied with the final product.

Ted Ashton Phillips, Jr., died barely an hour before sunrise on 17 January 2005. He had turned forty-five just two months before. He was survived by his parents, LaVonne and Ashton; his wife of nearly seventeen years, Janet; his younger brothers and sister, Mark, Al, and Sarah; and his daughters, Sarah and me. Together, with many of his friends from all across the world, we said goodbye to him at the gates of his silent city.

ACKNOWLEDGMENTS

When Ted Phillips died in January 2005, he had nearly completed the manuscript on which he had worked until illness stopped him. I have tried to follow his designs faithfully in seeing the book through to publication. Using materials that he had gathered, I finished the set of biographical profiles he had projected. I did not add to or subtract from that list. Ted's selection of subjects reflected his interests, and his ability to identify those names from the terse Magnolia burial register illustrated his familiarity with the Charlestonians who preceded him. In the copyediting process that Ted would have handled if he had lived longer, I have made every effort to preserve the author's characteristic voice and his historical and critical judgments, including those that I do not share. To maintain the informative yet informal tone that Ted sought, I have not introduced citations or a bibliography, though I have fact-checked the manuscript. As Ted indicated in the "Brief Note on the Biographical Subjects," he drew on standard reference works and newspaper obituaries as well as his decades of reading in South Carolina history, supplemented with more focused research in manuscript correspondence, city directories, census records, and other sources. Most entries mention any available recent full-length biographical treatments of the subjects.

While I am confident that this volume realizes Ted's plans for his book, I am sadly unable to complete one of the tasks that would have most pleased the author, acknowledgment of the many people who helped him along the way. I must limit myself to thanking those who have joined with me in tending to this part of Ted's legacy. His widow, Janet Hopkins, and their daughters, Alice and Sarah Phillips, warmly shared with me their inspiring devotion to the memory of Ted. His mother, LaVonne N. Phillips, generously showered her love on the project, as did Ted's siblings, Mark Phillips, Al Phillips, and Sarah Phillips Marshall. I am especially grateful for Gator's expressions of confidence in me in his capacity as the executor of Ted's estate. Josephine Humphreys has remained the great friend to Ted that she was during his life, as well as a wise and delightful friend to me. Beverly Donald, superintendent of Magnolia Cemetery, was exceptionally helpful to the project, particularly in the identification of illustrations and the preparation of the maps. Bob Ellis produced the superb index in addition to assisting in other ways with his usual combination of efficiency and good humor. Harlan Greene graciously shared his expertise in Charleston history and two works of art from his collection. Nichole Green provided photographs of the Old Slave Mart Museum, which she has so successfully invigorated. Henry Middleton Cheves kindly permitted the use of Charles Fraser's portrait of Langdon Cheves. Cynthia Jenkins of the Preservation Society of Charleston carefully read the entire manuscript and offered valuable suggestions and support.

I am sorry that Ted never had the chance to meet Carol Harrison, but he is deeply in her debt for all she has done for this book, as I am for that help and so much more. My parents, Lou and Helen Brown, and my children, Lucian and Veronica Brown, took an interest in the project that reminded me happily of their encounters with Ted. I very much appreciated the encouragement I received from many other mutual friends of Ted's and mine, including Elizabeth Barrett, Ward Briggs, Glen and Mary Fossella, Al Jean, Charles Kimball, Caroline O'Brien, Mike and Denise Reiss, Dale and Ted Rosengarten, and Rowan and Grace Wilson.

Although I had little contact with the Charleston Library Society, where Ted did much of the research for the book, I received vital assistance from Jennifer Scheetz of the Charleston Museum; Tom Spain of the Charleston *Post and Courier;* Lynnette Stoudt of the Georgia Historical Society; Sara Arnold and Joyce N. Baker of the Gibbes Museum of Art; Karen Brickman Emmons of the Historic Charleston Foundation; Alexis Thompson of the Historic Columbia Foundation; Lynn Robertson and Saddler Taylor of the Mc-Kissick Museum, University of South Carolina; Donna Wells of the Moorland-Spingarn Research Center, Howard University; Patrick Scott of Rare Books and Special Collections,Thomas Cooper Library, University of South Carolina; Jane Aldrich and Michael Coker of the South Carolina Historical Society; Beth Bilderback, Robin Copp, Brian Cuthrell, Graham Duncan, Craig Keeney, Lorrey McClure, and Allen Stokes, Jr., of the South Caroliniana Library, University of South Carolina; and Arthur W. Bergeron, Jr., and Clifton P. Hyatt of the U.S. Army Military History Institute.

The University of South Carolina Press has been an ideal partner in this venture. I thank the director, Curtis Clark, and the assistant director for operations, Linda Haines Fogle, for their enthusiasm for the book and their thoughtful planning for its success. Robert Pace made the wonderful maps. Alex Moore's faith in the project and exertions on its behalf have been absolutely extraordinary. Ted would have been thrilled to know that he received this editorial attention from a current representative of the grand tradition of South Carolina historians. I am immensely grateful to Alex for ensuring Ted's place in that constellation.

INDEX

Page numbers given in italic type represent illustrations.

ABOUT THE AUTHOR

TED ASHTON PHILLIPS, JR. (1959–2005),
was a resident and historian of Charleston,
South Carolina. A graduate of Harvard
College, where he wrote for the *Harvard
Lampoon*, Phillips was a trustee of Mag-
nolia Cemetery, a member of the Brown
Fellowship Cemetery Committee, and
an officer of the Preservation Society
of Charleston. He is buried in Magnolia
Cemetery with the subjects of his book.